Andrew H. Dent & Leslie Sherr

MCX
Material ConneXion®

MATERIAL INNOVATION
PRODUCT
DESIGN

355 color illustrations

Asra,

I know you are going to be so
successful in your business life ☺
I believe in you and anything
I can do to help please ask.

Sharon

P.S. Your mother is fantastic

Thames & Hudson

CONTENTS

A Note About Material Properties
Each project and material that appears in this volume is described according to its properties. Understanding a material's attributes is fundamental to its selection and to its role in fulfilling the needs of designers. While many material properties exist, this book highlights the following, which are currently at the forefront of innovation in product design: all-weather use, biomimicry, composite, compostable, durable, ergonomic, high strength, lightweight, nanotech, rapidly renewable resource, recycled, simplification, stain-resistant/ easy-clean, and sustainable solutions.

Material Innovation: Product Design © 2014
Material ConneXion Inc.

MCX
Material ConneXion®

A SANDOW Company

First published in 2014 in paperback in the United States of America by Thames & Hudson Inc., 500 Fifth Avenue, New York, New York 10110

thamesandhudsonusa.com

Library of Congress Catalog Card Number 2013950857

ISBN 978-0-500-29129-0

Printed in China by Shanghai Offset Printing Products Limited

PREFACE

BY MICHELE CANIATO
PRESIDENT, MATERIAL CONNEXION

Since Material ConneXion was founded in 1997 on the premise that the selection of materials able to give tangible form to a designer's vision is of paramount importance, the world has seen startling social change and scientific development. Technology now enables more products to be made and used than ever before in the history of man, transforming how we communicate with each other and relate to the material world. But many of these products have been of inferior quality and with little regard for their impact on the environment, whether in terms of production, use or disposal. This has triggered urgent questions about sustainability and natural resources. Our desires and concerns are reflected in the objects we make, a fact as true today as it was thousands of years ago. As our population grows and customization becomes commonplace, infinite cultural subtleties can now be reflected in the smallest detail such that design has become both an agent and a mirror of change, able to convey complex messages in the most basic, intuitive terms.

While this book is focused on product design, it is part of a series that encompasses multiple design practices because today modes of professional practice and ideas flow from one area to another and consumers and users do not compartmentalize designed goods and images in the same way as the manufacturing industry. Ideas generated within specialized design fields go on to influence others, with many designers believing that innovation can best be found by looking outside, rather than within, one's chosen creative discipline. Today, there is a fluid and pervasive overlap between architecture, identity, fashion, products, packaging, interiors, automobiles, computer interfaces, and so on. Recognizing this, we have sought to bring insights that come from considering design across a broad range of media and within a forward-looking context that acknowledges the field's shifting parameters.

Today, Material ConneXion offers a worldwide network of libraries and consulting teams that collaborate with an astonishing range of companies large and small, global and local, heritage brands and visionary entrepreneurs. For all these clients, design is integral to how they operate, facilitating innovation and creativity that allows them to deliver better products, and ultimately a better quality of life, to their customers.

This publication organizes by material type a select set of highly innovative products whose influence extends beyond their category and immediate purpose. While there are many publications about design as either a process or a set of intentions, here we define the attributes and benefits of each object, revealing how they are made, how they are different, and hopefully better, not just from an aesthetic point of view but as a way to inspire new ideas and applications. Some of these products we have been privileged to help develop, giving us a special insight into their unique attributes. For example, a recent collaboration with Logitech, a leading consumer electronics and accessories company, led to the launch of FabricSkin Keyboard Folio, the first iPad case made entirely of fabric (page 64). Designed to advance the consumer experience of digital tablets, the case uses a waterproof, touch-sensitive fabric that is available in six colors and suitable for both iPad 4 and iPad Air. Material ConneXion supported this project as a sourcing entity for the materials involved, working with the design agencies responsible for the style and look of the case to identify how they might best combine technology and familiar fabrics to trigger a warm, tactile, handcrafted feeling.

The act of designing, and the final designed product, make a cultural statement, one that refers to a way of life, how we engage with the world as we move through each day. In this broad sense, design is a dynamic process that reflects and shapes our existence, providing a bridge between creativity and consumption. Hopefully, this book will help readers think differently about designing—inventing around all the many aspects of products themselves from consumer usability to manufacturing to the after-use and, of course, the starting point: the material they are made from.

INTRODUCTION

BY ALLAN CHOCHINOV
EDITOR-IN-CHIEF, CORE77
CHAIR, SCHOOL OF VISUAL ARTS MFA PRODUCTS OF DESIGN

The field of product design is either very old or very new, depending on how you frame things up. If you're talking about ingenuity and invention and creating a better mousetrap, then no doubt its origins are as early as we can measure. (Indeed, the ability to use a tool has been posited as one of the main differentiators between humans and other animals.) If, however, you define product design as "industrial design"—one of the official monikers of its study and practice—then we're only talking several decades. Here, a primary definition of the practice is to innovate, through a repeatable process of design, new and notable objects that marry form, function, engineering, aesthetics, and business viability. When desire enters the picture, industrial designers can cynically be viewed as creating ever more pieces of stuff, feeding market demand and sometimes *creating* that demand through marketing, trends, and conspicuous consumption.

In fact, there are many other ways to characterize design and the products that result. Richard Tyson, systems thinker and design strategist, looks at products as "shadows of systems"; as embodiments that rest on the interconnected shoulders of so many elements of extraction, manufacture, shipping, usage, behavior, economics, and culture. I myself see products as "props in an experience," mediating interactions in ways as subtle as a couple of coffee cups changing the character of a "meeting" from official to social.

THE FORMS OF PRODUCT DESIGN

But what's particularly fascinating right now is the myriad forms that products can take. (Not *formal* as in shape or form, but rather how they find their way into the world and earn their keep.) From DIY hacks and mods to aeroponic urban farming machines, from shared libraries of digitally fabricated objects to speculative design gestures aimed at provoking dialogue and debate, the instantiations of products and product design are the broadest they've ever been: Bespoke Innovation's custom prosthetic fairings (page 104); Suzanne Lee's 'grown" textiles (page 20); Teague's 3D-printed headphones (page 102)… There are just so very many ways to think about what a designed object is and does.

A product can answer a question—*what would we need to create in order to solve this problem?* Or we can think of a product as a kind of delightful pursuit—*what could we furnish to celebrate and ennoble this event?* Or more, we could think of a product as something that enables something else—*what could we create in order to promote this kind of positive behavior?* Products are therefore situated along a continuum of intention: There are products that

opposite Bespoke fairings are made with sophisticated scanning, modeling, and 3D-printing technology to surround the owner's prosthetics and restore the lost contour with a product customized for his or her lifestyle and personality.

serve as a means to an end, and there are products that are an end in themselves. A 3D printer, for example, is a device that creates other items, but those items that result are then products in themselves. If it's the aforementioned bespoke prosthetic fairing that emerges from the 3D printer, that product functions to "dress" an engineered prosthetic leg underneath, "inviting an expression of personality and individuality that has never before been possible" (www.bespokeinnovations.com). At that point, we're talking about fashion and self-identity and dignity and a host of other characteristics that start to blur the line between an object and its purpose. In fact, if we think long enough, it can sometimes be hard to distinguish products from their function…in the same way that a set of Russian nesting dolls can be viewed as both container and contained. One of my favorite books to read to my daughter is *A House is a House* by Mary Ann Hoberman, illustrated by Betty Fraser. A representative passage goes like this:

A box is a house for a teabag.
A teapot's a house for some tea.
If you pour me a cup and I drink it all up,
Then the teahouse will turn into me!
And then . . .
Cartons are houses for crackers.
Castles are houses for kings.
The more that I think about houses,
The more things are houses for things.

(I thought the idea was so powerful that I started reading the story to my college students—storytime! They loved it as much as I did.) So products can be seen and held, but they can also enable activities. They affect behavior. They affirm life. This is one of the reasons why product design is so exciting: the notion that products are services, and that services are behaviors, and that behaviors are culture, and that culture is what designers seek to influence in the first place—it actually seems facile to think of products as just "products." They're so much more.

HOW PRODUCTS COME INTO BEING

Still, most people would define design as problem solving; as a way of improving the human condition and iteratively making the world a better place. Here, the design process

follows a more-or-less agreed-upon methodology: Research and discovery, insight gathering, problem definition, idea development, refinement, and finally production. This process seems linear and repeatable, but it can be much more effective if the phases overlap and feed back into one another, leaving room for a lot of induction and a little bit of serendipity. (Businesspeople don't like processes that aren't predictable, but designers *love* them.) This kind of product creation, then, uses external constraints as guardrails, and serves a concrete taskmaster: The design brief.

But another way of thinking about the creation of products is focusing in on their intrinsic, as opposed to extrinsic, demands. I've long encouraged design students to ask "what does the product want to be?" rather than "what do you want to make it?"—betting that if they can see things from the product's point of view, they would be able to innovate in a way that came from within; that didn't show the hand of the designer, but instead surfaced the unique properties of the product *as it could only be*.

A goal like this is ambitious, of course, but if you look around you, I'll bet that the products you most admire do

The Ganymed Walking Aid (on screen) was built with a novel S-shaped curve and pared down using software that relies on bionic engineering principles, to create a product that is lighter and feels more natural to use than its predecessors.

have a kind of "rightness" to them; that they have a signature characteristic that stands tall and proud, and in many ways *defines* the object. In this book, the combination of materials that results in the Ganymed Walking Aid (page 74) is a good example, or Julia Lohmann's Kelp Lampshades (page 28). And here I'd argue that materiality can be one of the most powerful drivers in defining a piece of design, determining its "thingness" and telling its story out loud.

THE MATERIAL'S THE THING

Designers choose materials they believe will best satisfy an object's requirements. Designers also employ materials to "rethink" and reimagine projects—say, changing a cellphone housing from injection-molded plastic to milled bamboo. Material manipulation can be targeted to save money, to save labor, to reduce ecological impact, or to simply refresh a brand. But perhaps the more ambitious (and even poetic) way to think about material is less ad hoc. Michelangelo famously remarked that his sculptures were already resident in the stone; that all he had to do was carve away everything else. With material choice, you can actually come at things from the inside out. What does this material want to be? What does it want to make? And, of course, what something is actually made of triggers an avalanche of dependencies and consequences: How does the material come into being—is it extracted from the earth or synthesized in a lab?

Material ConneXion's Tokyo location is part of a global network of libraries where product designers can search for materials alongside architects, engineers, and artists to find the perfect solution for their current project or an inspirational reference for future designs.

How is the material manipulated into its final form—is it the old "heat, beat and treat," or is it grown in a petri dish? How does the material serve its time in that form—how does it wear, shock-absorb, feel? And, of course, how does that material find its way *out* of the world—is it recycled, reused, composted, or landfilled?

We can even challenge the term "material *choice,*" since often the right material isn't necessarily chosen, exactly. It chooses *you*. You might be suspicious of such a thought, but as you enjoy the wonder-filled pages ahead, I'll bet that you vacillate between the notion that a material was selected for such-and-such a purpose, or that a material could not have created anything *but* the product that you are admiring. And what an amazing thing that is; that we are at the point in material science and technology where we can fit the right material to the job, we can fit the right job to the material, and, every so often, we can attain a match so ideal that we cannot imagine them apart. That's what designers shoot for a lot of the time, and the products in this volume are proof that very often, they succeed beautifully.

DAVID TRUBRIDGE

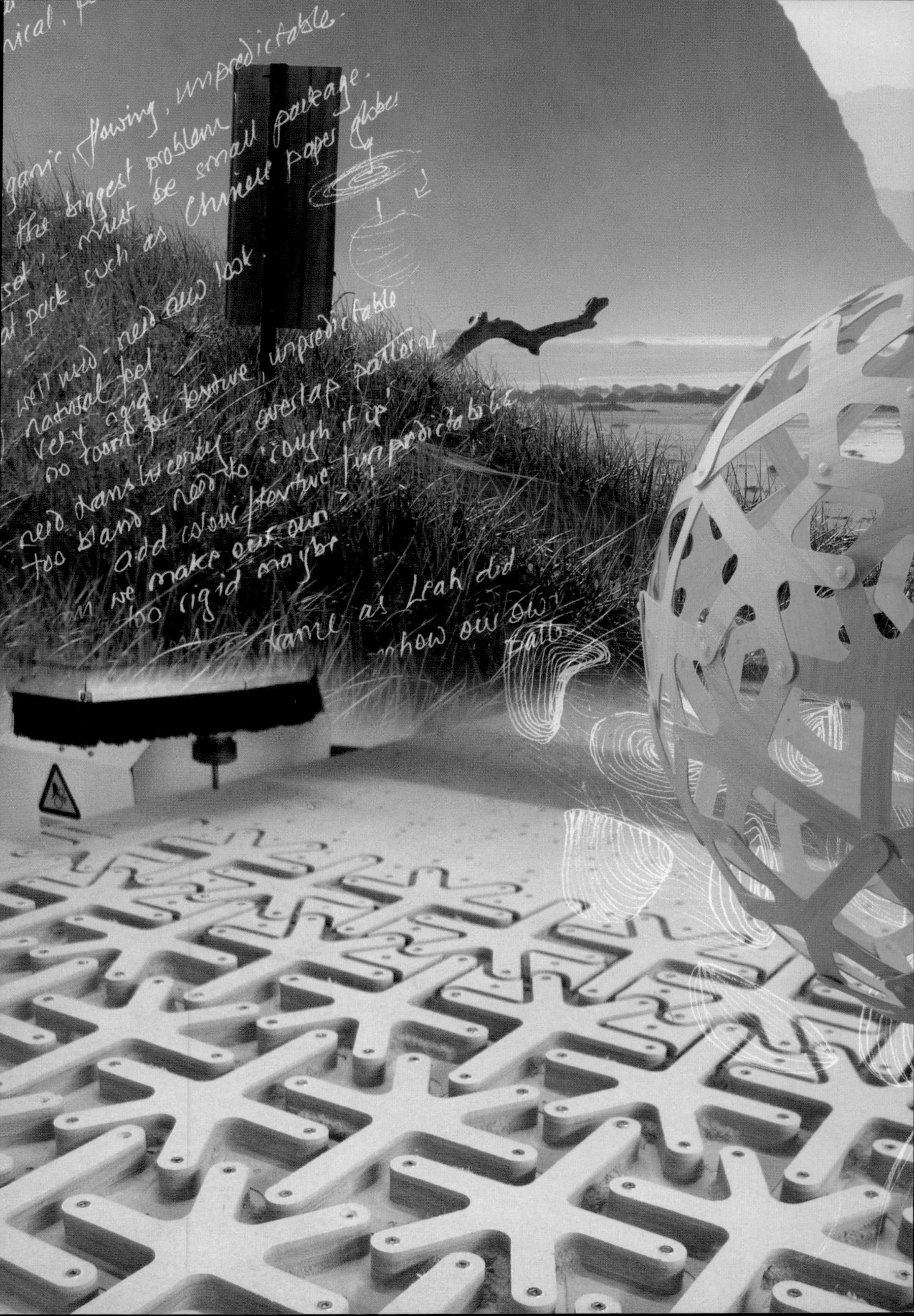

CHAPTER 1
GROWN MATERIALS

W

e have always grown materials. The majority of the human-manipulated things on this planet are from materials grown from the earth. However, these have been substances that then require more or less human effort to change them into usable materials, whether spun into yarn and woven into fabrics, hewn, cut and planed into lumber, or broken down into fibers and mulched into pulp. The material then needs to be used to create a product, requiring further synthesis, work, and energy. Nature needed to be harnessed, controlled, fought against to achieve these products; needed yet more energy, water, and other resources to do so.

There is a revolution going on in the twenty-first century that has at its forefront the idea that "nature knows best." There is an increasing belief that to produce more effectively, with fewer resources and less energy and resulting in a better end product, we need to work with nature rather than against it, using its best methods for furthering production not just of materials but of end products. Call it a version of "grow your own produce" that is using the latest advances in biotech as well as our fuller understanding of natural processes to envision a future where growing your own computer, teacup, chair, bike, car, and indeed home are the norm.

To get there, we need to overcome certain preconceptions about what our products should look like. We also need to bring together some newer production methods, and materials that are showing promise as alternatives to our twentieth-century thinking about how to make things and what they should be made of.

opposite Protocells can sense, move, and replicate, but they are not alive. The Amoeba Trainer promotes the concept of bioengineered materials that can be 3D printed protocell by protocell in the shape of a runner's foot, then "turned on" with the user's movement, causing them to flock to areas where the most support is needed.

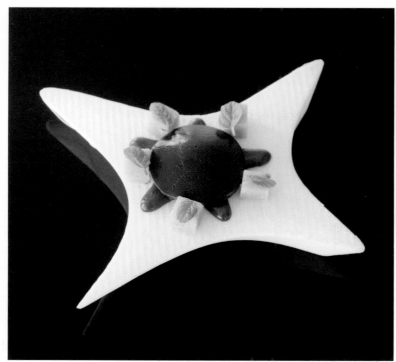

Robots in Gastronomy is a research group based in Spain, where chef Paco Morales and architects at GGLab have successfully 3D printed crockery and food.

3D PRINTING OF FOOD

There are some similarities between the growing of products and the current revolution in 3D printing. Though this phenomenon will be covered in more detail in the "Additive Manufacturing" chapter of this book, the idea of "growing" a substance through the cumulative adding on of material offers some great ways to manipulate biological materials not possible previously. Indeed, the successful production of 3D-printed food (www.robotsingastronomy.com) suggests that we are not far away from the blurring of the lines between grown and printed things.

CHEMISTRY OF PLASTICS: NATURAL VS PETRO

We know that almost all of the plastics utilized in the products we use in everyday life derive from oil. This oil, as we know, is the combination of many long-dead plant and animal species from prehistoric times. It is possible therefore that we could manufacture all the plastics we need from natural sources—grow them—as is shown by the currently large range of bioplastics we use. We need to move quickly to a "third stage" of bioplastics, those made from large-scale production of plant species that are neither a food source for humans nor require the displacement of food crops (this topic is examined in the discussion of "Altered Naturals" in the *Architecture* book in this series). This third-stage production is exemplified by such sources as switchgrass (though even this produced on a large scale could affect local ecosystems), algae, bacteria, and to a certain extent, waste streams from the production of food from crops, though care must be taken that these wastes could not be effectively turned into food sources of some kind. Beyond this third stage is the potential to produce plastics from the carbon from CO_2, and there are some companies (for example, Bayer in collaboration with RWE, a power generator, of Germany) that will be bringing this production on line in 2015. Getting this production to the efficiency and cost effectiveness of our current oil-based solutions will take some work, but is possible, and viable.

Thinking beyond the simple replacement of oil-based plastics with those from bio or waste sources, there have been some effective forays into using biological sources to "grow" our products. Suzanne Lee's BioCouture fabrics and products show how it is possible to use warm kombucha tea to create fabric-like materials that can be sewn together, dyed, and made into clothing (though of an indoor sort, as they are yet to be made fully waterproof).

On a more conceptual level, the Biolace project (www.carolecollet.com) from Carole Collet is investigating the possibility of biological manufacturing through "exploring the cellular programming of morphogenesis in plant systems." Combining food production with textile production, fruits and vegetables such as strawberries, basil, spinach, and tomatoes are engineered to also produce couture lace from their root structures. Similarly, Shamees Aden and Dr. Martin M. Hanczyc have proposed the use of "protocells," "a form of synthetic biology that blurs the gap between the non-living and the living," which they aim to use to develop a high-performance running sneaker that has visual similarities to the Vibram FiveFingers so beloved of barefoot runners but that also actively adapts to the requirements of the user's foot.

And it is such examples as this that show that, unlike the relatively basic chemistry of the majority of the plastics we use on a daily basis, there is a complexity in living systems that is both more responsive and also more susceptible to the ecosystem around it. Some of the biggest challenges to biomimicry today revolve around the weakness of natural solutions when taken out of the ecosystem in which they evolved. Spider silk is, weight for weight, three times stronger than steel, but expose it to certain adverse conditions and it suddenly fails—we need to adapt the basic advantages of the combination of amino acids and protein crystals to a more robust solution that can work in a wider range of applications.

So when we design using biological systems, we need a much greater understanding of their advantages and limitations, something that will inevitably require a certain change in the way we think about our relationship with the products we use. Nature produces beauty very easily, but not uniformity. When "growing" products, inevitably we will see slight variations in their formation, which in today's industrially produced world are seen as imperfections but in the natural world are, rather, variations on a theme of perfection. No one worries that no two apples look alike or that the wood grain in a table does not repeat perfectly. Thus we will need to adjust our viewpoint on products that are "grown" to appreciate the infinite variety of nature. Some might say that with the current trend in mass customization—wanting our very own version of a shoe, phone, bag, bike, or car—we are primed for this variation in every product already. Add to this the rather ephemeral nature of a lot of the products we consume—for many their life span is from six months to a few years—and the idea that anything so transient should be made from materials that can last hundreds of years seems counterproductive.

Of course, it is no accident that this revolution in "grown" materials and products aligns well with our concerns over environmental impact. Products such as Mushroom Materials from Ecovative (www.ecovativedesign. com), a packaging, insulation, and construction material from agricultural waste and mycelium, exemplify this, very effectively following the "Cradle to Cradle" principles that are the ideal of sustainable production. However, it is not just the "natural" aspect of this material that makes its development so influential: the fact that it uses nature's own preference for low-energy manufacture puts it at a massive advantage over other grown materials such as cotton that require intensive farming to produce high yields—Mushroom Materials require no water, light or fertilizer, and grow to inches of thickness in a few days. That the production can also happen at the location it is needed (Dell has been piloting a process that "grows" its laptop packaging needs in the basement below the computer production facility) leads to greater chances for localized production, reducing further the impact of shipping.

This is the opportunity that grown materials and grown products offers—the evolution to a lower impact, localized, more beautiful range of products, that last only as long as we need them, can be used at the end of their useful life to feed future products and truly work with natural processes and cycles to satisfy our needs and desires. Who would not want that?

As a final thought, it should be noted that for this revolution to work, we will need the involvement of big chemistry and big agriculture. Though the creative breakthroughs, the "a-ha" moments may well come from inspired individuals starting up companies, the mass-production work to ensure that the revolution becomes a reality will likely be from faceless multinationals that many in the localization movements rail against. This is because to feed and produce for the currently seven billion on this planet, it is the organizations already set up for this type of mass production that will make the grassroots development possible on a workable, successful, global scale.

HEMP CHAIR

DESIGNER / MANUFACTURER
Studio Aisslinger
www.aisslinger.de

MATERIAL
Acrodur (binder)

MATERIAL MANUFACTURER
BASF

DESIGNER BIOGRAPHY
Berlin-based Werner Aisslinger delights in making use of the latest technologies, helping to introduce new materials and techniques to the world of product design. His unique gel furniture that defines the "Soft Cell" collection and the "Soft" chaise for Zanotta from 2000 stand out, as does the "Juli" chair for Cappellini, which introduced a new "polyurethane integral foam" and became the first chair by a German designer since 1964 to enter the permanent collection of the Museum of Modern Art in New York.

MATERIAL PROPERTIES
Sustainable Solutions, Rapidly Renewable

A monobloc stackable armchair, especially one as thin as the Hemp Chair, needs reinforcement to keep its shape. Designs with similar engineering are made with reinforced plastics. This chair utilizes the high stability and light weight of the hemp fibers that comprise 75 percent of its composition.

Werner Aisslinger has spent a great deal of time thinking about hemp, by necessity. For two years he worked to develop a stackable, monobloc chair made from natural fiber, and as with so many things he touches, the design of the Hemp Chair for the Italian furniture company Moroso elevates this humble material to new heights of style and innovation.

Stackable chairs, going back to grade school, are so pervasive that most people barely give them a second thought. But crafting an entire chair from one single piece of material is an exceptionally challenging process, particularly at a time when the furniture industry is moving away from plastic and metal toward natural, sustainable alternatives.

With its curvaceous, cantilevered form, the Hemp Chair echoes Verner Panton's overtly futuristic "S" chair, the first single-form, injection-molded plastic chair from 1960. But unlike its sleek predecessor, Aisslinger's design gives new life to one of the world's earliest domesticated plants—*Cannabis sativa*. Hemp has been grown for millennia in Asia and the Middle East, and its documented use not just as a mind-altering drug but for such items as rope, sailcloth, shoes, and paper dates back at least to the Iron Age.

Much of Aisslinger's work, and rightly so, rests on the belief that visionary and pioneering designs emerge from the transformation of materials and technology into a new context. Here, he has looked outside of furniture design to repurpose a technology common to the automotive industry and revived an age-old material, all toward charting a new path forward.

MATERIAL INSIGHT

This Hemp Chair combines two innovative materials for chair production in one unique design. A one-piece fibrous panel from hemp is heat-formed to create the chair's final shape, utilizing the strength of the hemp fibers to ensure

a stiff yet compliant structure. BASF's Acrodur, a solvent-free water-based resin system, is used as a compatible binder for the fibers, and is a low-environmental-impact alternative to epoxy. The binder system can be pigmented any color but the hemp fibers will always add a more earthy hue to the composite. Alternatively, as is the case for the Hemp Chair, the surface can be color-coated. This hemp fiber/Acrodur binder combination creates a system that offers a truly new way of creating stackable furniture that utilizes natural materials and a low-toxicity process.

above Containing no phenols or formaldehyde, Acrodur is used by car manufacturers to make resin-impregnated fiber mats for interior door trims. The Hemp Chair shows just how thin Acrodur parts can be made, and at a lower weight and cost than reinforced plastic.

BIOCOUTURE

DESIGNER / MANUFACTURER

Suzanne Lee
biocouture.co.uk

MATERIAL

Grown, molded, and hand-sewn microbial cellulose fermented in green tea

DESIGNER BIOGRAPHY

BioCouture is a pioneering design consultancy focused on bringing living and biobased materials to fashion, sportswear, and luxury brands by collaborating with innovative creatives in design and science. Founder Suzanne Lee's book *Fashioning the Future: Tomorrow's Wardrobe* was the first to map out the future landscape of technological innovation in fashion, from spray-on dresses to talking T-shirts. From 2000 to 2011 Lee was Senior Research Fellow in the School of Fashion and Textiles at Central Saint Martin's College of Art and Design, London. A TED Senior Fellow, she lectures, curates, and exhibits work internationally.

MATERIAL PROPERTIES

Sustainable Solutions, Rapidly Renewable, Biodegradable/Compostable

Update your spring outerwear with . . . bacterial cellulose? In shades of beetroot and green tea? It is not so far-fetched an idea if, like eco-fashion designer Suzanne Lee, you believe biology may hold the key to "Fashioning the Future"—the title of her seminal text on how to harness new materials and processes to help safeguard our precious natural resources through sustainable apparel.

Lee's aim, to discover if synthetic biology can develop organisms capable of growing consumer products, is pursued through decidedly humble materials. By allowing green tea, sugar and microbes to ferment, tiny cellulose threads form to become a mat that, as it dries and knits itself together, can conform to 3D shapes or be cut and sewn into garments. The cellulose is highly absorbent, making it receptive to experiments with color and pattern using natural dyes. The garments are naturally biodegradable, bound for the compost bin rather than the dump.

Fashion encompasses a wide range of industries, from agriculture to artisans to architecture, and therefore has a huge global impact on labor and the environment. Pushing past the cliché of hemp dresses and cork sandals to produce, with needle and thread, beautiful, sustainable clothes in such a trend-focused, seasonally driven industry is no small feat. The excitement for Lee is the ability to imagine growing a whole range of applications through highly efficient microbes that produce no waste. Ultimately the material may not be bound for the dressing room, but the exciting possibilities resulting from her experiments offer an elegant model for updating our views on lasting environmental change, not just our wardrobes.

MATERIAL INSIGHT

A truly "grown" fabric that moves beyond our traditional concepts of how apparel should be constructed and look

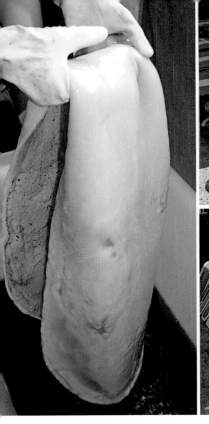

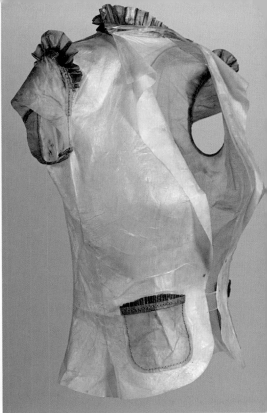

above and below After two weeks microbial cellulose forms a sheet where liquid meets air. Bacteria on the surface extrude chains of molecules that group into microfibrils and bundle to form the ribbons of the sheet.

above center top A mini "fabric farm" ferments multiple sheets of microbial cellulose cultures in a static system of plastic containers.

above center bottom After harvesting, the wet material is laid out on wooden boards to air-dry.

above The Bio Ruff Jacket is molded and hand-sewn from grown microbial cellulose fermented in green tea. The body is molded over a wooden dress form when wet, allowing seams to bond with evaporation. The collar, sleeves, and pockets are sewn when dry.

above The Bio Bomber Jacket features an engineered print using vegetable pulps: beetroot, blueberry, and raspberry are applied through laser-cut stencils.

opposite Color and structure work organically in Suzanne Lee's designs. The seams around zippers as well as the studs of the Bio Biker Jacket are visible because of the density of the material, which also indicates added strength.

more akin to the technologically advanced polyurethane membranes. These sheets of material have been produced through the action of bacteria on sugary kombucha tea. Naturally amber in color and translucent when sufficiently thin, the material can have graphics, textures, pigmentation and shapes incorporated into it as it grows, offering the chance for one-piece structures and one-of-a-kind production. As with many organic materials, this material has limited durability in certain environments, with water being its main enemy, a limitation that the designer is working hard to overcome by potentially using coatings or treatments to the surface.

BOGOBRUSH

DESIGNER
John McDougall
www.bogobrush.com

MANUFACTURER
Do., LLC outsources custom manufacturing
to multiple suppliers

MATERIAL
Bamboo and Tynex fine filaments,
made from nylon 6

MATERIAL MANUFACTURER
DuPont

DESIGNER BIOGRAPHY
John McDougall is an award-winning industrial
designer who has worked for Fisker Automotive,
Peugeot, General Motors, and Dean Kamen.
In 2010, he co-founded Bogobrush with his
sister, Heather, on a mission to bring social and
environmental values into people's daily routines.

MATERIAL PROPERTIES
Sustainable Solutions,
Rapidly Renewable, Ergonomic

Made with water-based dye
and sustainable materials, the
Bogobrush has a cylindrical shape
designed to fit any size of hand and
be held comfortably in any position,
which benefits both the buyer and
the person to whom a second
brush is donated.

For the modern minimalist, the Bogobrush rings every bell. Combining the basic geometry of a sleek, cylindrical handle with an elemental material—in this case sustainable bamboo, whose innate form seems ideally suited to a toothbrush handle—this humble design delivers a prototype par excellence. A color-dipped base and matching bristles add graphic appeal, whether in basic white or a pop of turquoise.

This smart collision of eco-consciousness and elegance, however, also comes with a generous heart, attributed to both the designer and the user. Today, many people are without access to basic oral healthcare. For those who live in rural areas where a dentist is not available or those who cannot afford treatment, taking good care of their teeth can be difficult. So, North Dakota siblings Heather and John McDougall put in place a buy-one-give-one system designed to ensure that this is "the first toothbrush you will actually care about." For each Bogobrush that is purchased, another one is donated through a network of philanthropic partners to someone who lacks proper care.

While nuanced innovations come and go, the toothbrush remains a disposable tool, a prime example of built-in obsolescence, as dentists recommend changing brushes every three months. While bamboo is more durable than the average oral-care tool, it is also biodegradable:

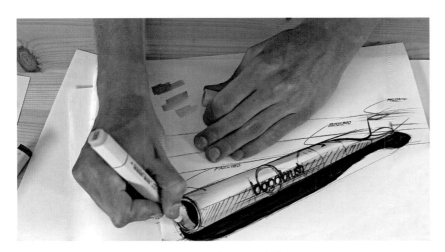

You simply pull out the nylon bristles with a pair of pliers and compost it. Which, in an age of excess with its emphasis on consumerism, allows the socially minded Bogobrush to thumb its nose at landfills not once, but twice.

MATERIAL INSIGHT

Adding to the seemingly endless number of applications for which bamboo can be effectively used, these toothbrushes offer a low-environmental-impact alternative to many existing solutions. The advantages of the fast-growing plant, together with its stiffness, ease of processing, and natural antibacterial properties make it ideal for this use. Though the polymer bristles need to be removed prior to discarding, at least 95 percent of the product (the bamboo) can in fact safely biodegrade. Tynex is used for the bristles, as a potentially biodegradable version, nylon 4, is not yet suitable for use in toothbrushes. The rapid growth of bamboo means that it is classed as "rapidly renewable," growing to harvestable size within ten years.

above McDougall's sketch shows early plans to make an ergonomic bamboo handle but it was a challenge to find a manufacturer that could execute the complex multi-curvature of the brush.

below and right As a Class I Medical Device the humble toothbrush bristle demands durable and well tested material. Bogobrush founders tried natural fibers and animal hairs, then nylon 4—which has shown promise in research—before settling on Tynex.

GORD BOTTLE

DESIGNER / MANUFACTURER
Jerry Mejia
www.jerrymejia.com

MATERIAL
Gourd fruit grown in a mold

DESIGNER BIOGRAPHY
Jerry Mejia's early knack for observation, eye for detail, and sensitivity to his environment have served him well as a multidisciplinary designer whose skills include industrial design, product development, 3D modeling, and graphic and website design. The native New Yorker and Parsons School of Design alumnus is a design engineer at Nulux, an architectural lighting manufacturer whose clients include the Museum of Modern Art, the Metropolitan Museum of Art, Prada, and Chanel. In 2009 he opened Jerry Mejia Design Studio, and has appeared in such publications as *Surface*, *Interior Design*, and *Metropolis*.

MATERIAL PROPERTIES
Sustainable Solutions, Rapidly Renewable, Durable

The Gord bottle positions itself between organic vessels used for thousands of years and products made with lightweight plastic constructions today. The concept strikes a balance between the natural and the processed, yielding a product with a smaller carbon footprint than other portable water bottles.

The appeal of spring water, with its promise of pure refreshment and healthful properties, may be the single most decisive factor in the quest for reusable water bottles. In 1856, Saratoga Springs, New York, among the most popular early water sources, was producing more than 7 million bottles of water annually. In 1908 the San Pellegrino mineral water distribution network stretched from Italy to the United States, China, and Australia.

In the intervening century our desire hardly seems to have been sated. Billions of plastic water bottles are discarded annually. But consumers have become concerned that chemicals used in plastic packaging, especially bisphenol A, or BPA, an estrogen-mimicking industrial chemical, can leach into consumable products, prompting beverage makers to revert to glass containers. The primary drawback is, of course, that glass breaks.

Jerry Mejia hopes to change that with the Gord bottle. Gourds are among the earliest domesticated plants, grown for both ornamental and utilitarian purposes. Mejia's ingenious design fuses natural systems with contemporary needs, producing a reusable water bottle that grows inside a mold to become a simple sleek container that is as dense as wood with a similar warm, organic feel.

While gourds are consistently prized for their interesting shapes, new contours are possible simply by tying soft string or bands around the young fruit. Mejia has gone a step further by providing options for customization. "The gourd fruit can be stained and carved," Mejia explains. "The bottle's logo is also designed into the mold, resulting in a debossed detail as the fruit hugs every possible surface."

MATERIAL INSIGHT

Going beyond just growing materials, this concept considers growing the product itself. Using the ancient water container solution of a gourd, the innovation is in the control of its

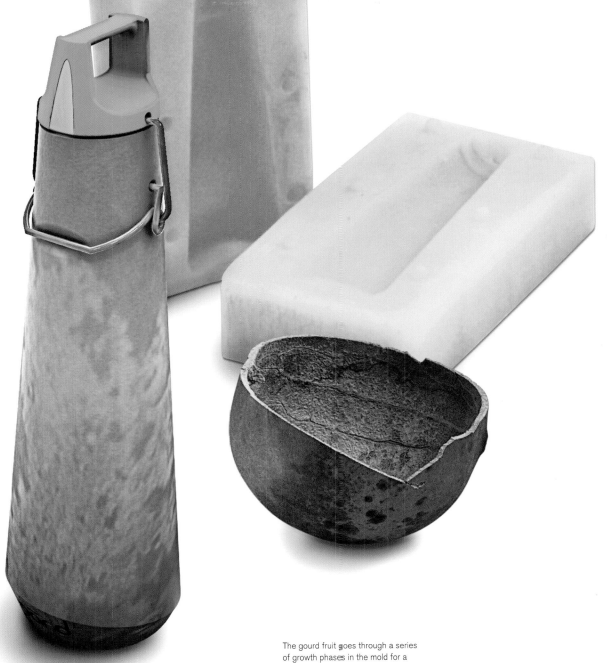

growth by the use of a shaped mold to create a standardized yet unique bottle. The texture and pattern on each bottle is dependent upon the growing pattern of the gourd, while the drying of the shape renders the shell as tough as wood. Since only the vine needs sunlight, and not the fruit (gourd) itself, the mold does not need to transmit light.

As with many aspects of nature, the process involves a slower production timeline than the plastic water bottle alternative—the gourd grows in approximately 120 days and takes a few months to dry—but the result is a more durable, uniquely grown product.

The gourd fruit goes through a series of growth phases in the mold for a couple of weeks. It is removed at the end of the growing period to prevent ongoing expansion outside of the mold, which may cause warping.

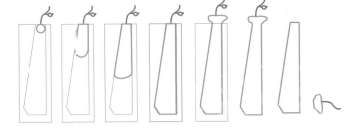

KELP
LAMPSHADES

DESIGNER / MANUFACTURER
Julia Lohmann
www.julialohmann.co.uk

MATERIAL
Laser-cut kelp sheets

DESIGNER BIOGRAPHY
Julia Lohmann is a professor of design at
the University of Fine Arts in Hamburg. She
has taught the MA Design Products course
at the Royal College of Art in London,
where she is engaged in a PhD studentship
in conjunction with the Victoria and Albert
Museum. Lohmann's objects and installations
are exhibited worldwide and in private and
public collections, including the Museum of
Modern Art, New York.

MATERIAL PROPERTIES
Sustainable Solutions, Rapidly Renewable,
Biodegradable/Compostable

opposite Julia Lohmann
began to work with *naga-
kombu* kelp from Hokkaido
when she was an artist-in-
residence in Sapporo, Japan.
In 2012, she brought her
experience with kelp to Vienna
Design Week, where she laser-
cut the leaves to showcase
process-oriented work
positioned between graphic
design and product design.

Early lampshades, rather than acting as screens,
functioned like reflectors, directing and amplifying
the light from the flames of oil lamps. With the
arrival of the electric light bulb in 1879, the shade
evolved into something more befitting its name, softening
and modulating the bright filament like a scrim.

With this invention came lampshades in a variety
of materials: silk, tole (painted tin), paper, largely inspired
by Japanese lanterns, and glass, in particular the designs
of Louis Comfort Tiffany, whose stained-glass lamps
depicting natural motifs became icons of American
decorative arts.

Today, London-based designer Julia Lohmann
continues the thread of handmade lampshades with designs
that do not merely reflect the natural world but speak
to its protection. In 2007, during a residency in Japan,
Lohmann produced "The Catch," an installation composed
of towering waves made from empty wooden fish crates
inspired by Tokyo's Tsukiji fish market. The installation,
as Lohmann explains, "probes our fatal beliefs in endless
supplies of marine life, in inflated fishing quotas and our
reluctance to act on scientific research."

Building on this aquatic theme, the following year
at the Salone del Mobile in Milan, Lohmann held a "Kelp
Constructs" workshop during which kelp from Japan and
Ireland was crafted into finished lighting designs. Visitors
could see the working process and touch the sustainable
material in different stages of production: dried, rehydrated,
stretched, varnished, and unvarnished.

Lohmann has since repeated the workshop for such
companies as Audi, and refined her use of kelp through
the fashioning of delicate, laser-cut lampshades that upend
the aesthetic and technical conventions of translucent
materials and propose a reevaluation both of kelp and
of lighting as we know it.

MATERIAL INSIGHT

Kelp has a surprisingly large range of applications, including emulsifying or bonding agents for toothpastes, shampoos, salad dressings, puddings, cakes, dairy products, frozen foods, and pharmaceuticals, and even as a source for renewable energy. It is fast-growing (some types can grow up to half a meter a day) and is commercially harvested globally in such locations as Norway, California, and China. Here, Julia Lohmann is using the translucent properties of its dried surface as a "grown" lampshade, with the frond easily manipulated into different shapes when wet, then drying into a rigid form. Laser-cutting of the kelp adds a technical aspect to the organic nature of the product.

Kelp, like other brown algae, stores energy in a different way from plants. Instead of starch (polymers of glucose), kelp produces laminarin chains of glucose and mannitol, which regulates water retention. Kelp cell walls also contain algin gum, a thickener and emulsifier used in the food and cosmetics industry. Julia Lohmann takes advantage of these algal attributes by manipulating kelp in its wet stage when algin is still elastic.

YULEX R2 FRONT-ZIP FULL SUIT

DESIGNER / MANUFACTURER
Patagonia and Yulex Corporation
www.patagonia.com
www.yulex.com

MATERIAL
Yulex biorubber (derived from guayule plant)

MATERIAL MANUFACTURER
Yulex Corporation

DESIGNER BIOGRAPHIES
Jason McCaffrey is the Director of Surf at Patagonia, where he has worked for more than fifteen years. He has an MBA from Pepperdine University's Graziadio School of Business and Management in California.

Jeffrey A. Martin is President and Chief Executive Officer of Yulex Corporation. Martin launched the sales operations of London Rubber Company's (Regent Medical) US startup in 1986, which subsequently became a global leader in the surgical glove market. He has held positions in both R&D and sales with the Professional Healthcare Group of the Kimberly-Clark Corporation, and the Ethicon division of Johnson & Johnson, Inc. in the Polymer Development Department.

MATERIAL PROPERTIES
Sustainable Solutions, Ergonomic, All-Weather Use

After ripping down a wave's face, then looping around in a series of spectacular S-turns, a surfer's exhilarating ride has often been accompanied by a whiff of petrol. The culprit was neoprene, a synthetic petroleum-based rubber invented by DuPont in 1930 that is commonly used in aquatic sports equipment because it is flexible and resilient and provides excellent insulation against cold.

Patagonia, however, thought they could do better. Begun by alpinists and surfers, the elite outdoor clothing company excels at harnessing design and innovation at the same time as searching for high-performance solutions to environmental problems. To significantly reduce the impact of fossil-fuel-based wetsuits on the environment, they knew that rather than merely improving on neoprene, they would need to replace it with a completely different material. After four years of experimentation, Patagonia introduced the results of their collaboration with Yulex, a clean-technology company developing agricultural-based biomaterials for a range of products.

Together they developed a unique biorubber made from the flowering guayule shrub, a plant indigenous to the arid southwestern United States, that resulted in a

60 percent plant-based wetsuit. While there are still strides to be made in eliminating neoprene, the partially "grown" suit has 30 percent more stretch than the average top-of-the-line wetsuit, dries faster, and is warmer. And while the human sense of smell is often seen as insignificant, in this case the pleasing aroma of eucalyptus and pine that results from the guayule sap is yet another way the suit stands out.

MATERIAL INSIGHT

The performance of this wetsuit is really the combination of numerous materials working in harmony together. The core of this alternative to neoprene is Yulex, a bio based rubber extracted from the guayule plant, which has 30 percent better stretch, excellent recovery, UV resistance, and durability. The Yulex is combined with a crumb rubber, then processed into sheets of the material. It is backed with a 25 percent recycled polyester fabric that offers insulation, as well as a top layer of super-texturized nylon spandex for strength and durability. Though currently forming only 60 percent of the rubbery neoprene alternative, the company is working to increase this to 100 percent.

opposite from left to right
Yulex harvests guayule from arid regions in the USA and separates the rubbery stems, which are milled into slurry. The milled stems are pressed to release pourable rubber-rich liquid and then centrifuged and purified into a biorubber emulsion that can be further processed into solid sheets.

right Latex allergies are caused by tropical allergenic proteins contained in natural rubber from *Hevea* latex Guayule is not only more elastic and often stronger than natural rubber, it also contains none of these proteins.

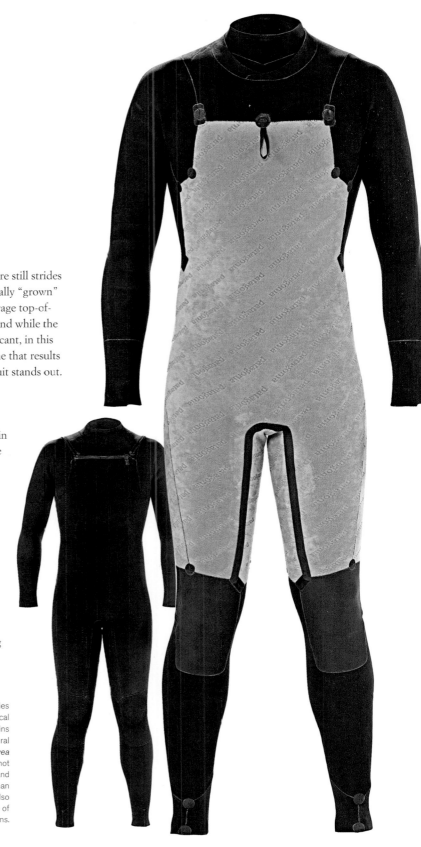

iNATURE iPHONE COVER

DESIGNERS

Luca Torresi and Carlo Vecchiola
www.lucatorresi.com

MANUFACTURER

Biomood Srl
www.inature.it

MATERIAL

Apinat

MATERIAL MANUFACTURER

API SpA

DESIGNER BIOGRAPHIES

Luca Torresi was born into a family of Italian shoe manufacturers; he left university to continue the family factory, F.lli Gismondi di Gismondi Gastone & C. In 2007, he bought a 25 percent stake in the Montegranaro-based TNT Group, which produces leather and textiles for shoes. In 2010 he and Paolo Pallotta launched Biomood Srl, producers of the iNature brand, where he serves as CEO.

Paolo Pallotta began his career selling plastic shoe soles in Monte Urano. He is now product manager at iNature, where his focus is to produce zero-impact products that possess exceptional design and workmanship befitting the "Made in Italy" slogan.

MATERIAL PROPERTIES

Sustainable Solutions, Rapidly Renewable, Stain-Resistant/Easy-Clean, Biodegradable/Compostable

Despite the vast options for customization, iPhone cases (rather than the phones themselves) have become commonplace objects, rarely the focus of innovation. Two Italian companies—Biomood and API—have leveraged their individual expertise in durable goods and thermoplastic compounds to form a partnership called iNature (playing on the theme of "me and nature"), where Italian design and innovative research have led to the first 100 percent biodegradable iPhone case. The secret is Apinat, a fully recyclable and biodegradable bioplastic that offers a level of flexibility and softness beyond anything else currently available. The case even gives off a fresh aloe/lemon scent. iNature biodegradable cases are available in a vast range of non-toxic colors.

Once they have been sent to be composted, the material quickly biodegrades by as much as 90 percent in approximately 180 days, a huge advance when you consider that petroleum-based plastics such as PET do not decompose in the same way organic material does simply because the micro-organisms responsible for biodegradation do not recognize it as food. But while the iNature cover readily breaks down in high-heat compost, it holds its shape with extended use and comes in a range of elegant neutrals and juicy bright colors.

Since zero environmental impact is the goal, all the packaging and display materials are also 100 percent biodegradable. The box is made with recycled cardboard and the inks are water-based.

iNature's cases and cable tidiers are made with Apinat, a range of fully recyclable bioplastics that can biodegrade in an aerobic environment.

MATERIAL INSIGHT

The world's first European-certified compostable elastomer
resin was used to create these shock-absorbing iPhone
accessories. The resin has much the same properties as
rubbery resins used for sports equipment, consumer
products, and electronics, but will decompose safely into
biomass and water in 180 days when subjected to industrial
composting conditions. In its natural state it is a white color,
so can be colored any hue but cannot be made clear. It is
also available in a range of hardnesses from rubbery to quite
stiff and can be molded by any of the current processes
used to create parts. The availability of this rubbery resin
widens the range of synthetic materials that are industrially
compostable; a great addition to the toolbox of quickly
biodegradable materials for the designer to select from.

Because it can be
processed, colored and
even scented like so
many traditional, polluting
materials, iNature's
biodegradable plastic is
easily adopted into existing
manufacturing chains.

COCO MAT
BOARD

DESIGNER
NSP / Global Surf Industries
www.surfindustries.com

MANUFACTURER
Cobra International
www.cobrainter.com

MATERIAL
Coco Mat technology

DESIGNER BIOGRAPHY
NSP is the largest global supplier
of surf and stand-up paddleboards.
The development of the Coco
Mat technology redefined the
strength-to-weight ratio and allowed
NSP to offer a product globally
that was strong, light, and more
environmentally friendly.

MATERIAL PROPERTIES
Sustainable Solutions,
Rapidly Renewable, Lightweight,
All-Weather Use

The Coco Mat boards
have a responsive,
fluid ride with great
flex characteristics.

For anyone passionate about surfing,
the pursuit of the perfect wave is
more than a mere sport. It takes
quiet, focused attention to read
the surface of the water and ultimately
become one with the ocean. A surfboard
offers the promise of this deep connection
with nature, while also reminding us of a
timeless truth: that the best way to move
something of any weight from one place to
another is to float it. This is as true today
as it was in 1778 when Captain James
Cook and his crew sailed to the Hawaiian
Islands aboard HMS *Resolution* and first
witnessed the locals riding in to shore on
long wooden boards without fins.

Given the sport's origins, there
is something intuitively obvious about a
surfboard made from the husk of a coconut.
This tropical, naturally buoyant "drift" fruit
is among a remarkable flotilla of plants that
travel across the earth's oceans, impervious
to salt water and fond of sandy soil. Yet it
has taken designers hundreds of years to
incorporate the coconut's thick fibrous husks
into surfboard designs.

Global Surf Industries (GSI), a young,
dynamic company whose motto—"Life is better
when you surf"—sums up its commitment to board
design, has developed a proprietary technology that is,
literally, at the core of "the lightest, strongest surfboard
on the market today." GSI is at the vanguard of surfboard
designers shaping new materials into families of dynamic,
flowing forms. The Coco Mat board's earthy palette stands
in direct contrast to the jazzy, neon aesthetic that is typical

of surf culture, and evokes the kind of sun- and sand-filled days that make surfing such a carefree dream.

MATERIAL INSIGHT

Coconut fibers, also known as coir, have been used for centuries as upholstery padding and for floor mats, brushes, rope, and string. The Coco Mat surfboard uses these fibers as an alternative to glass fibers to create a natural-fiber-based surface that is lighter in weight than standard boards. Although coir fibers are not quite as stiff individually as glass, they are combined with epoxy resin into thicker mats that create a stronger board overall. The fibers are a by-product of the food industry, require minimal processing, and in the case of this board manufacturer, are harvested locally to the board production site. Though not easily pigmented, the natural color of the fibers gives a unique golden hue to the board.

The natural fibers of the coconut are readily available, need minimal processing, and come from local self-sustaining crops.

CLEAR RESIN FLUID FINISH

FIBERGLASS

NATURAL COCONUT HUSK

FIBERGLASS

SECURE CELL E.P.S. CORE

FIBERGLASS

NATURAL COCONUT HUSK

FIBERGLASS

The most impressive characteristic of the coconut-husk fiber is its incredible strength-to-weight ratio. Integrating random discontinuous fibers into the lamination makes for an incredibly light and strong surfboard.

CORKY WATER BOTTLE

DESIGNER
Ruben Marques Pedro

MANUFACTURER
Polisport Plásticos
www.polisport.com

MATERIAL
Cork composite

MATERIAL MANUFACTURER
Amorim Cork Composites

DESIGNER BIOGRAPHY
Following an early career in communication
design, Ruben Marques Pedro earned a degree
in industrial design and joined GranDesign,
developing work for Philips, Swatch, and
BH Fitness, among others. Since 2010, he
has worked at Polisport, where he develops
bicycle and motorcycle products, while also
collaborating with such clients as KTM,
Husqvarna, Gas Gas, Rieju, and Decathlon.
He is passionate about sustainable mobility
and body-protection gear, both areas where
Polisport is currently developing new designs.

MATERIAL PROPERTIES
Sustainable Solutions, Lightweight,
All-Weather Use, Durable

When Portuguese product designer Ruben Marques Pedro, as part of his work for Polisport, a European leader in parts and accessories for bicycles and motorbikes, went looking for a solution to the waste piles of plastic water bottles generated by recreational cyclists, he turned to a material that is at the heart of Portugal's cultural heritage and a natural resource with excellent thermal properties: *Quercus suber*, or cork oak.

Cork oak forests cover nearly 2.7 million hectares (6.7 million acres) of Portugal, Spain, Italy, France, and North Africa. The harvesting of cork offers one of the finest examples of traditional, sustainable land use. Every ten years, foresters strip off the outer layer of bark with short-handled axes. The trees are then left with bare, reddish trunks revealing where the bark was shorn away. Properly done, the bark will grow back so that it can be harvested again in a decade. But to grow cork requires a long view, since new trees need twenty-five years or more before the first harvest.

The aptly named Corky is an outwardly modest but environmentally significant design that delivers a better-

In the spring or summer the soft layers of cork come away easily from the trunk. The virgin surface is soon covered with a new layer of bark that will protect it during the winter. Trees are harvested every nine to twelve years. The estimated lifespan of the most common species of cork oak is 200 years.

performing bottle by capitalizing on the inherent strengths of the thick, spongy bark while also cutting down on the emissions in the manufacturing process. The outer shell is composed of a mix of plastic and cork, resulting in a lighter product with a tactile appeal, rather than one derived from fossil fuels.

MATERIAL INSIGHT

The use of cork granulates for this bottle casing both reduces the amount of plastic needed, as well as the overall weight—cork is typically a quarter of the weight of most plastics. Add to this the improved thermal insulation, good hand feel, and impact resistance of cork, and this product offers significant improvements over standard plastics. The proportion of cork can be varied from a few percent to up to 60 percent and the plastic can be colored to give a specific overall hue to the composite. Cork/elastomer composites have been successfully used for the grips of screwdrivers, though only for sections of the handle, so this completely overmolded water bottle shows the extent to which these forms can be achieved by the material.

A cubic centimeter of cork bark contains approximately 40 million fourteen-sided cells, making for a highly insulating material. Many of these cells maintain their structure and thermal properties even after being ground up and mixed with resin for the final product.

SAMUEL WILKINSON

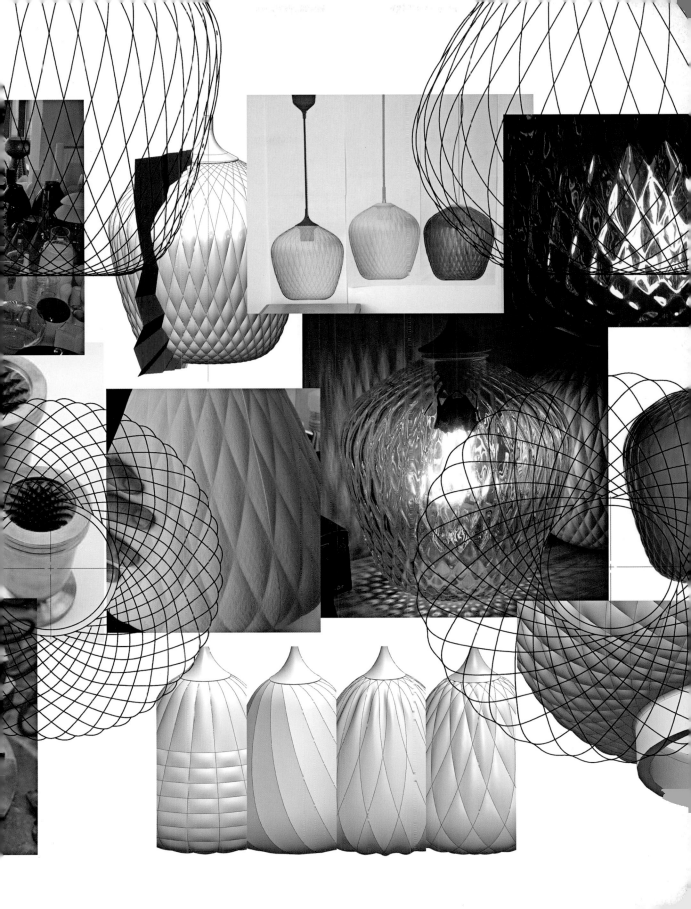

CHAPTER 2
SURFACE PROTECTION

W e want the real thing, but we also want it to look good forever. Very few modern products age well; we need to protect them, but not so much that the protection becomes obvious. The resultant "authenticity," stemming from the desire to have the real material shown as its authentic self, whether metal, natural or even plastic, is really a sham. Real woods are varnished to maintain their natural look, many metals are plated or coated to keep from staining, plastics are often painted to give a more even color, and any fabric that offers "performance" has typically been treated with some chemical to make it so. So we should be circumspect when considering "authenticity" with any modern material or surface, and accept that to keep the "real" look, it is likely that you are actually touching something else.

MULTIFUNCTIONAL COATINGS

Coatings are essential to the majority of our products, offering multiple functions: to protect—from water, staining, sun, corrosion, fingerprints, slipping; to enhance the look and feel of the product; but also, increasingly, to offer improved mechanical properties. The new era of structural coatings uses the coating process as a way of creating a higher-performing product, or simply enabling the use of a lower-cost substrate. Many of these come closer to approximating composites, with their intimate bonding with the base material and their ability to offer a stiffening component to the match. Some of the standout versions of these include the original Curran coating developed by CelluComp, which offers stiffnesses close

opposite Ampacet Corporation's masterbatch color for PET molding resins lends metallic hues to these bottles while eliminating many of the processes involved with traditional colors and additives, to produce a lower-cost alternative to metal.

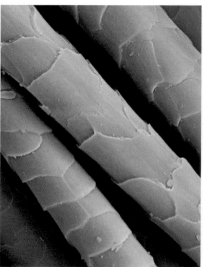

left An ultra-thin layer of Nanopool Liquid Glass is composed of silicon dioxide (SiO_2) extracted from quartz sand. When sprayed these molecules self-organize and interlink to create new surface properties, such as hydrophobicity shown here. This coating will cling to any surface (wool fiber pictured **above**) and seal it at a micro level.

to that of carbon fiber for a carrot-based dip coating; and the Nanovate coating from Integran, which uses a relatively thick nanostructured coating to offer much-improved stiffnesses for plastic parts. Also added to this list should probably be the amorphous zirconia metal coatings from Liquidmetal Technologies that use specific formulations of zirconium alloy to give super-hard surfaces for medical and sports equipment and high-end consumer products. The most scratch-resistant of all are still the diamond and DLC (diamond-like carbon) coatings, which are deposited by PVD (physical vapor deposition), putting down the structure atom layer by atom layer. Though of limited flexibility, they are transparent if laid down thin enough, and you cannot get anything harder.

As coatings for protection have evolved, in the same way that composite materials have superseded monomaterials, new finishes combine the durability of a metal or ceramic with the ease of deposition and flexibility of a plastic. Metal and ceramic particles loaded into liquid-deposited coatings give greater hardnesses and durability, and the appearance of metal—with the ability to polish or

tarnish like a metal—or ceramic. Ceramic-loaded paints such as Cerakote, and the range of metal-like coatings from PS Oberflachen and Luminore, are showing that it is possible to create ostensibly ceramic or metal surfaces without the challenges of depositing these high-performance surfaces.

Protection does not always have to be hard and structural. Despite being glass-based, some of the new silica nanocoatings such as Liquid Glass from Nanopool offer incredible flexibility, thanks to their thinness (glass fiber when sufficiently fine is flexible enough to knit). Suitable for coating and protecting fabrics, food preparation surfaces, automotive interiors and building exteriors, these breathable, transparent surfaces bond through quantum forces and give stain and water resistance to anything they coat.

BIOMIMICRY

In our desire to mimic nature, the self-healing coating—which acts like skin and heals itself after damage—is something that scientists have been trying to perfect for a number of years. Scott White's team at the University of Illinois has had perhaps the greatest success, but we are still some way from a repeatedly healing surface that can repair all damage. Some of the automotive topcoats rely on a viscoelastic film "reforming" after being scratched, sometimes with a little help from a heat gun or the sun.

P2i and other plasma-deposited fluorocarbon (the chemistry of Teflon in non-stick pans and Gore-Tex membranes) water-resistant coatings have been successful at offering "total product" water resistance, including those products that have intricate parts and small holes, as the plasma gas process infiltrates the inner workings of the product to protect even the insides from water damage. Debuted on Timberland's Earth Keepers boots, the process is being used ubiquitously to coat cell phones and other small consumer electronics. Looking beyond these, some of the most advanced stain-resistant coatings offer a surface so slick that almost nothing will stick to them. These "superhydrophobic" coatings use nanotech, an example being Ultra-Ever Dry from Resource Energy Group that is both hydro- (water) and oleo- (oil) phobic, repelling paints, greases, glues, oils, sugars, and of course water.

Biomimicry has also made some progress toward solving the problem of stain and water resistance. Inspired by the way in which the lotus leaf self-cleans (micro hairs on its surface cause water to roll off and take with it dirt and debris), micro- or nanotextured surfaces are being created to achieve similar results. These can be molded into the surface of the part, as produced by companies such as Hoowaki, or applied as edible, non-stick coatings to the insides of condiment bottles as seen for Liquiglide. This mechanical solution (rather than chemical as for the fluorocarbon Teflon coatings) is a more elegant alternative, though, like the lotus leaf, can sometimes suffer from limited damage resistance.

So, in response to our desire to have all of our products be authentic but also look good for ever, coatings are evolving to become thinner, more flexible and less noticeable and to offer greater protection, with some of the latest solutions mimicking nature by becoming self-cleaning and antibacterial through structure alone. Coatings are turning out to be the best thing about our products that you never knew was there.

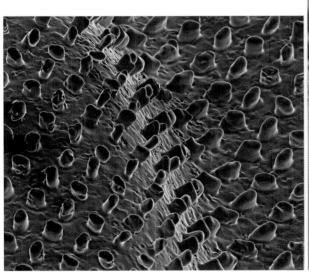

VOYAGER LEGEND

DESIGNER / MANUFACTURER
Plantronics
www.plantronics.com

MATERIAL
Splashproof nanocoating

MATERIAL MANUFACTURER
P2i

DESIGNER BIOGRAPHY
Plantronics Design treats the human form as a canvas from which to begin the design process of creating advanced products that look beautiful and become extensions of the body. To achieve this, Plantronics's vice president of Corporate Design, Darrin Caddes, has assembled a world-class team of industrial design professionals from diverse backgrounds and design companies. Each member of the Plantronics Design team brings a special expertise, which collectively inspires innovation and creative breakthroughs, ensuring Plantronics stays at the forefront of customers' taste and marketing needs.

MATERIAL PROPERTIES
Lightweight, Stain-Resistant/Easy-Clean, All-Weather Use

The headset is protected from moisture by a coating whose thickness is equivalent to one thousandth that of a human hair.

To the uninitiated, it can seem as though wireless headsets do not evolve much from year to year. The basics may look nearly identical, but in the world of wireless handset accessories, the biggest advances are often incremental and inconspicuous. Most headset innovation has been focused on streamlining devices with nanotechnology while enhancing their performance.

As pragmatically conceived as it is elegant, the Voyager Legend seems poised to live up to its name. The mobile Bluetooth headset system enhances the management of mobile and desk phone calls through a simple yet technologically sophisticated solution, but also goes a step further. Voyager Legend headsets are protected against moisture damage by technology from P2i. The nanocoating results in invisible liquid-repellent properties that make the headset more reliable.

Putting the headset on will answer an incoming call, or transfer one that is in progress from a phone to the headset. Taking off the headset will transfer the call back to the phone or pause audio. A tap on the voice command button is all that is needed to check the battery level or the connection status. Beyond these benefits, sports enthusiasts and active wearers would be wise to take note: human sweat contains a high amount of salt and minerals, which work as corrosive agents. The coating guards against this, a real plus as commuter bikes thrive.

MATERIAL INSIGHT

Water and electronics do not mix. Water damage is the number one reason for malfunctioning phones (mostly dropped in toilets) and a constant concern for newer lifestyle products that are expected to go everywhere we do. PTFE- (polytetrafluoroethylene, or Teflon) type coatings have been the solution for water repellency for many products but are challenged with concerns over the "slick" feeling of the

material, and the use of large amounts of fluorocarbons. In addition, they are unable to cover the complex surfaces typical of products such as this headset. The coating from P2i is a revolution in water resistance in that it uses plasma—the fourth state of matter that is a gas-like cloud of atoms—to infiltrate tiny crevices so that even the sensitive electronics inside the product are made resistant to water. The process uses a vacuum chamber, in which every surface of the product is able to be coated.

The nanocoating developed by P2i covers every crevice of the headset, making it less vulnerable to reduced performance or even malfunction after exposure to humidity, rain, or the inevitable coffee spill.

MICRALOX COATING ON ALUMINUM

DESIGNER
Dr. Mike Sung, Sanford Process
www.sanfordprocess.com
www.micralox.com

MANUFACTURER
D-CHN
www.d-chn.com

MATERIAL
Micralox® aluminum oxide coating

MATERIAL MANUFACTURER
Sanford Process

DESIGNER BIOGRAPHY
Technical manager Dr. Mike Sung led the Micralox development team as the project's lead researcher and is the principal author of the patent applications. Sung completed his PhD in Chemical Engineering at the University of Illinois, Chicago, in 1993. Before joining D-CHN in 2007, he worked for Oxford Instruments, Waters Corporation, and Millipore Corporation in technical and product development. Supporting Sung in the development of Micralox were Jack Tetrault, President of Sanford Process Corporation, and Tim Cabot, head of D-CHN, the parent of Sanford Process.

MATERIAL PROPERTIES
Nanotech, All-Weather Use, Durable, High Strength

Materials come in all shapes and sizes. The tendency is to think of them as discrete entities waiting to be given a purpose, molded into a form or a product. Sometimes, though, materials are best served as companions, adjuncts to another material, without which both would be decidedly less, their full potential far from realized.

Micralox, a revolutionary aluminum coating, is one such example. Micralox creates an extraordinarily resistant barrier to various forms of aluminum corrosion, which makes it ideally suited to tough environments where a long-lasting, virtually indestructible surface is needed. Unlike a conventional amorphous anodic coating (a surface treatment that increases resistance to corrosion and improves adhesion for paints and glues but which can also be brittle and susceptible to fissures), Micralox offers a unique microcrystalline barrier that makes it especially suitable to aggressive environments where new approaches to finishing equipment made from aluminum are needed.

When you take into account factors such as the weight, thermal conductivity, strength, and cost of products made from aluminum, as a base material it is clearly preferable to stainless steel or plastic. Micralox reinforces the metal's role as an excellent alternative to more expensive options, especially in situations where disinfection and repeated cleaning is a requirement. Micralox is able to protect equipment from corrosion due to harsh chemicals and cleaning detergents, such as sterile medical devices or food-processing equipment, both of which require absolute cleanliness.

In automotive and, especially, in marine environments, where salt water is ever present, Micralox is also appropriate, providing a potent reminder of how a single material innovation can have broad-reaching implications that directly affect daily life.

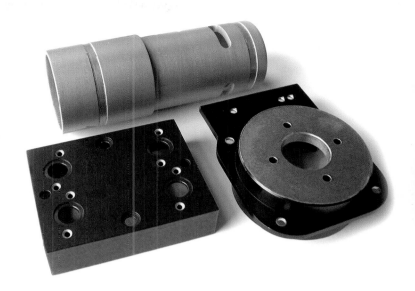

MATERIAL INSIGHT

Aluminum is a high-performance metal that offers great machinability, stiffness, and thermal conductivity and can easily be alloyed to further enhance its properties. However, it has had limited application in certain industries because of its susceptibility to strongly acidic and alkali solutions. Anodizing can offer protection, but even this does not fully protect the surface. The Micralox coating creates a highly ordered, microcrystalline anodized surface that protects the metal even in corrosive environments such as dishwashers, sterilization procedures and sanitization cleaning, enabling it to be used for medical equipment.

opposite Color can be embedded with specialized ink into the microcrystalline surface of these Micralox-anodized parts with Sanford Print technology.

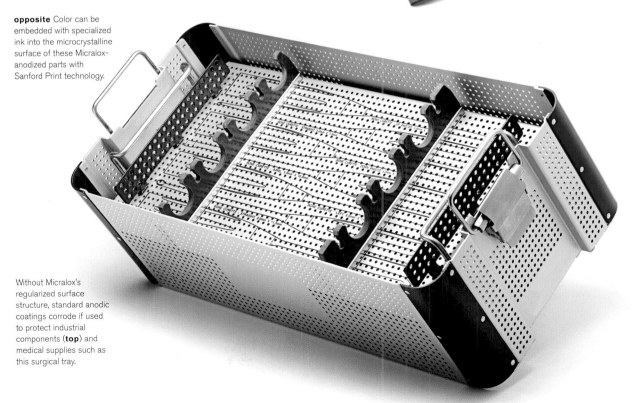

Without Micralox's regularized surface structure, standard anodic coatings corrode if used to protect industrial components (**top**) and medical supplies such as this surgical tray.

BLOOM COOKWARE

DESIGNER
Enrico Azzimonti
www.enricoazzimonti.it

MANUFACTURER
Pavoni Italia
www.pavonitalia.com

MATERIAL
Liquid-crystal polymer (LCP)
and platinic silicone

DESIGNER BIOGRAPHY
Enrico Azzimonti studied at the Polytechnic
University of Milan where he obtained a degree
in architecture in 1993. The following year he
founded his own studio, focusing on architectural
and industrial design. In 1995, he received his
Master's in Design and Management at the same
university. He has held workshops at several
universities including the IUAV of Venice, the
IUAV of San Marino, La Sapienza University
of Rome, the Istituto Marangoni in Milan, and
the European Institute of Design in Milan.

MATERIAL PROPERTIES
Lightweight, Stain-Resistant/Easy-Clean, Durable

opposite Bloom cookware is
protected by silicone-coated
LCP, which is packed with
fibrous polymers that retain
their structure to temperatures
as high as 450° C (840° F).

The Italian designer Enrico Azzimonti is known for sexy, well-crafted product designs. These include a curvaceous line of suspended lamps for Zava; the witty Ruota del Tempo ("wheel of time") perpetual calendar composed of elegant ceramic discs for Diamantini & Domeniconi; Flutter, a sleek iPad stand for BLM Group; and the whimsical Bateau Ivre ("drunken boat") sugar cubes that he conceived with collaborator Jordi Pigem for pastry chef Ernst Knam.

For Pavoni Italia, leaders in kitchenware and tools, he designed Bloom, a line of cookware made of an LCP technopolymer coated with platinic silicone, which allows for a lush range of colors and finishes. With typical intelligence, Azzimonti abandoned the standard set of pots and lids in different sizes, replacing it with a versatile, interchangeable system in which each component can be used on its own or in combination to create different volumetric forms. Pans become a cake tin become cocottes, and so on, all of them working in conventional ovens and microwaves, in the fridge, and on the table. Both the name and the distinctive scallop rim inject innovation with *joie de vivre*.

MATERIAL INSIGHT

Plastics are inexorably taking over many of the accepted roles for metals and ceramics, whether in planes, cars, sports equipment, or, now, cookware. This collection of Bloom cookware utilizes two of the plastics best suited to the high heat and corrosive environment of modern cooking. Liquid-crystal polymer (LCP) is used to create the form of each of these products, since it can easily withstand oven temperatures and is resistant to corrosion from acids and alkalis. Silicone, that other synthetic wonder-material now ubiquitous in cookware, is used to coat the LCP, giving it a high-gloss surface, saturated color, and easy cleanability from the non-stick surface.

MC METAFUSE BINDING LINE

DESIGNER / MANUFACTURER
Union Binding Company
www.unionbindingcompany.com

MATERIAL
Nanovate CoP

MATERIAL MANUFACTURER
Integran Technologies

DESIGNER BIOGRAPHY
The Union Binding Company is an independent brand whose goal is to produce the best bindings on the planet for snowboarders who thrash their gear and expect it to survive. Notable for its use of innovative materials, it is the first and only company in the snowboard industry to employ MetaFuse, following three years of intense research and design.

MATERIAL PROPERTIES
Nanotech, All-Weather Use

The plastic highback of the MC MetaFuse binding is buffered from the damaging contortions of boarders' shifting weight with a fine-grain metallized Nanovate coating.

Since the Christmas morning in 1965 when Sherman Poppen cross-braced two inexpensive skis together, stood at the top of his backyard hill and started sledding down while standing up, snowboarding has grown into a multi-million dollar business. While the commodification of snowboarding's indie spirit has muted its edgy brilliance, the sport remains a source of energy and invention. Today, most of the sport's advances spring from innovative materials, in a perpetual quest for lightness, strength, and flexibility.

Unlike many brands, Union Binding's sole focus is the crucial point of contact between rider and board. If well matched to a rider's board and riding style, snowboard bindings can have a decisive impact on the quality of the ride by swiftly initiating the transfer of energy and response from the smallest bodily shifts of weight and thrust.

Of all the bindings that Union makes, the MC MetaFuse binding possesses the most material-driven advantages. Nanometal heelcups are exceptionally light and strong. The highback, a vertical plate that rises from the ankle to help control the board's rear edge, is symmetrically shaped with asymmetrical openings of full carbon. The hardware throughout the binding is crafted from CNC-anodized aluminum to further enhance lightness, while a carbon-fiber accelerator transmits power from heel to toe.

Snowboarding is among the most dynamic of sports, from free riding off-piste to freestyle jumps, spins and tricks, and the MC binding streamlines the sport so there is less material, less weight, and fewer restrictions.

MATERIAL INSIGHT

Most metallic coatings for plastics offer two advantages—protection and aesthetic enhancement. The Nanovate nanostructured coatings change the idea of a traditional coating into something

that provides additional structural strength. Increasing the
thickness of the metal layer gives the part—in this case the
back sections of snowboard bindings—improved stiffness
and greater resistance to failure, because the coating is now
taking a lot of the strain. It is as though the plastic is simply
a substrate onto which the coating is laid down, enabling
greater complexity of design for the part than would be
possible with standard casting. The nanostructured form
of this nickel- or cobalt-based alloy also enhances its strength
when in such thin sections.

Increasingly thin elements
could break if not protected
by the more resilient
nanocrystalline metal
coating from Integran.

CST-01

DESIGNERS
Jerry O'Leary and Dave Vondle

MANUFACTURER
Central Standard Timing
www.centralstandardtiming.com

MATERIAL
E Ink segmented display

MATERIAL MANUFACTURER
E Ink Corporation

DESIGNER BIOGRAPHIES
Central Standard Timing was founded by Dave
Vondle, an interaction designer and electrical
engineer, and Jerry O'Leary, an industrial
designer and mechanical engineer, while
both were working at IDEO. Together, the
founders have a combined twenty-four years
of experience in inventing, engineering, and
designing products for the world's top brands.

MATERIAL PROPERTIES
Lightweight, Stain-Resistant/Easy-Clean

At 12 grams (0.42 oz),
the CST-01 watch uses
E Ink to achieve the "most
minimal expression of
a timepiece" described
by its creators as "time
embedded in a band."

It is not often that a typeface inspires a product but
such is the nature of the design process that a solution
for one project frequently begets another. In this case,
one with a strikingly superlative claim: the thinnest
watch in the world.

The CST-01 was designed by David Vondle and Jerry
O'Leary during their off hours from working for IDEO,
a global design and innovation firm. Based in Chicago
(hence CST for Central Standard Time), they were
inspired by the capabilities of E Ink's electronic paper
displays—exceptional thinness, legibility, robustness,
flexibility, and ultra-low power. With that as a starting
point, they experimented with adhering the digital display
to a metal spring strap, ultimately arriving at a solution
that involved laminating all the components—the interface
screen, the electronics and the thin-film battery that powers
the watch—into a 0.7-millimeter (0.03-inch) pocket in
a 0.9-millimeter (0.04-inch) titanium band.

To power the watch, a prototype charger base
station was 3D printed and fitted with a mini
Arduino board that enables an embedded
solid-state, thin-film battery to charge in twenty
minutes, last for more than a month, and
deliver a lifetime use of fifteen years, which
almost eliminates the need ever to change
a battery.

With watchmaking, advances are often
incremental and inconspicuous. The CST team's
outsider status freed them from having to follow
the strict codes of established watch design. Materials,
technologies, and processes new to the industry fully
deliver on the design's techno-futurist vibe, and helped
turn the duo into savvy entrepreneurs when they posted
the design on Kickstarter.com and far surpassed their
funding goal.

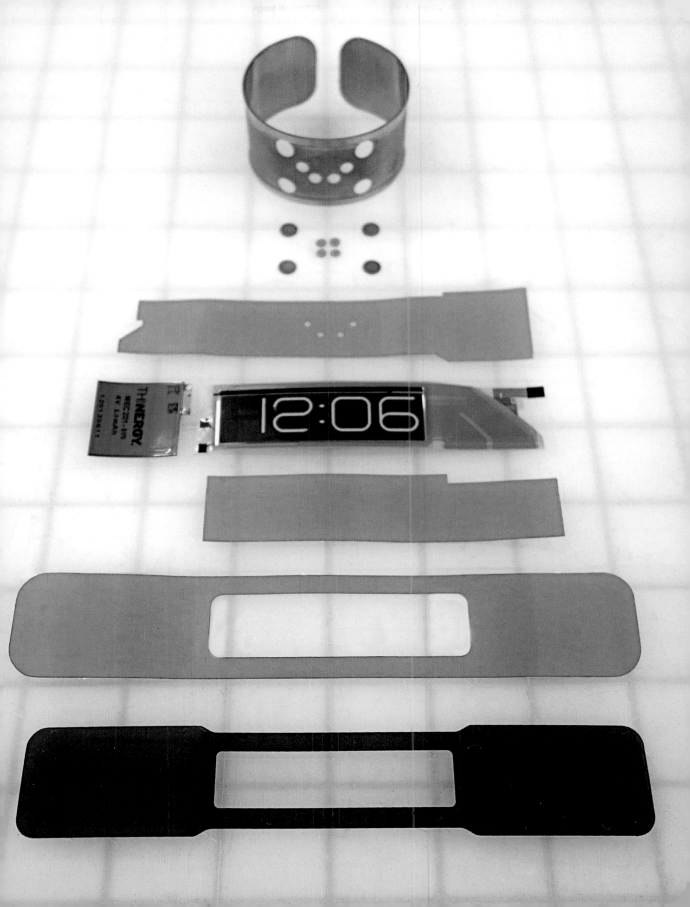

MATERIAL INSIGHT

Presaging the move toward slimmer and more flexible electronic devices, the CST-01 watch cleverly combines thin components into a titanium band that has had a 0.7-millimeter (0.03-inch) deep trough cut into it. A solid-state, thin-film battery, rechargeable 10,000 times during its fifteen-year lifespan, a system on a chip processor, and an E Ink display, all separated by wafer-like insulating layers, are combined within the trough, with charging and time setting achieved using a docking station. And it is this symbiotic relationship between the larger data-storage and powering part and the superlight portable device that currently shows the direction of such products, looking toward options that are more lifestyle objects than traditional electronics devices.

The watch uses energy only once a minute, when white and black particles migrate to opposite sides of the microcapsules that make up the segmented display.

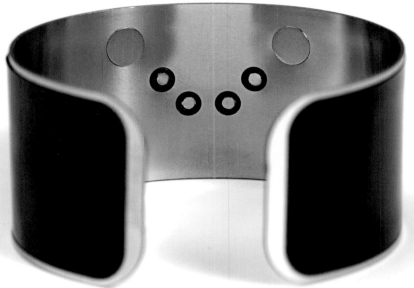

Thinner than a credit card, the CST-01 packs a microcontroller from Seiko. With a thin-film battery, charging takes a mere twenty minutes.

UE BOOM

DESIGNER
NONOBJECT
www.nonobject.com

MANUFACTURER
Ultimate Ears
www.ultimateears.com

MATERIAL
Water-resistant acoustic skin

DESIGNER BIOGRAPHY
NONOBJECT was founded in 2006 by Branko
Lukic, an acclaimed design visionary and former
lead designer at IDEO and frog, and Suncica
Lukic, an award-winning graphic designer and
brand strategist. The following year they were
joined by Steve Takayama, a renowned master
craftsman and former lead designer at IDEO.
Today, Branko Lukic and Takayama are the
creative partners behind NONOBJECT's design
practice, and Suncica Lukic directs the studio's
branding practice.

MATERIAL PROPERTIES
Stain-Resistant/Easy-Clean, All-Weather Use

The Swiss possess a graphic design heritage that
makes a trip to Basel akin to a pilgrimage. But,
compared with their German and Italian neighbors,
product design has not historically been their
strong suit. Logitech, a product design company based
in Morges, Switzerland, whose designs are now sold
worldwide, has been chipping away at this, first with the
computer mouse and now with a portfolio of interface
devices that include an entire category dedicated to music
and home entertainment.

Making stereo-quality sound portable has long been
a preoccupation of music lovers. The UE Boom (UE stands
for Ultimate Ears, a brand of custom in-ear monitors used by
musicians that Logitech acquired) Bluetooth speaker is small
enough to hold in one hand and has a tiny footprint. Unlike
most portable speakers, it is designed to stand upright rather
than on its side. Billed as the first social music player, it
delivers what Logitech calls 360-degree sound, accessible
via a smartphone or laptop.

The cylindrical shape is modeled on a bottle of water
and the styling has a similarly light, low-tech touch. Aside
from its vibrant array of colors—black, white, red, blue,
pink, and moss green—what stands out is the specially
developed acoustic skin, which is both water-resistant
and stain-resistant, giving the simple and elegant
device a quiet ruggedness.

When two Booms are paired up through the
company's free UE Boom app for iOS and Android,
the dream of anytime, anywhere wireless stereo that
can be shared with others is at last possible.

MATERIAL INSIGHT

In developing a truly portable wireless speaker for
the Millennial Generation, UE had the challenge
of creating a completely new category—high-quality

sound from a device that could be thrown in a backpack, rolled along a sticky bar or coffee table, or placed close to the water at a pool party. To do this they needed a speaker fabric that was at the same time splash-resistant, durable, and sufficiently sound-transparent not to reduce the impact of the speakers beneath. The resulting product used the type of mesh fabrics more often found on high-end office chairs, ingeniously wrapped around a cylindrical shape and tucked into shock-resistant ends molded from TPSiV, a silicone-containing rubber that gives a unique soft-touch surface.

right Armored with water-resistant and sound-translucent mesh, the UE Boom's surface is designed to be roughed up, so the colorways will not fade or scratch.

below, left and right The speaker's rugged, airtight, and water-resistant shell will not allow water to penetrate, yet is transparent to Bluetooth signals that connect users.

THE
GLIDER

DESIGNER / MANUFACTURER
Kammok
www.kammok.com

MATERIAL
Amphibiskin

MATERIAL MANUFACTURER
Kammok

DESIGNER BIOGRAPHY
Greg McEvilly is the driving force behind Kammok, an
adventure brand that is revolutionizing products for the
social good. Since its inception, Kammck has become a
vehicle for sustainable giving and broad social impact by
partnering with aid organizations such as Malaria No More,
1% For The Planet, and Comfort the Children International.
McEvilly and his team are working to expand the Kammok
brand, to push beyond the boundaries of "business as usual."

MATERIAL PROPERTIES
Nanotech, Lightweight

The Kammok Glider
is a tenacious piece of
equipment reinforced with
fibers that hold the unique
shape of the covering,
complete with gutters to
collect rainwater.

Humble design elements make a powerful statement
in the Glider, a portable weather shelter that also
does duty as a water-collection system. Motivated
by a far-from-humble goal—"to change lives"—
Kammok founder Greg McEvilly explains that the idea
for the Glider grew out of the aftermath of the 2010 Haiti
earthquake, which saw both flooding and a lack of clean
drinking water.

The unadorned, waterproof and heat-reflective design
incorporates an adjustable suspension system that holds the
tarp in place and allows rain gutters to form. These channel
water toward the corners, where BPA-free plastic connectors
create funnels for collection bottles that can be stored or
used for immediate drinking.

As a brand, Kammock is exemplary in that its
"why"—"to equip and inspire for life-changing adventure"—
informs every "what" that it makes. Through its partnerships
with selected aid organizations, it provides a model for how
a commercial venture can realistically be a driving force for
social good.

MATERIAL INSIGHT

A simple and elegant solution for collecting rainwater
and overnight condensation, this fabric has multiple
functional coatings that reduce weight, maintain
strength, and provide an almost lotus-leaf-
like water resistance to the outer surface.
The design of the six catenary curves that
aid the collection of the water is based on the sugar glider,
a marsupial that resembles a flying squirrel; and the fabric
itself, called Amphibiskin, combines a durable base
layer of nylon Cordura, a silicone lamination layer, and
a proprietary heat-reflection and waterproof coating.
The Glider can be used dark side or reflective side up
to either absorb or protect from the sun's warming rays.

LOGITECH FABRICSKIN KEYBOARD FOLIO

DESIGNER / MANUFACTURER
Logitech
www.logitech.com

MATERIAL
Coated elastomeric textile

DESIGNER BIOGRAPHY
Mike Culver, Vice President and General
Manager of Mobility at Logitech, is responsible
for its worldwide tablet business, with more
than twenty years of experience in consumer
technology. Prior to joining Logitech in
January 2008, he was co-founder of the
Sightline Group, a management consulting
company, where he had engagements with
various consumer electronics companies.
Culver holds BSEE and MBA degrees from
Purdue University, Indiana.

MATERIAL PROPERTIES
Stain-Resistant/Easy-Clean, Ergonomic

The FabricSkin
Keyboard is protected by
a stretchy textile with a
water-repellent coating.
This combination, often
seen in swim caps and
performance apparel,
provides a soft, durable,
and spill-resistant
casing material.

For all the wonder of the iPad, people still prefer to type rather than tap. More specifically, they want the blend of laptop-like productivity in a super-lightweight package—the essence of the mobile office. But it is not all about fingers flying over keypads. Touch has transformed the experience of the computer from a large block of hardware accessible by a clicking keyboard into a digital companion that fits in a purse or a pocket and goes anywhere.

For designers, touch is a critical and often overlooked opportunity to create connections between people and products: consumers today use their hands to access not just objects but brands. Different tactile sensations—softness, flexibility, weight—can lead users to interpret and interact with products in different ways.

Enhancing the total "feel" of a product in order to increase user satisfaction has been underemphasized in much design. Logitech is among the exceptions. The Swiss-based company uses the power of touch to convey important product attributes, delivering experiences that help set its products apart by fulfilling its focus on the "last inch between you and your computer."

In the world of the ultra-thin and ultra-light, the latest version of the Logitech FabricSkin Keyboard Folio extends the iPad Air's touch-driven capacity with a single, continuous piece of fabric that is protective covering, keyboard and tablet rest in one. The soft, rubbery surface of the embedded Bluetooth keyboard is water-repellent and large enough for typing, making a tactile impression on the user for reading, viewing, communicating, and playing.

MATERIAL INSIGHT

The first real combination of functional consumer electronics and fashion fabrics that does not sacrifice performance, the FabricSkin has solved the challenge of typing quality and

woven surface. The keys of this iPad accessory
keyboard have been integrated seamlessly into the
Lycra-based, polyurethane-coated stretch skin while being
connected to the electronics beneath; Bluetooth is used to
connect to the tablet itself. This inner fabric has also been
bonded onto a highly durable woven outer skin that protects
the iPad, with both fabrics treated with a hydrophobic
coating to resist spills. Magnets integrated into the semi-
rigid back panel enable multiple stand geometries.

The sophisticated
yet streamlined case
construction integrates
a keyboard, magnetic
locking system, and
USB port.

Pinarello's Dogma Carbon
60HM1K road bicycle utilizes
elastomeric Nanoalloy to bind
fibers together without sacrificing
impact resistance for weight.

CHAPTER 3
ADVANCED COMPOSITES

In the creation of a new product, there are four main considerations for the selection of a material: aesthetics, cost, performance, and, more recently, environmental impact. Depending on its function and on other expectations for the product, each will have a different level of priority. Most materials for consumer products tend to chart a middling course, offering a reasonable combination of the four. For advanced composites, however, it is all about performance.

The drive for almost all new composite development is an increase in some form of performance, predominantly through the holy grail of better strength to weight. It is no wonder, then, that the leading industries driving composite technology forward are aerospace, high-end automotive, wind turbines, and sports equipment. Advanced composites are at first glance ugly, expensive, and an environmental nightmare. But closer scrutiny shows that some of the hand lay-up and filament-wound composite parts can have their own beauty, the reductions in weight, material volume, and fuel can make them cost-effective, and the latest predominantly composite-based planes can offer a lesson in how reductions in weight can save millions of gallons of CO_2-producing fuel.

CARBON FIBER

Carbon-fiber-based composites, those that use a woven structure whose filaments run the entire length of the part, still reign supreme in the strength-to-weight competition. They have also gained their own particular beauty based on an appreciation of

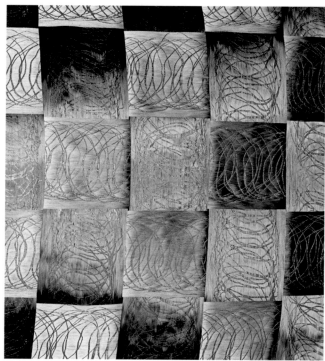

Ridea Touring Skis are made with Textreme spread-tow carbon fabrics, which achieve a flatter profile, with thin fibers woven tightly in longer spans to deliver both lighter weight and less drag.

their performance-led attributes. New weave constructions and finer tows (filament thicknesses) enable thinner and thinner composite sections for lighter and lighter products (the ISPO-2013-winning world's lightest touring skis from Ridea are a great example of this). Combinations with other fiber materials such as Kevlar (for Fox Racing's V3R Carbon motocross helmet) or the polyethylene super fibers such as Dyneema or Spectra can add a resistance to impact that increases the toughness of the part (Dimension Polyant's GXLD 60 Composite Sails).

Improved resins (the "glue" that holds the fibers together) are being developed that further reduce overall composite weight, thickness and susceptibility to the elements, as well as offering faster curing times and better surface quality, enabling them to be used without painting. A recent innovation in this area is Nanoalloy, a nanostructured mixture of polymers that enhances the resin used as a binder for carbon-fiber composites. Formulated by Toyobo, it has been commercially successful in the Pinarello Dogma Carbon 60HM1K road bicycle. The Nanoalloy is a dispersion of "nanoscale elastomers between the carbon fibers—these elastomers have the ability to absorb impacts and prevent the propagation of cracks as they occur." The result is, Pinarello claims, that the Dogma frame weighs about 860 grams (30 ounces), 40 grams (1.4 ounces) less than a comparable frame, but is 23 percent more resistant to impacts. There is also a lot of promise in the area of biobased binders, with products such as Acrodur from BASF and SuperSap from Entropy Resins beginning to offer comparable performance to petroleum-based solutions, and giving the opportunity for 100 percent renewably resourced and completely biodegradable performance composites.

NATURAL FIBERS

Flax retains its pre-eminent position in the world of natural fibers for composites thanks to its high stiffness-to-weight ratio, and a number of the product selections in this chapter use it with different binder resins. The alternatives, which include jute, hemp, kenaf (bast fibers), and coir (a fruit fiber), all offer some advantages, such as low cost, light weight or fire retardancy, but since composites are predominantly about strength performance, they remain less-used options. The main areas of growth for natural-fiber composites include sports equipment, automotive interior panels, construction, and consumer electronics, as well as some furniture parts for interiors.

SELF-REINFORCED POLYMER COMPOSITES

Still within the arena of advanced composites are the lesser-known self-reinforced polymer composites. Rather than using a different material for the fiber or fabric, such as glass, these polymers use a different form of the same polymer for the stiff fiber part. Typically, the stiffer polymer section is in the form of a woven fabric, similar to carbon or Kevlar composite products. The most widely used is self-reinforced polypropylene (SRPP), as in the Samsonite Cosmolite and TUMI Tegra-Lite suitcases. The suppliers of these SRPPs include Milliken (Tegris), Propex (Curv), Don and Low (Armodon), and Pure Composites (Pure), each having its own particular advantages and processing challenges. Academic studies have also been conducted on other plastics including nylon, polyethylene, and polyester (PET) but currently not with the same success as for polypropylene. The two biggest advantages for these new materials are that the bonding between the matrix and the fiber is exceptionally good (they are basically the same material) and that they can be recycled together. The cost is also significantly lower than most advanced composites, though processing is often a challenge and can increase cost.

By the mere fact that they use two dissimilar components—fibers and resin—the challenge with the recycling of composites remains with us; currently only the self-reinforced polymers are easy to put back into the resource stream. In the *Architecture* book of this series the potential recycling of certain glass-reinforced polymer composites (GRPCs) was offered through new resins that could be "activated" by specific conditions such as certain wavelengths of light, certain vibration frequencies, or heat and pressure to release their fibers and be effectively separated. This development is still in its infancy, but Boeing, for example, has claimed that it intends to make

its composite parts more recycled than aluminum within the next thirty to forty years.

Other innovative solutions to this end-of-life problem are being created. Polyfloss is a process that uses a simple process similar to making candyfloss to separate thermoplastics from their glass-fiber reinforcements. Heated and semi-molten plastic exits using centrifugal force through tiny holes in a drum containing the composite, leaving the too-big glass fibers stuck inside. The plastic is collected on plates outside the drum for processing into pellets for reuse. Though still only suitable for thermoplastics and not thermosets (which cannot be remelted by heating), it shows some significant steps in the right direction.

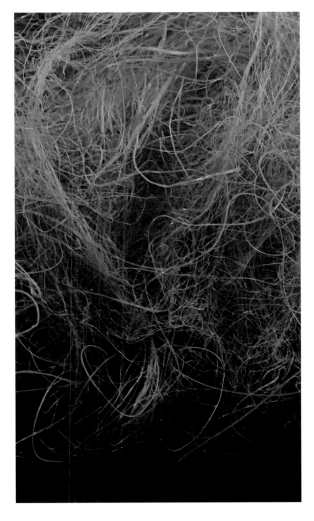

Polyfloss, described as "plastic wool," offers a creative way of recycling polypropylene into fibrous insulation, or if reprocessed, into new solid parts.

TEGRA-LITE

DESIGNER / MANUFACTURER
Tumi
www.tumi.com

MATERIAL
Tegris®

MATERIAL MANUFACTURER
Milliken & Company

DESIGNER BIOGRAPHY
Tumi is among the leading international brands for premium travel, business, and lifestyle accessories. Its heritage of design excellence over the past three decades can be traced to its continual focus on its founding principles of functional superiority, technical innovation, and high quality. The Tegra-Lite® collection is exclusive to Tumi.

MATERIAL PROPERTIES
Lightweight, Durable, High Strength, Composite

In the badlands of baggage handling, two things count: weight and strength. Now, with the invention of a thermoplastic composite called Tegris that is the innovation behind Tumi's Tegra-Lite suitcase line, recyclability can be added to this. This revolutionary material was originally used in lifesaving armor, NASCAR race cars and NFL (National Football League) protective gear, where it is prized for its stiffness and advanced impact properties.

Tegris was invented by Milliken, a company founded in 1865, with a long reputation for innovation in manmade textiles. The name, from the Greek for "you are protected," reflects the material's role in shielding and armor, and the material allows for designs of impressive mobile chic. Like all composites, Tegris is made of two different components: polypropylene-based tapes feature a strong center core sandwiched between a lower-melt polypropylene copolymer, which is co-extruded as a film and slit into strips to create a yarn that can be woven into a fabric. The luggage is made through compression-forming, in which the materials are pressed together and heated to form a single piece.

At first glance the exterior looks like most other hard-shell luggage. The impassive envelope is, however, exceptionally agile thanks to its featherlight weight and the modest effort required to maneuver it. While the color palette is discreet, in keeping with the brand's sophisticated customer base, the material also takes well to pattern, providing plenty of options for creative customization.

MATERIAL INSIGHT

The Tegris material used as the outer skin of this line of luggage gives a much stiffer and tougher shell than standard polycarbonate, and at two-thirds the density, is a lighter-weight solution. Although 100 percent polypropylene (PP), it is a combination of higher-molecular-weight, stiffer

polypropylene woven yarns within a tougher PP matrix. The advantage of this combination is that there is excellent bonding between the fibers and the matrix, a key aspect of strength in these materials. One limitation, however, is that the stiffer fibers do not stretch easily when heated, so, unlike standard plastics, are harder to form over compound curves such as the corners of suitcases. This can be seen in the decision to reinforce these areas of the Tegra-Lite line with a thermoplastic.

Tumi made its name with its lightweight and durable luggage made of ballistic nylon in the 1980s. The Tegra-Lite range promises continued high performance using Tegris, which has fifteen times the impact resistance of typical thermoplastic composites. This material can take harder hits than carbon fiber and its polypropylene construction makes it recyclable too.

GANYMED WALKING AID

DESIGNER
Karen Ostertag and Dr. Sigmar Klose

MANUFACTURER
Ganymed GmbH
www.ganymed.eu

MATERIAL
Grivory GVX

MATERIAL MANUFACTURER
EMS-GRIVORY

DESIGNER BIOGRAPHY
Karen Ostertag has worked in both two- and three-dimensional design. She is an accomplished photographer and graphic designer, recipient of the Kodak Culture Award for creative photography and a photography educator at the University of Ulm, Germany. A member of the German Society for Photography and a Board Member of the BFF (Bund Freischaffender Foto-Designer) in Germany, her photographic work has appeared in numerous publications and exhibitions. Today she is also recognized for the Ganymed line of barrier-free mobility product designs.

MATERIAL PROPERTIES
Lightweight, Ergonomic, High Strength, Composite

The functional and democratic potential of design is amplified in products that provide mobility and freedom to those who are injured or impaired. Distinguished by its fretwork handle and ergonomic hand rest, the Ganymed Walking Aid is an elegant modern reworking of the longstanding forearm crutch.

With the Ganymed, a series of structural and detail-driven improvements has led to a widely celebrated design; awards include a 2010 Good Design Award from the Chicago Athenaeum in the United States and a 2012 German Design Council Award.

The S-shaped crutch design extends along the forearm, allowing for better stability, directional control, and less pressure on the palm of the hand. Advances were also made to the overall weight of the crutch. "One of our challenges was keeping Ganymed super-lightweight," said designer Karen Ostertag. "This required the use of a brand new plastic with 65 percent fiberglass and a special software for the simulation of bionics that occur in natural phenomena." The sleek, resilient telescopic tube ends in an oval-shaped foot that can be adjusted for either hard or soft contact with the ground, depending on the terrain and the rotation that is needed. Interchangeable handgrips offer further customized comfort. By marrying biomorphic

form to sensitively crafted details, the Ganymed replaces
awkwardness with agility and ease.

MATERIAL INSIGHT

The use of two different composites, one for the stiff yet
compliant frame and the other for the cushioning handgrip,
shows the breadth of application possible with these
materials. Cork has an excellent hand feel and is used in
the handgrip: molding particles of this
sustainably sourced natural material
with rubber of a mid-range
hardness gives an ergonomically
shaped form with water, oil,
and dirt resistance. It can be
injection-molded in a similar
way to standard rubbers, with
cork concentrations of up to
approximately 50 percent.

    The stiffer formulation
of polymer and glass-fiber
composite frame enabled the
creation of a "cut-out" structure,
reducing weight and promoting
an improved walking gait.

opposite The S shape enables
"quadrupedal posture" so that
the user can walk naturally
without putting undue pressure
on their palm, or raising their
shoulder as they would with
perpendicular supports.

Nerve damage can occur
when one needs to tightly
grip a walking aid on a regular
basis, so Ganymed carefully
designed the handle with soft
materials that require less
pressure to hold.

THE
LIGHT ROOM

DESIGNER / MANUFACTURER
Bram Geenen
www.studiogeenen.com

MATERIAL
Dyneema and glass-filled nylon

MATERIAL MANUFACTURER
DSM Dyneema

DESIGNER BIOGRAPHY
Bram Geenen of Studio Geenen designed the Gaudi Stool, a super-lightweight piece of furniture internationally recognized as uncompromising and technologically advanced. The stool has been exhibited widely, including in Cologne, New York, Prague and Milan, and in the permanent collection of the DHUB Design Museum Barcelona. The design exemplifies the studio's desire to create furniture based on advanced materials, new technologies and high-end techniques.

MATERIAL PROPERTIES
Lightweight, High Strength, Composite

opposite top, from left to right Gaudi Stool, Dyneema Chair, Tensile Table, Grid Shelf, and SLS-Chair (**also bottom**). SLS stands for Select Laser-Sintering, a type of 3D printing.

The Light Room designed by Bram Geenen, of Amsterdam-based Studio Geenen, carries us far from conventional concepts of furniture and interiors. The name refers not to luminosity but to weightlessness, as if the very notion of solidity were in question. The "room" is composed of five signature furniture designs—the 3D-printed SLS-Chair, the Dyneema Chair, the Gaudi Stool, the Tensile Table, and the Grid Shelf—arranged on a low, biomorphic platform. While most furniture emphasizes permanence, the Light Room seems constructed from milky panels and elegant, attenuated membranes, an impression reinforced by the fact that altogether the furniture weighs a mere 7.5 kilograms (16.5 pounds), the usual weight of a single chair.

Airy, yet seeming to respond to gravitational forces, the designs are decidedly architectural, taking on the feel of a small cityscape. The ultimate purpose of the vignette, though, is to bring attention to lightness as a sustainable solution. As Geenen explains, "By stripping down a piece to its lightest value, the energy consumption in its creation is lowered [and] transport costs are also reduced."

MATERIAL INSIGHT

The Light Room consists of furniture designed with no other goal than getting as light as possible. The carbon-fiber shell of the Gaudi Stool was hand laid-up using a woven fabric and epoxy resin binder. The complexity of the underlying beam grid structure was first formed using rapid prototyping, with Freedom of Creation assisting in the development. Glass-filled nylon was used as the resin, improving on the stiffness compared to the virgin resin typically used in additive manufacturing. The Tensile Table is a unique mixture of Kevlar and silk. The Dyneema Chair uses both knit and woven Dyneema yarn (ultra-high-molecular-weight polyethylene) for stiffness and comfort.

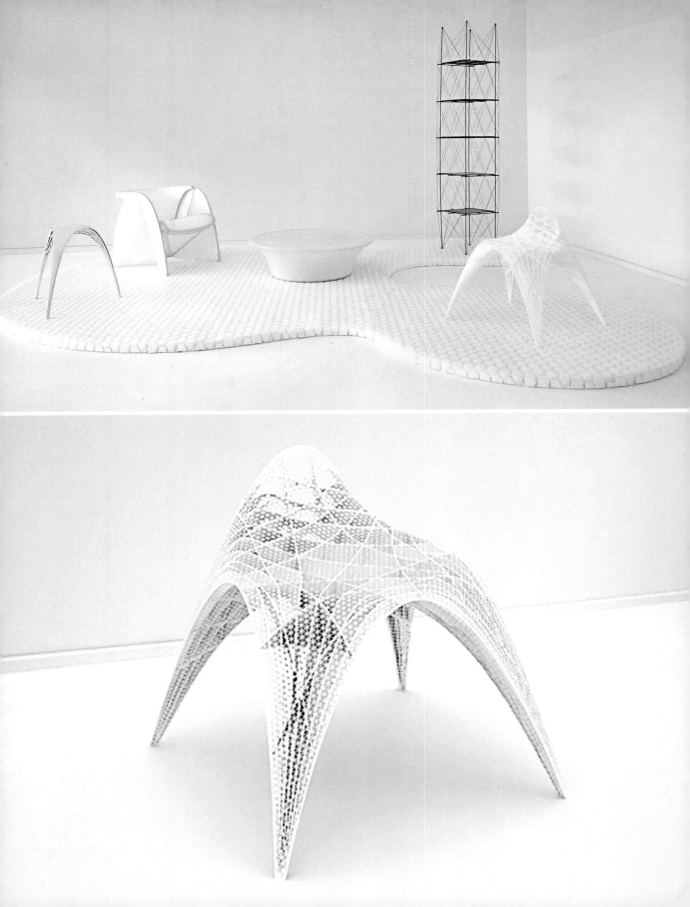

ERGON SR2 BIOCOMP CONCEPT SADDLE

DESIGNER
Ergon Werksdesign
www.ergon-bike.com

MANUFACTURER
Ergon / RTI Sports GmbH, Bcomp Ltd
www.ergon-bike.com, www.bcomp.ch

MATERIAL
AmpliTex fabrics

MATERIAL MANUFACTURER
Bcomp

DESIGNER BIOGRAPHY
Ergon's in-house design team develops
ergonomically advanced solutions for
bike riders. Its interdisciplinary approach
incorporates a strong focus on material
research. At Ergon designers, engineers,
professional cyclists, and sports ergonomists
seek to optimize performance and comfort
through points of contact between human
and machine.

MATERIAL PROPERTIES
Lightweight, Ergonomic, High Strength, Composite

Even with their simple form and mechanics, bicycles offer a unique challenge to designers. To power each two-wheeler, rider and machine must meet at three critical contact points: the saddle, the handlebars, and the pedals. Ultimately, the degree of integration between these elements determines the vehicle's performance and comfort. Of these, the saddle is the most important component to get ergonomically correct since it carries and distributes the weight of the upper body, positions the rider over the pedals, and helps control the bike. Thus, the ergonomics of the saddle directly influences how efficiently muscle power translates to motion and speed.

Against this backdrop, German bicycle innovator Ergon has jump-cut to the future with the SR2 BioComp saddle. While typically the craft of bicycle building involves extensive metalwork—bending, welding and carving such materials as steel, titanium, aluminum and carbon—the SR2 BioComp introduces upgrades with completely new materials that optimize saddles for not just weight and comfort but also sustainability. The SR2 BioComp is made with 95 percent natural flax fibers to give the saddle outstanding vibration-dampening properties, superior lightness, and an innovative aesthetic. This revolutionary saddle sheet concept is the result of a year-long collaboration between Ergon and Bcomp—a Swiss company that specializes in natural-fiber composite solutions—providing Ergon with structural engineering, prototyping, processing, and optimum fabric solutions that translate to less weight and more performance in a sustainable way.

For Franc Arnold, founder of Ergon, the focus on sustainable materials is exemplified by the company's Greenlab, a product development initiative whose goal is to boost product performance while optimizing environmentally conscious design by replacing resource-intensive materials with biobased alternatives.

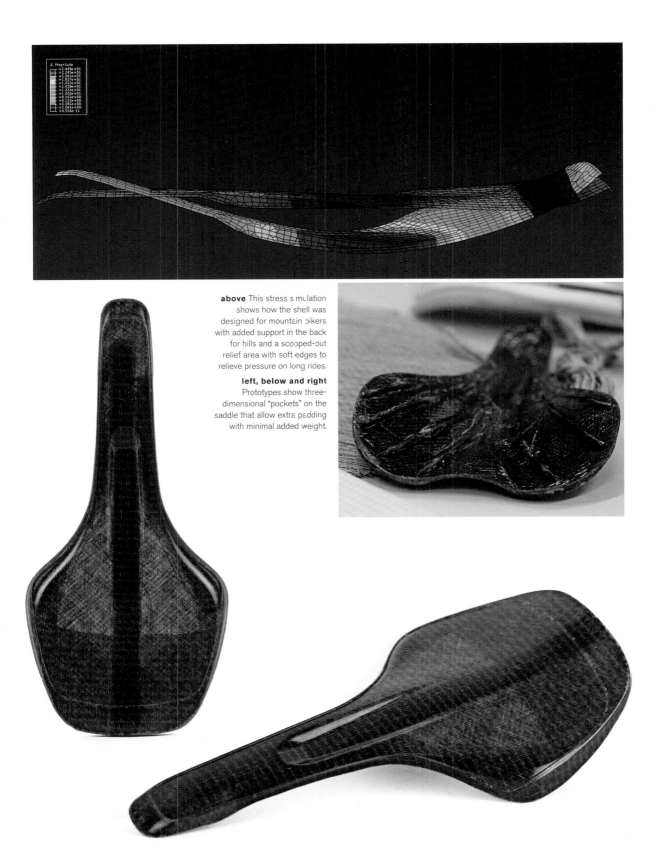

above This stress simulation shows how the shell was designed for mountain bikers with added support in the back for hills and a scooped-out relief area with soft edges to relieve pressure on long rides.

left, below and right Prototypes show three-dimensional "pockets" on the saddle that allow extra padding with minimal added weight.

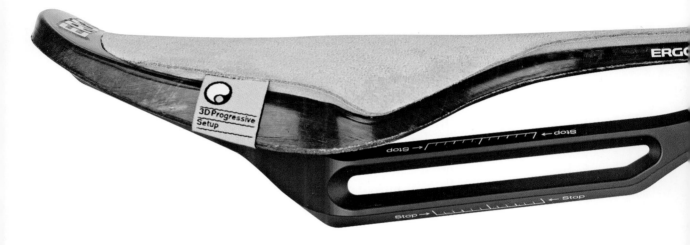

BioComp follows Ergon's 3D Progressive Setup, which applies harder padding to the vibration-dampening flax-composite shell and elastic comfort padding on top.

MATERIAL INSIGHT

AmpliTex is a revolutionary internal structure used in biobased composites that increases strength without significantly adding to weight. A substructure latticework of additional biobased composite twisted yarns gives the saddle stiffness in the directions it is most needed. Carbon-fiber filaments can be incorporated into these yarns for increased performance. These are bonded to the main structure as a form of reinforcing brace, with their angle and yarn density dependent upon the part's stress requirements. The flax fabric used in the main section of the seat provides additional vibration dampening beyond that found in other advanced composites, and has a stiffness equivalent to glass fiber but with half the density.

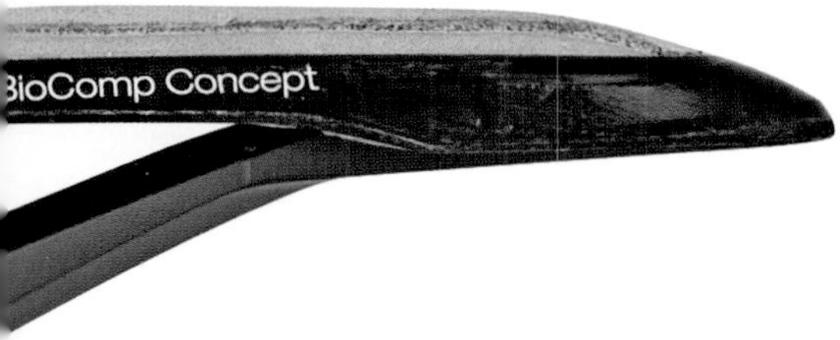

BioComp Concept

ERGON

FU LEI ZHI SEAT

DESIGNER / MANUFACTURER
Vivian Chiu
www.vivianchiudesigns.com

MATERIAL
Twintex

MATERIAL MANUFACTURER
Owens Corning

DESIGNER BIOGRAPHY
Vivian Chiu was born in Los Angeles and raised in Hong Kong, and currently works in Brooklyn, New York. She studied Furniture Design at Rhode Island School of Design, where she discovered a passion for making and building things. Hard work and pushing herself mentally and physically form the philosophical foundation that drives many of her designs. Her work aims to combine sculpture and function to create a visually stimulating object.

MATERIAL PROPERTIES
Lightweight, High Strength, Composite

Conceived as part of a collaborative experimental learning project between Massachusetts-based Klinger Engineering and students at the Rhode Island School of Design, the Fu Lei Zhi bench by RISD graduate Vivian Chiu displays the hallmarks of Twintex, an advanced composite that is both strong and malleable. The bench's simple conception, articulated through the negative space that fills its rectangular volume, contrasts eloquently with the wrapped, porous, tensile frame, which reads like a web or cage. Since the threads are wrapped randomly, the design gives the impression of having been handcrafted, lending it an air of provocation and fun that suggests inventive possibilities for Twintex far beyond its patented, engineered origins.

Fu Lei Zhi represents the next step in a series of conceptual designs by Chiu that involve cutting, torqueing, layering and bending, usually from wood or paper, shapes that are both organic and geometric. Here, black threads composed of glass and polypropylene create a dynamic composition that is as much about sculptural form as sinuous line. But they also reveal the exciting structural possibilities inherent in new composite materials where a wide variety of knits are possible and where the surface material and the structural frame are able to function as one.

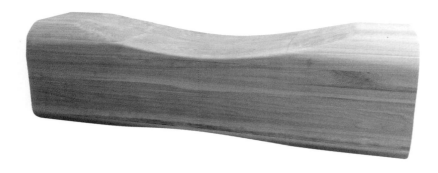

The form was not fixed until the fiber-wrapped wooden mold (**left**) was stood up on its end (**opposite**) so that every surface would be evenly heated when in the kiln. Unlike many composites, Twintex can be recycled, because this heating process is reversible.

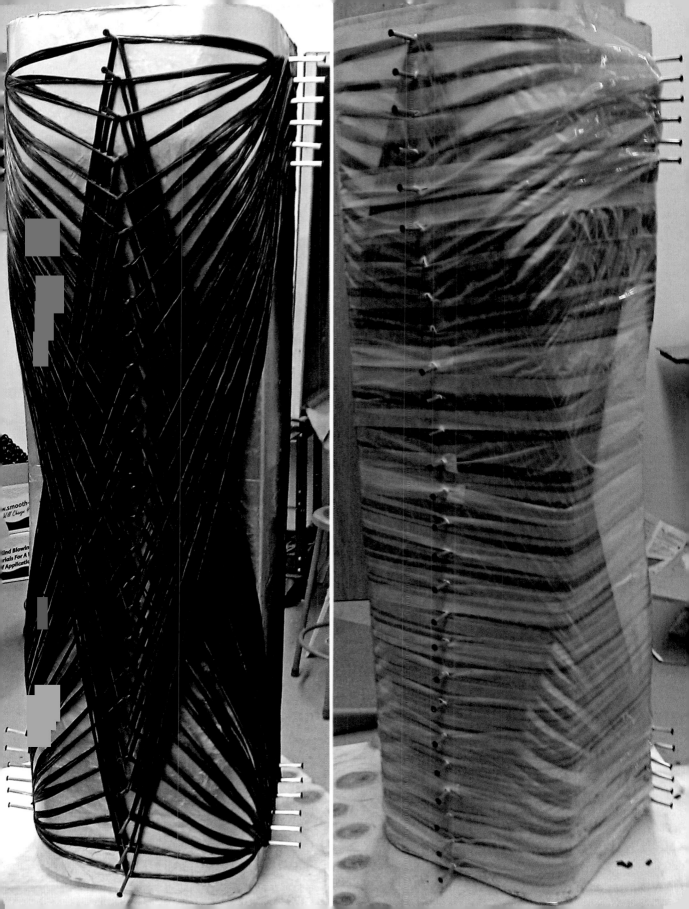

MATERIAL INSIGHT

Twintex is a roving (yarn for composite manufacture) made from commingled glass and polypropylene yarns. This combination is intended to improve conformability, and does not require additional resin in order to be formed into composite structures. Consolidation is achieved by heating the Twintex to just above the melting point of the polypropylene: 180–230° C (360–450° F). The mixture has been designed with excellent mechanical properties; it offers an improved stiffness-to-weight ratio with superior impact properties over traditional fiberglass, and lends itself to the type of forming used for this structure.

Chiu developed a system for weaving a seat with Twintex yarn. The glass fibers lend strength while the polypropylene, once heated and cooled, provides stability.

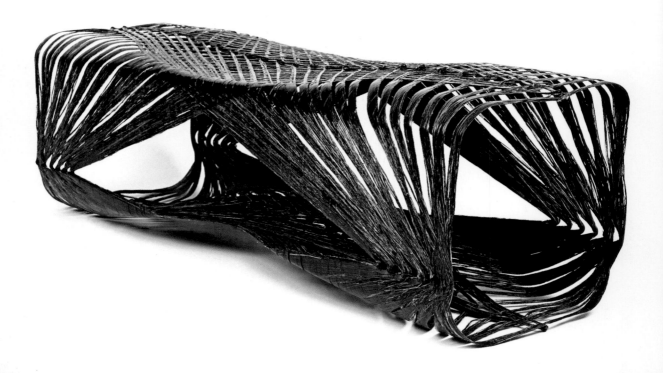

FORNIX SKI HELMET

DESIGNER / MANUFACTURER
Fredrik Hallander and Jan Woxing,
POC Sports
www.pocsports.com

MATERIAL
Kevlar

MATERIAL MANUFACTURER
DuPont

DESIGNER BIOGRAPHIES
Jan Woxing, an industrial designer,
is co-founder and design director at
POC. Fredrik Hallander, a material and
engineering expert, works in research
and development.

MATERIAL PROPERTIES
Lightweight, Ergonomic, All-Weather Use,
Composite

Advances in equipment that allow even recreational skiers to move at much faster speeds, plus a series of high-profile ski accidents, have made helmets the headgear of choice on the slopes. Early helmet designs had a hard shell and a soft liner that were hard to penetrate but heavy and did not absorb impact well. Molded helmets with a thinner shell of hard plastic that covers the ears and the back of the neck were an improvement but not good at absorbing repetitive shocks, a requirement in ski racing, where athletes repeatedly hit gates at high speed.

Enter POC Sports: This Stockholm-based company has leveraged Sweden's expertise in safety, healthcare, and product development into a line of lightweight, high-performance gear for gravity sports athletes that protects against injury through a focus on superior impact absorption and penetration resistance.

POC's sophisticated, patented designs draw on cross-disciplinary research involving engineers, material specialists, industrial and graphic designers, neurologists, and back specialists. Among their most enviable inventions is the Aramid Penetration Barrier—APB—which enables massive energy dispersion upon impact while allowing the helmet shell to remain lightweight and comfortable to wear, a key advantage of the Fornix ski helmet. POC's helmets come in a range of juicy, vibrant colors that make them fun to wear.

Molding the EPS foam core and exterior polycarbonate shell together in one process saves on production time and costs with injection-molded helmets such as the Fornix.

Helmets today also come with adjustable features. A distinctive element of the Fornix is its ventilation system: six elongated tear-shaped vents radiate out from the crown to help keep the skier's head cool and goggles clear of fog.

MATERIAL INSIGHT

The aramid (Kevlar) composite bridge construction on the front of this helmet provides a good dissipation of impact energy during a collision. (Kevlar has the highest energy absorption of all the super fibers.) This composite is molded together with an expanded polystyrene (EPS) foam core to create improved impact resistance. The technology is a crossover from the company's successful mountain bike helmet range. In conjunction with MIPS (Multi-Impact Protection System), a technology that allows the outer shell of the helmet to slide slightly across the inner EPS core (similar to a membrane between brain and skull that enables the brain mass to shift and absorb shear when hit), these two materials reduce significantly the chance of concussion through impact in a collision.

With five times the strength of steel on an equal-weight basis, aramid, when placed between the foam core and the outer shell, makes this ski helmet more impact-resistant and improves the durability of injection-mold construction.

MOJO
UFO TENT

DESIGNER
Vincent Mares

MANUFACTURER
Sierra Designs
www.sierradesigns.com

MATERIAL
Cuben fiber

MATERIAL MANUFACTURER
Cubic Tech Corporation

DESIGNER BIOGRAPHY
Vincent Mares is a design manager at
American Recreation Products in Boulder,
Colorado. Educated at the California
College of the Arts, he specializes in soft-
goods design with a focus on the outdoor
recreational and military/law enforcement
markets. A skilled backpack designer,
he has been part of the design and
development teams at Camelbak and
Gregory Mountain Products.

MATERIAL PROPERTIES
Lightweight, All-Weather Use, Composite

When it is the middle of the night and you are
curled up like a human chrysalis, clinging to
a windy ridge, your tent is your best friend.
Sierra Designs, one of the most forward-
thinking brands in the outdoor gear industry, understands
this. Its track record for innovation in lightweight tent design
was well established long before the arrival of the Mojo
UFO, a featherweight dwelling consisting of an exceptionally
tough membrane of shimmery silver walls that takes the
category a step further.

The name, part slang, part space age, speaks to the
product's twin attributes: comfort-driven design married to
state-of-the-art materials. Cuben fiber is both extraordinarily
light and virtually indestructible, allowing the 213 x
127-centimeter (84 x 50-inch) two-man tent to consume
a mere 760 grams (1.68 pounds) of carrying weight while
delivering the requisite protection in extreme conditions.
Fully assembled, the high-performance, rip-resistant fabric is
suspended with an ExoFusion carbon-fiber pole design that
forms a sunflower hub that extends down to locking pole
tips. When it is time to move on, the tent folds up into an
ultra-light envelope.

MATERIAL INSIGHT
Cuben fiber is a flexible, non-woven but directionally laid
laminate made from a mixture of ultra-high-molecular-
weight polyethylene Dyneema yarns sandwiched between
thin films of polyester and fluoropolymer membranes.
A technology transfer from the yacht sail industry, the
Dyneema fibers are laid in non-bias and bias configurations
in a variety of weights depending on the requirements of
the sail. Here in the Mojo UFO tent, the fibers are run in
the direction of the longest sections of the tent fabric.

Carbon-fiber tent poles are a clear choice to reduce
the weight further.

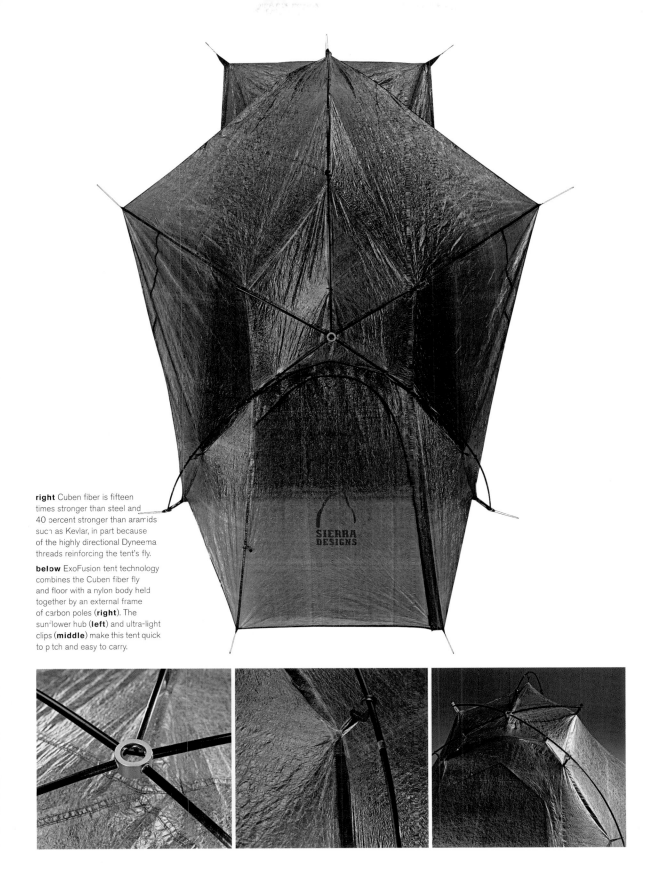

right Cuben fiber is fifteen times stronger than steel and 40 percent stronger than aramids such as Kevlar, in part because of the highly directional Dyneema threads reinforcing the tent's fly.

below ExoFusion tent technology combines the Cuben fiber fly and floor with a nylon body held together by an external frame of carbon poles (**right**). The sunflower hub (**left**) and ultra-light clips (**middle**) make this tent quick to pitch and easy to carry.

SIERRA DESIGNS

BERING SLEEPING BAG

DESIGNER
Sarah Groth

MANUFACTURER
Nordisk Company
www.nordisk.eu

MATERIAL
Thermo Dry (filling)/20D Airtastic Nylon
with Black Yarn Technology (shell)

MATERIAL MANUFACTURER
Advansa (filling) and Nordisk (shell)

DESIGNER BIOGRAPHY
Since completing a bachelor's degree in
Industrial Design at Denmark's TEKO
design and business school, Sarah Groth
has worked in fashion and textile as a
designer and design manager with a
focus on brand positioning, market
research, and product development.
In New Zealand and then in Denmark,
she designed children's wear, workwear,
underwear, accessories, womenswear,
and outdoor gear. At Nordisk Company
she has helped to reposition the brand
through designs for sleeping bags,
mattresses, tents, bags, and cookware.

MATERIAL PROPERTIES
Lightweight, Composite

opposite bottom Soft synthetic
filling in the Bering -3° sleeping
bag is engineered with a thick
layer of ultra-fine microdenier
fibers, which trap warm air near
the skin, and hollow fibers, which
sustain loft and durability. Unlike
feathery down, they maintain their
structure when wet and stay warm.

Abundant natural beauty plus a century-long
design tradition that links aesthetics with craft
make Denmark an ideal location for Nordisk,
a specialist in outdoor equipment since 1901. Its
mastery of tent design, including the old-fashioned cotton
kind that evokes childhood memories of sleeping out on
warm summer nights, speaks to a typically Danish approach
toward beautifully made objects for everyday use. These
qualities are especially evident in Nordisk's Bering sleeping
bag, which the won'mark (a contraction of "Wonderful
Denmark") blog singled out for its emphasis on quality,
clarity of purpose and graceful, organic shape.

What further sets the Bering apart
from other mummy bags is Black Yarn—
a revolutionary fabric made of carbon particles
melted on to nylon fibers. This results in
the bag's exceptional ability to absorb and
retain heat for longer inside while drawing
moisture to the outside. The bag is also filled
with Thermo Dry Soft polyester, a synthetic
that offers an advantage over down because
it stays warm when wet, allowing the tough,
tear-resistant bag to perform in a range of
temperatures and conditions with exceptional
breathability and comfort.

Sleeping bags have evolved dramatically
from the early folded woolen rugs used by
armies and missionaries into ergonomic cocoons
that can be stuffed down into a small sack weighing
as little as half a kilogram (16 ounces). The organic
design idiom combined with high-performance
materials captures the functional essence of gear
created to bring us closer to the natural world
while optimally catering to the practical needs
of the human form. If the result is that more

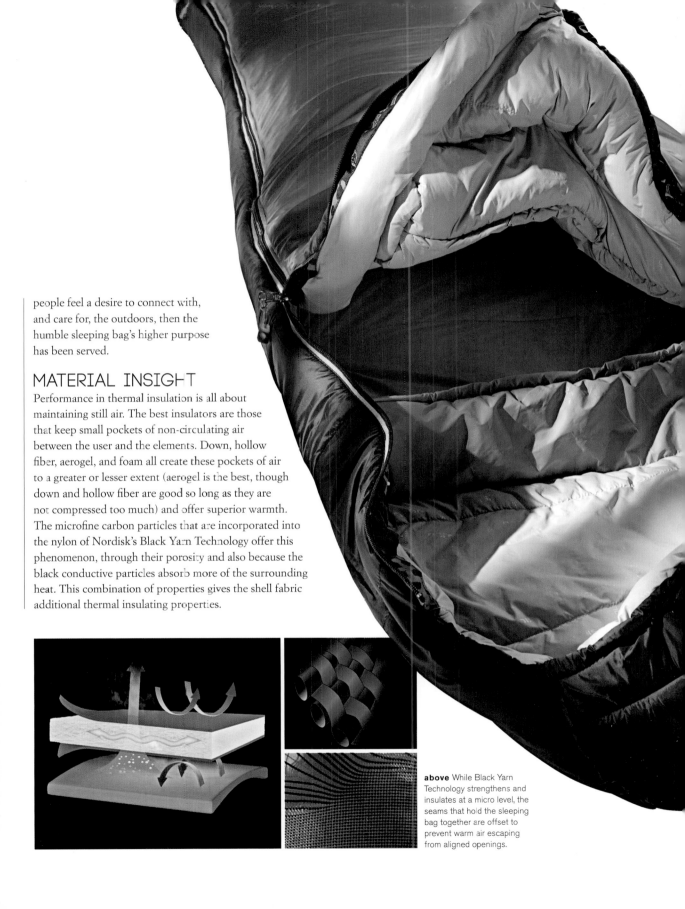

people feel a desire to connect with, and care for, the outdoors, then the humble sleeping bag's higher purpose has been served.

MATERIAL INSIGHT

Performance in thermal insulation is all about maintaining still air. The best insulators are those that keep small pockets of non-circulating air between the user and the elements. Down, hollow fiber, aerogel, and foam all create these pockets of air to a greater or lesser extent (aerogel is the best, though down and hollow fiber are good so long as they are not compressed too much) and offer superior warmth. The microfine carbon particles that are incorporated into the nylon of Nordisk's Black Yarn Technology offer this phenomenon, through their porosity and also because the black conductive particles absorb more of the surrounding heat. This combination of properties gives the shell fabric additional thermal insulating properties.

above While Black Yarn Technology strengthens and insulates at a micro level, the seams that hold the sleeping bag together are offset to prevent warm air escaping from aligned openings.

W127 LAMP

DESIGNER
Dirk Winkel
www.dirkwinkel.com

MANUFACTURER
Wästberg
www.wastberg.com

MATERIAL
Ultramid S Balance

MATERIAL MANUFACTURER
BASF

DESIGNER BIOGRAPHY
Dirk Winkel is a Berlin-based product designer who specializes in lighting and furniture design. He has an MA in Design Products from the Royal College of Art, London, and teaches Design Construction at the Universität der Künste Berlin (Berlin University of the Arts), where he also studied. His work has been honored with awards and nominations from Good Design (Chicago Athenaeum), Swedish Design Award (Svensk Form), and Designs of the Year (London Design Museum).

MATERIAL PROPERTIES
Rapidly Renewable, High Strength, Simplification

The w127 lamp was built for a lifetime of use with non-mineral-oil-based plastics and gas-powered springs often used in the automotive industry, prized for their lifespan of more than 50,000 compressions.

Sometimes, innovation strikes twice. In the case of the Winkel w127 lamp, a dimmable table lamp designed by German industrial designer Dirk Winkel in collaboration with the Swedish lighting brand Wästberg, a minimally elegant design offers both technical and tactile performance.

Winkel's challenge was not merely to extend the possibilities of form and function but to give an entirely new dimension to a material known for its lightweight, moldable properties: plastic. "One of the greatest things I was missing in typical designs made of plastic was a significant impression of substance, of materiality," he explains. "The next step could only be a design that celebrated the material as it is, straightforward, solid and honest, hiding nothing while showing its innermost values to the outside."

The recyclable lamp is made out of a biopolyamide based on renewable sources and equipped with a warm-white LED, whose glow is modulated by a reflector and glare protection. The fiberglass-reinforced material possesses a unique tactility, while the solid arms give the lamp a substantial look and feel. The mechanics are based on micro gas springs for smooth movement.

MATERIAL INSIGHT

One of the first commercial examples of a biocomposite that uses castor oil as a raw material, this lamp is a combination of glass fiber and a biopolyamide, an engineering nylon resin produced from oil from the castor plant as at least 60 percent of the entire volume. This annually harvested oil is already used industrially for adhesives, brake fluids and dyes. The castor-oil-based nylon is chemically and performatively equivalent to standard nylon but has a lower environmental impact. The resin has been colored so that no paint is required, highlighting the aesthetic qualities of well-engineered plastics.

LYNX SKI

DESIGNER / MANUFACTURER
Thomas Greenall

MANUFACTURER
Idris Skis (Thomas Greenall and
Kiyoko Yamaguchi)
www.idriskis.com

MATERIAL
Super Sap 100/1000

MATERIAL MANUFACTURER
Entropy Resins

DESIGNER BIOGRAPHY
Born in 1973, Thomas Greenall began skiing at the age of six
and in his teens competed for two years on the Welsh Junior Ski
Team, roughly the same time that he built his first snowboard. He
earned a BEng degree from the University of Salford in England
and in 2004 began designing skis, working for PM Gear on the
Bro Model. In 2006 he built his first prototype ski and three years
later launched his first commercial ski.

MATERIAL PROPERTIES
Sustainable Solutions, Lightweight, High Strength

In late 2001, Thomas Greenall, a former member
of the Welsh Junior Ski Team and with a degree
in engineering, moved to Chamonix in France's
Haute-Savoie region, one of the country's oldest
ski resorts, whose access to Mont Blanc attracts extreme-
sport enthusiasts year round. He began designing skis, and
eventually founded Idris Skis. Like early mountain artisanal
skis, the simple, classic designs are handmade using locally
sourced, renewable materials wherever possible.

Among the tiny company's five signature designs
is the Lynx, named for the solitary wildcat that thrives at
high altitudes. With local mountain guides as his test case,
Greenall designed a ski able to handle a wide range of
conditions: "I use the real world—the Haute Route, the
North Face of the Aiguille du Midi and the top of Mont
Blanc—for evaluating a touring ski, not a laboratory." Long,
broad-shouldered tips taper gently over the ski's length,
allowing the skier to float through powder, with thick bases
and edges to cut through crust and turn easily on hard, steep
slopes. As Greenall sees it, a ski should "work
well in places it was never intended
to go, not just the places it was
designed to handle."

The Lynx comes
reinforced with fiberglass
and epoxy resin, but the
environmentally preferable
choice is the company's
cutting-edge flax and bio-resin
option, which promises the same
weight, strength, and performance as
the traditional alternative. The international sports business
network ISPO was equally impressed; the Lynx was an
award winner in the Off Piste Ski segment while also earning
top marks for environmental excellence.

The Lynx ski has a polyethylene
core strengthened with flax-based
reinforcement, secured with
bamboo, and is finished with oak
to make a fully sustainable
sporting good.

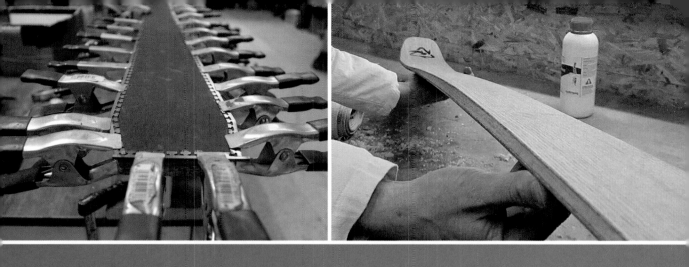

MATERIAL INSIGHT

Comparable in stiffness and responsiveness to other carbon-
or glass-fiber composites, these eco-friendly performance
skis use a combination of woven flax fiber and a biobased
resin. To complement this renewably resourced core,
sustainably harvested oak veneers are used as the topsheet
and sidewalls, and bamboo inserts are incorporated for
greater strength in screw-holding areas beneath the bindings.
The biobased resin, called Super Sap, was developed by
Entropy Resins in California and is the first US Department
of Agriculture (USDA) Bio-Preferred epoxy resin. The flax,
supplied by Bcomp of Switzerland, is sustainably sourced
in Northern Europe, creating a truly renewably resourced
competition ski.

top left and top right
Biobased Super Sap can be
used like traditional epoxies. It
is derived largely from naturally
occurring pine oil, which has
better elongation properties than
petroleum-based products.

ERIC CHAN OF ECCO DESIGN

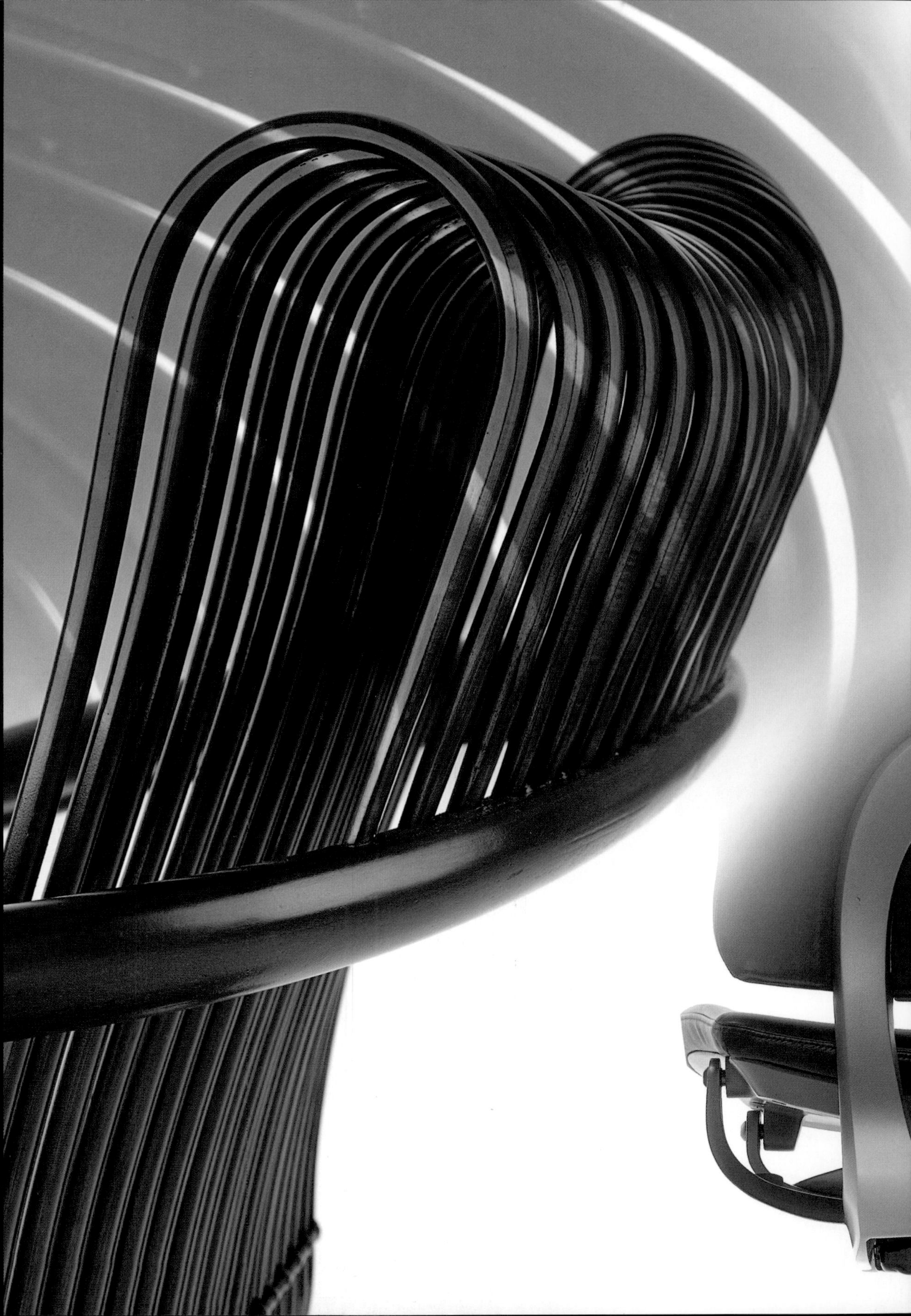

CHAPTER 4
ADDITIVE MANUFACTURING MEDIA

Additive manufacturing (aka 3D printing) is the new catch-all term for the range of technologies that add materials layer by layer, guided by a software program that renders from a 3D image. Touted by some as the "next industrial revolution," it has evolved from prototyping process to commercially viable manufacturing method in only a few years. The number of different techniques also continues to grow, using wire, powder, UV-cured liquid, and laminated layers as the base materials from which products are created. The techniques include various methods for product consolidation such as fused deposition modeling (FDM), which lays down semi-molten material in layers; electron beam melting (EBM), direct metal laser sintering (DMLS) and selective laser sintering (SLS), which melt metal or plastic powders layer by layer with an electron or laser beam; and stereolithography (SLA), which uses UV light focused onto light-curable materials to solidify successive layers to build up an object.

PUSHING PAST POLYMERS

To this list must be added some of the other methods of building up a product through adding material. The "Endless Furniture" series by Dirk Vander Kooij uses a basic extrusion technique to translate layers of material into stools and tables, while the evolution of 3D knitting allows fully formed three-dimensional objects, such as chair backs or car doors, to be created from yarns.

Compared to most conventional manufacturing methods, all these additive processes produce little or no waste, enable mass customization from individual part to part, and offer a one-step

opposite The plate of Nike's Vapor Laser Talon cleat was sintered together layer by layer to achieve a complex support structure designed to help football players launch into a drive faster and maintain their stance longer.

process for the putting together of many complex parts made from different materials. This allows for a much more iterative approach to manufacturing and enables the user of the product to influence its performance and aesthetics within certain boundaries. The fear that once we can all produce our own stuff using these machines we will no longer need brands, however, is to misunderstand the value of a brand. It is likely that brands will offer licenses of their

creative output to commercial additive manufacturers or individually to customers, creating brand value through initial forms that can then be customized. After all, many of our current beloved brands no longer make their own products anyway.

The range of material types that can be effectively printed or added is increasing, with more refined ways to consolidate them, enabling quicker and cheaper production. From the original starch, nylon and ABS plastics, metal alloys are commonplace, as are some ceramics, stone, conductive polymers, rubbers, and mixtures of more than one material at a time via multiple deposition heads. Ultra-fine metal powders can be efficiently consolidated using high-powered lasers, giving almost 100 percent dense net-shaped parts that need only minor final surface preparation to be usable. This makes the production of unique jewelry and anatomically exact medical implants out of silver or titanium a much easier prospect. It also enables the production of alloys of metals that traditionally have been hard to produce because the constituent materials do not mix well together (an analogy might be oil and water), and on levels that allow the close control of microstructure and thus performance. One challenge in the future in which all things are manufactured this way is the handling of potentially hazardous materials by users. Fine powders can be potentially explosive if left in the open (aluminum

above The proposed Landscape House's artificial limestone shell is printed in horizontal layers complementing the structure's continuous form. Reinforced-concrete filling adds a vertical load to make complex structures such as stairs simultaneously with walls and fittings for utilities.

below The Urbee car by KOR Ecologic, printed in ABS plastic with Dimension 3D Printers. The designers pledge that the Urbee 2 will cross the United States on 45 L (10 gal.) of gas, in part because of its lightweight, digitally optimized shell.

powder is used as a rocket fuel), and some combinations of chemicals could cause adverse reactions. Clearly as this technology develops and more become users and producers, some basic guidelines will become essential. This intimate mixing of materials even lends itself to the printing of food, engineering new tastes and textures by the combining of ingredients in fine striations impossible to make until now.

The scale of products that it is possible to create varies more widely in additive manufacturing than in other processes, with millimeter-sized parts commonplace, but also entire buildings being printed using fast-setting concrete pumped out of a hose.

THE MAKER COMMUNITY

It may be because of the accessible nature of many of the additive manufacturing processes (there are many desktop 3D printers but nothing so portable for injection molding or blow molding) that a lot of the advancements are coming from individual inventors and from the "maker" community, aided by the open-source way in which they are sharing ideas and solutions. This has led to a much faster evolution and maturity in the discipline than in many others, and heralds a new way forward for product development.

Though many of the developers of these processes consider faster, larger-scale manufacture a goal, there is the potential, at the other end of the scale, that new discoveries may be made at the micro and even nano level. There is a chance that additive manufacturing and nanotechnology might meet somewhere in this move toward closer control of making things. Controlled placement of material, layer upon layer, is what nanotech is all about, offering the chance to mimic nature in the way that it evolves and grows, and to tune performance and function on a ultra-small scale. Indeed, carbon nanofibers are already being used as a strengthening material included as part of the printed piece.

So is additive manufacturing the next industrial revolution? Certainly it has had a rapid rise in popularity and in only a few years we have seen commercial products such as jewelry, kitchen and bathroom hardware, medical implants and prosthetics, even shoes (such as the Nike Vapor Laser Talon), be successfully printed using these processes. This evolution will likely result in its being a viable method for producing many consumer products, especially those that offer a degree of customization and design adaptation, but the slower speed compared to other processes such as injection molding and the "one at a time" current manufacturing will keep it as a more bespoke, higher-end way of creating the products we love.

below left Designed by Belgian firm Unfold and Tim Knapen, "L'Artisan Électronique" creates pots from rolls of clay in real time with direction from remote users' hand movements through a sensor.

below right The seamless, hinged organic form designed by Patrick Jouin equips the BLOOM table lamp with printed petals to release or contain light. The material is fire-resistant polyamide.

13:30
HEADPHONES

DESIGNER / MANUFACTURER
John Mabry, Teague
www.teague.com

MATERIAL
ABS plus TM-P430 thermoplastic

MATERIAL MANUFACTURER
Stratasys (Dimension 1200ES Series 3D printer)

DESIGNER BIOGRAPHY
A senior designer at Teague, John Mabry has
spent the past decade working in the consumer
goods and tech space with such clients as
Intel, Microsoft, HP, Starbucks, and Xbox. He
previously designed everything from televisions
to toys for Kodak, RCA, Xerox, and Fisher-Price.
A graduate of Rochester Institute of Technology,
New York, he has earned numerous utility and
design patents for his work.

MATERIAL PROPERTIES
Sustainable Solutions, Lightweight, Simplification

opposite

top left The tapered, thin-walled parts of
the 13:30 headphones, including a flexible
strap and semi-articulating cans, were
designed to be printed.

top right ABSplus offers the widest range
of colors available with FDM technology.

bottom The set of fifteen parts can be
assembled without any tools and fitted with
readily available electrical components.

Driven by design as much as acoustics, headphones
and other listening devices have become mainstays
of today's mobile consumer electronics arena.
Teague, the Seattle-based design firm founded
by design legend Walter Dorwin Teague, is recognized for
commercializing groundbreaking technology, including
its work with Samsung and Panasonic. Senior industrial
designer John Mabry carries this legacy forward with
13:30, a pair of 3D printable headphones that is completely
functional yet easy to assemble and recycle.

Seeking to challenge the convention of mass
production that drives the consumer electronics market,
13:30 embraces the idea of printed prototypes as actual
products. "What if once off the print bed an object could be
assembled without any tools yet made functional by readily
attainable components?" Mabry wondered. To encourage
collaboration, he released the designs, component list, and
instructions to enable anyone to make their own working
version, an equivalent product to what is commercially
available, only "made on demand—just for you."

MATERIAL INSIGHT

ABS, the go-to plastic resin for consumer electronics for
the past twenty years, was the obvious choice for these
headphones. The material has good durability, is elastic
enough to work well for the head band, and is suitably stiff
so that the parts snap together easily and securely. It was
produced on an FDM (fused deposition modeling) machine
and the whole printing procedure took thirteen and a half
hours (hence the name 13:30). Made using a professional
Dimension 1200ES machine, two of the critical parts relied
heavily on soluble support printing that this machine
specializes in, so Mabry is working on newer versions that
are more easily replicable on a more accessible machine such
as a MakerBot Replicator.

BESPOKE FAIRINGS

DESIGNER
Scott Summit, Bespoke Innovations
www.bespokeinnovations.com

MANUFACTURER
3D Systems
www.3dsystems.com

MATERIAL
DuraForm impact-resistant engineering plastic

MATERIAL MANUFACTURER
3D Systems (sPro SLS Production Printer)

DESIGNER BIOGRAPHY
With more than twenty years of experience and research in design and additive fabrication, Scott Summit, co-founder of San Francisco-based Bespoke Innovations, seeks to connect complex human needs with design and technology solutions. Bespoke was founded in 2010 with the simple idea that an integrated approach connecting design, medicine, and new technology can offer more meaningful and individualized solutions for many current challenges. His clients have included Apple, Nike, Palm, and Silicon Graphics, among others. Bespoke was acquired by 3D Systems in May 2012 and now drives its medical solutions research.

MATERIAL PROPERTIES
Ergonomic, Durable, High Strength

Lightweight fairings from Bespoke Innovations are made of impact-resistant plastic that can be plated with chrome. The fretwork is more than decoration: it reduces the weight of a standard fairing to a mere 190 g (6.6 oz.).

Whether their condition is congenital or the result of trauma, those with a prosthetic limb are often acutely aware of being perceived as different. Most attempts to grapple with this involve moving among the able-bodied as unobtrusively as possible. Bespoke Innovations, by contrast, views prosthetics as an opportunity for self-expression, even a form a connection with others.

For the designer, it begins with seeing those without a limb more deeply and with less judgment than most able-bodied do. It is an acute lesson in reaching beyond the pride of one's own creations to all the possible variations of the end user, managing not just to improve their functional experience but to ennoble a handicap. To achieve this, Bespoke designed the fairing, a specialized covering that surrounds an existing prosthetic leg and, through a three-dimensional scanning process, recreates the leg's unique shape with a strong, flexible, and lightweight polymer that restores the lost contour and introduces an expression of personality. The individualized application of materials, patterns, and graphics to the fairing helps erase the awkwardness that can distance amputees from their surroundings.

Most manufacturers start with a product and end with the user; Bespoke starts with the user and ends with the product. Founders Scott Summit and Kenneth B. Trauner and their team are part of a movement toward personalized medicine that is the opposite of mass production. The aim is to aid well-being not through an engineering-driven mindset but by accepting that our true self lies in our uniqueness, idiosyncrasies, tastes, and quirks.

MATERIAL INSIGHT

Fairings that can be easily swapped out on both the shin and the calf sections of a prosthetic leg are produced to order in virtually any material. Using scanning technology to create a 3D rendition of the other leg, a mirror design is made, and once the scanning process is complete, customization of the fairing is possible by selecting from an array of form templates, patterns, tattoos, materials, metal plating, and graphics, using an online tool called the "Configurator," which allows users to explore and apply a range of design styles to see how the end result might appear. The 3D-printed part can be manufactured from plastics, ceramic, and metals such as steel, titanium and others; and also painted or plated to create decorative effects.

TITANIUM JAW

DESIGNER

Biomed Research Group of the University of Hasselt, Xios Hogeschool, Xilloc Medical BV, and the Catholic University of Leuven

MANUFACTURER

LayerWise
www.layerwise.com

MATERIAL MANUFACTURER

LayerWise NV (titanium) and Cambioceramics (coating)

DESIGNER BIOGRAPHY

LayerWise is the first production center in Belgium that exclusively focuses on the additive manufacturing (AM) process for metal parts. The company was founded by Jonas Van Vaerenbergh and Peter Mercelis, both of whom were closely involved in the development of selective laser melting (SLM) at the Catholic University of Leuven, an important collaborative partner.

MATERIAL PROPERTIES

Ergonomic, Durable, Composite

The custom-built implant fits exactly to the patient's existing bone structure and weighs approximately 107 g (3.8 oz.), with highly polished rims for nerves and cavities for facilitating muscle attachment and ingrowth.

A truly ephochal moment in the quest for patient-specific bone implants came when an eighty-three-year-old Dutch woman received a new lower jaw made from titanium powder that had been heated and fused, a layer at a time, by a 3D laser printer. Unlike earlier versions of implants that would have required multiple metalworking steps to craft, the total lower jaw implant was produced by a single company, LayerWise, a Belgian facility with expertise in metal additive manufacturing, or AM.

A high-precision laser selectively fuses together layers of metal particles, eliminating the need for any glue or binder while enabling complex freeform geometries to be produced as a single part. To achieve this a 3D digital design is split into 2D layers that are then read as cross-sections by the printer. Thirty-three layers equal 1 millimeter of height, with many thousands of layers needed to construct the entire jawbone. A marvel of efficiency, it took a matter of hours to print, and dramatically reduced the time needed for the reconstructive procedure. "The use of such implants yields excellent form and function, speeds up surgery and patient recovery, and reduces the risk for medical complications," explains Dr. Peter Mercelis, co-founder of LayerWise.

The launch of LayerWise's 3D-printed implants caps an extensive development process involving intense collaboration among researchers, engineers, surgeons, and material scientists. As LayerWise continues to push the boundaries of AM technology, made possible in part by a commitment to systematically invest in research and development, the promise of patient-specific implants applied to body organs comes into focus, a testament to today's enthralling advances in healthcare technology.

MATERIAL INSIGHT

The use of fine metal particles enables metals to be rendered using additive manufacturing. The particles melt and fuse together to create the overall form. Thanks to its resistance to corrosion and compatibility with the human body, titanium is the typical metal used in medical implants, and can be effectively produced in complex parts using additive manufacturing. By having full control over the part consolidation process, the geometry of bone can be replicated exactly and reproduced with titanium alloy for similar material properties, including absolute density, hardness, strength, elongation, and modulus when compared to cast or even wrought material.

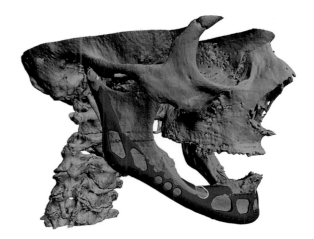

Maikel Beerens, CEO of Xilloc Medical, led the design stage with the patient's surgeons and SLM engineers at LayerWise. Tomography (CT) scans—2D images built up into a 3D model—were crucial for designing a prosthetic to replace the entire jawbone.

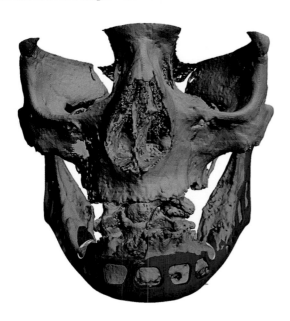

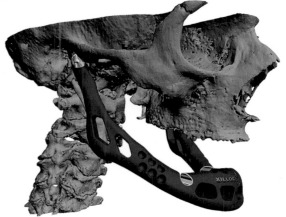

STAINLESS STEEL BONE CUFF

DESIGNER
Nervous System
www.n-e-r-v-o-u-s.com

MANUFACTURER
Shapeways
www.shapeways.com

MATERIAL
Stainless steel alloy (40% bronze)

DESIGNER BIOGRAPHY
Jessica Rosenkrantz, Creative Director, and Jesse Louis-Rosenberg, Chief Science Officer, founded Nervous System in 2007. Jessica graduated from MIT in 2005 and holds degrees in Architecture and Biology. Afterwards, she studied architecture at the Harvard Graduate School of Design. Jesse also attended MIT, majoring in Mathematics. Before co-founding Nervous System he worked building modeling and design automation for Gehry Technologies. They have given talks on their generative design process in many forums, including MIT and Carnegie Mellon and design conferences such as the Eyeo Festival, Minneapolis.

MATERIAL PROPERTIES
Durable, High Strength

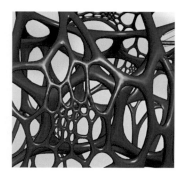

Nervous System's Cell Cycle tool is a web-based design app that customers can use to shape, twist, and subdivide their own physible--a program that instructs a 3D printer about form, color, and material-- to see parameters such as price change in real time.

The jewelry and housewares designed by Jessica Rosenkrantz and Jesse Louis-Rosenberg of the design practice Nervous System comprise a uniquely advanced cabinet of curiosities. Their poetically futuristic creations play at the edge of abstraction but never stray far from the natural phenomena that inspire their work—radiating tendrils of algae adorn ear lobes, the aggregate growth of corals and crystals shimmers along a neckline, pollen and seeds inspire spherical lamps that cast a constellation of shadows around a room.

It is a testament to their combined degrees in architecture, biology, and mathematics that their creative approach "focuses on generative design methods using both algorithmic and physical tools," yet reverberates with the intricacies of the natural world. Their iterative methodology begins with an initial concept, from which they write a pattern-generating algorithm that allows them to further explore ideas and formal possibilities before arriving at a finished product. As an extension of their process, they have developed web-based generative design apps that allow users to create their own unique patterns and products.

For the lattice-like Porous Cuff, the team looked to Radiolaria, amoeboid protozoa that possess intricate skeletons of often perfect geometric form and symmetry. These microscopic creatures are the silent partner in an open-weave bracelet design that can be executed in endless permutations, either organic or geometric. The design is built up layer by layer through a 3D-printing process that gives the piece its airy form, arresting nature's ephemeral quality in steel, bamboo, or felt.

MATERIAL INSIGHT

The jewelry is sintered from fully alloyed stainless steel powders that can be produced in parts with a minimum wall thickness of 0.3–0.4 millimeters (0.01–0.02 inches).

The steel powder is melted in the sintering process using a high-powered 200 watt Yb-fiber-optic laser, typically building up layers approximately 20 microns thick. No further tooling is required to create the fully consolidated part. The surface of the part is typically shot-peened down to a roughness of 1–50 microns and then polished to a mirror finish. Various alloys of stainless steel are available, with 316L being the most often used owing to its good combination of corrosion resistance and strength.

The stainless steel material, sourced from Shapeways, requires carbide bits to mill and drill it, yet a laser can steadily sinter these otherwise impossible forms to save time and material.

ENDLESS FLOW ROCKING CHAIR

DESIGNER / MANUFACTURER

Dirk Vander Kooij

www.dirkvanderkooij.nl

MATERIAL

Reused plastics from recycled refrigerator interiors

DESIGNER BIOGRAPHY

Studio Dirk Vander Kooij works at the intersection of design, craft, and production with the belief that a new production technique is as interesting as an entirely new design. Following Vander Kooij's graduation from the Design Academy in Eindhoven in the Netherlands, the Endless Flow Rocking Chair design was included in the Design Academy exposition in 2010, and displayed at the Salone del Mobile, Milan. He returned to the fair the year after with a complete furniture collection, which caught the attention of the Stedelijk Museum in Amsterdam, the Vitra Design Museum in Germany, and the Museum of Modern Art in New York.

MATERIAL PROPERTIES

Sustainable Solutions, Recycled, Simplification

Vander Kooij wrote the code for and repurposed a robot so he could evaluate his design by looking at, sitting in, and adjusting it. After fifty-four prototypes he achieved a comfortable shape and continued to explore different colors and patterns in the "Endless" process.

For the Arts and Crafts movement of the late nineteenth century, the humanization and democratization of design offered a beacon of hope, inspiration and meaning in an increasingly industrialized world. More than a century later, product designers such as Dirk Vander Kooij are exploring anew the possibilities of design, craft, and production, this time with the benefit of predecessors like Ray and Charles Eames who, among other twentieth-century pioneers, introduced innovative aesthetic ideals for furniture and products made possible by techniques and production processes from other fields.

The Eindhoven graduate's Endless Flow Rocking Chair shrugs off the notion that a prototype must be perfect before it can be produced and, instead, revels in the quirks and inaccuracies, as well as the discoveries and refinements, that emerge from rapid prototyping made possible with 3D printing. The name "Endless" refers to the thin continuous strand of synthetic thread, built up layer upon layer, that the chair is made with, as well as the endless variations that are possible by modifying each piece of furniture, with no additional expense. A computer-programmed robotic arm repurposed as a large-scale "printer" deposits recycled bits of refrigerator interiors in a single strand of plastic. The execution suggests new possibilities not only for meaningful design but also for an ongoing legacy of process innovation.

MATERIAL INSIGHT

In a similar process to more well-known additive manufacturing, this chair uses thicker, continuous lines of recycled plastic, extruded rather like toothpaste from a repurposed industrial robot. The recycled material is laid down in semi-molten colored strips that build up to form the furniture, adhering to each layer below. The additive manufacturing process enables the product to be tweaked as more are made, customizing for fit, design, and color.

IRON MAN 2 BODY ARMOR

DESIGNER / MANUFACTURER

Jason Lopes, Legacy Effects

www.legacyefx.com

MATERIAL

Objet precision photopolymers

Stratasys (Objet Eden 260V)

DESIGNER BIOGRAPHY

Jason Lopes is the lead systems engineer at Legacy Effects, a special effects company that has worked on some of Hollywood's biggest blockbusters. His credits include *Terminator Salvation*, *2012*, *Avatar*, *Thor*, *Iron Man* and *Iron Man 2*, and *Cowboys and Aliens*. Lopes is a strong advocate of 3D printing as an invaluable tool along with 3D scanning, 3D design and 3D modeling. He has used Stratasys's Objet 3D-printing technology to produce stunning visual effects along with consumer printers such as the MakerBot Replicator 2 to see how they might support the earlier stages of workflow.

MATERIAL PROPERTIES

Ergonomic

Droplets of photopolymer UV-cured into thin layers ensured that every copy of the glove had a high enough resolution to be smooth to the touch and primed for a coat of chrome paint.

The beauty of 3D printing is that a solid object of virtually any shape or size can be quickly made from a digital model. Eliminating the time involved in cutting, drilling, or gluing to assemble a design, 3D printing's additive process allows creative disciplines, especially those that rely on effectively conveying visual ideas, to work three-dimensionally from the start.

Since 3D printing appeared in *Jurassic Park 2: The Lost World*, the technology has come into its own in the world of film special effects. This is especially the case with live-action movies where real stunt work calls for endless identical, often customized props that need to be produced in multiples for repeat takes.

For the *Iron Man* film series, lead character Tony Stark (played by Robert Downey, Jr.) is an industrialist and master engineer who constructs a powerful exoskeleton that is able to transform him into the technologically advanced superhero Iron Man. The plot line and film production mirror each other, both driven by advanced technology that seeks to bring the mythology of Marvel Comics action heroes into a believable present-day reality.

To meet the film's production demands involving grueling fight scenes, a 3D printer by innovation leader Objet Geometries collaborated with the movie's production company Legacy Effects to scan the actor who would wear the costume, producing anthropomorphic components sized to human proportions for the creation of the Iron Man suit, as well as the armature worn by his arch-nemesis Whiplash. The body armor for both characters is truly "print-to-wear"—taking us at once into a world that is futuristic yet ancient, heroic yet elusive, tangible yet dramatic.

MATERIAL INSIGHT

The Eden printers from company Objet use PolyJet 3D technology, printing, and photopolymer resins with an

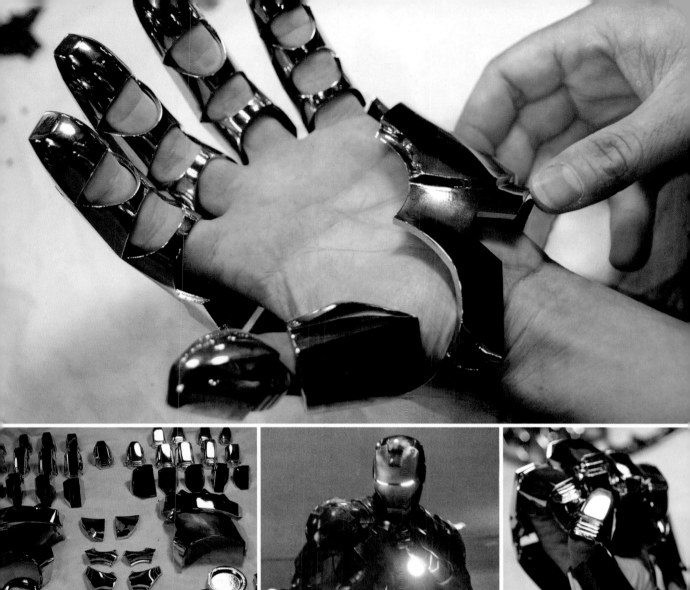

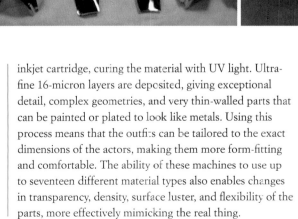

inkjet cartridge, curing the material with UV light. Ultra-fine 16-micron layers are deposited, giving exceptional detail, complex geometries, and very thin-walled parts that can be painted or plated to look like metals. Using this process means that the outfits can be tailored to the exact dimensions of the actors, making them more form-fitting and comfortable. The ability of these machines to use up to seventeen different material types also enables changes in transparency, density, surface luster, and flexibility of the parts, more effectively mimicking the real thing.

Each glove has twenty-five parts. Plates lock around the wrist and back of the hand and fingers are printed with channels that designers threaded together with wire. The final product survived challenging stunt work with a flawless appearance that required little digital touch-up.

Bottom row center image
© 2010 Marvel Studios

MATERIAL INSIGHT

The additive manufacturing process used to create the Flyknit is an update on existing knitting processes such that more complex shapes (a shoe upper) with multiple patterns, yarn materials, and constructions such as loops, holes and hardware can be constructed. The knitting proceeds in one continuous step, with several spools of yarn of different materials incorporated at once, even in a tube construction. Each part can be customized during manufacture, offering one-of-a-kind designs similar to the way rapid prototype products are made. Areas of the sneaker can be stiffened through a fusing process, giving the shoe upper differing areas of hard and soft sections where needed.

The Flyknit process saves material because there are virtually no scraps to cut off in this additive design. Nike further lowered the environmental impact of the Flyknit Lunar1+ by using water-based glue on components of the shoe and laces made with 100 percent recycled polyester.

3D-PRINTED OPTICS

DESIGNERS
Karl D. D. Willis, Eric Brockmeyer, Ivan Poupyrev, Disney Research; www.karlddwillis.com, www.ericbrockmeyer.com, www.ivanpoupyrev.com
Scott E. Hudson, Human Computer Interaction Institute, School of Computer Science at Carnegie Mellon; www.hcii.cmu.edu

MANUFACTURER
Disney Research
www.disneyresearch.com

MATERIAL
Objet's VeroClear photopolymer

MATERIAL MANUFACTURER
Stratasys (Objet Eden series)

DESIGNER BIOGRAPHIES
Karl D. D. Willis, Eric Brockmeyer, and Ivan Poupyrev are members of the Interaction Group at Disney Research, a diverse group of interaction designers, scientists, technologists, and artists. Scott Hudson is a professor in the Human Computer Interaction Institute at Carnegie Mellon University, and was founding director of the HCII PhD program.

MATERIAL PROPERTIES
Simplification

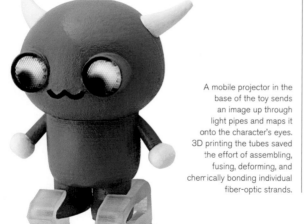

A mobile projector in the base of the toy sends an image up through light pipes and maps it onto the character's eyes. 3D printing the tubes saved the effort of assembling, fusing, deforming, and chemically bonding individual fiber-optic strands.

Witnessing the end result is easy, but what actually goes into the creation of a 3D-printed object, especially one with interactive capabilities? Printed Optics, an innovative 3D-printing approach pioneered by Disney Engineering, enables the form and interactive functions of an object to be created simultaneously, thereby paving the way for new manufacturing techniques. Drawing on art and science, design and technology, the entertainment giant has devised a way to embed specially shaped "light pipes" into an object so that light can circulate around it, respond to external triggers, and emit graphic displays of symbols and text.

Beyond the dynamic possibilities this opens up for 3D printing, among the chief benefits of this approach is speed. Creating prototype toys on 3D printers means that a working design can be generated within minutes, rather than the time it would traditionally take to retool in a factory. With shorter prototyping cycles comes greater flexibility to experiment, model new ideas, and consider new features that were not part of an original design.

To achieve true innovation requires vision and conviction. While 3D printing may still be in its infancy, Disney's research efforts show what dedication to the "how" of toy making, confidence in an ability to overcome obstacles, and pure creative fun can produce.

MATERIAL INSIGHT
The power of this work by Disney Research and their collaborators at the Computational Design Lab at Carnegie Mellon University is that additive manufacturing is being used to solve design problems that are a step beyond mere complex part forming. Using a material called VeroClear, a clear photopolymer designed for creating transparent parts, the researchers were able to build optical pipes and guides with small toy parts. These optical guides could then be used

to channel projected light to create additional animation and information on the toys. There were some challenges with printing fully optically clear parts, because the process inevitably creates variations in material properties that lead to reductions in clarity, but these are being worked through. One major advantage with this process is that as the technology develops, the ability to dynamically control optical properties such as the refractive index, reflectivity, transmittance, absorption, and diffusion will enable an even richer design space for sensing, display, and illumination.

VeroClear has optical properties similar to those of PMMA (Flexiglas), but easier to manipulate at this scale in ultra-thin layers. Light pipes were printed inside chess pieces (**top left**) that channeled light from the board at a right angle. Custom lenses were printed with long "beamsplitters" that have blade-like prisms (**top right**) and dot-shaped air pockets (**bottom**).

MYLON GLASSES

DESIGNER / MANUFACTURER
MYKITA
www.mykita.com

MATERIAL
Polyamide-based MYLON with hydrophobic nanocoating

DESIGNER BIOGRAPHY
MYKITA has been supplying handmade eyewear since 2003. A constant search for intelligent technical solutions, the creative use of materials, and a wealth of experience in eyewear design are the defining elements behind its collections. A key factor in the company's success is its holistic business philosophy, which unites all departments and the in-house workshop under a single roof, the MYKITA HAUS, in the heart of Berlin.

MATERIAL PROPERTIES
Sustainable Solutions

While optical lenses designed for visual acuity are among the modern era's most important inventions, well-fitting eyeglass frames remain a challenge. The earliest designs were made from natural materials, including wood, horn, shell, and bone. Later, more durable versions were rendered in metals, such as brass, silver, gold, and steel. In the twentieth century, improved plastics introduced a new era in frame styling, which endures today.

But no matter the era or the material, comfortable, well-functioning frames depend on the shape and position of the wearer's nose and ears, with their myriad variations in size, firmness, and symmetry. Additionally, the lenses must sit perpendicular to the arms that they depend on for support. And while designers mastered early on getting the lens positioned squarely in the line of vision, challenges linger since the eyes are constantly moving, as focusing distance and direction shifts.

Berlin-based MYKITA has developed Mylon, which takes a decisive step toward resolving these variations. In 2007, Mylon began experimenting with a polyamide material, aiming to introduce the next wave in eyewear. Polyamide, or nylon, is extremely tough and resistant to oils and bodily solvents, like sweat—ideal for daily use.

Several years of research led to a complex, patented process by which selective laser sintering (SLS) enables objects to be created in every possible geometric configuration, making 3D designs out of layers of superfine polyamide powder. MYKITA's exclusive process results in

a set of frames that are highly customized, lightweight, and durable, all optimal qualities for sports gear and everyday accessories

MATERIAL INSIGHT

One of the first commercially available consumer products that has been constructed using additive manufacturing, the Mylon frames are produced using selective laser sintering (SLS) of nylon. This process potentially enables the glasses to be individually constructed for the user based on their head shape, precise eye location, and desired comfort. The characteristic slight surface roughness found in SLS-produced parts is here classed as a unique visual and tactile effect. The lenses themselves are not produced using additive manufacturing, as they require an optical clarity that is currently hard to achieve using this process, though light transparency is possible.

After any remaining uncolored nylon-based powder has been removed from the frames they are submerged in dye and readily absorb color. Screwless hinges and logos are affixed, then every surface of the glasses is plasma-sprayed with a hydrophobic coating.

CHAPTER 5
RECYCLED MATERIALS

Absolutely everything on the surface of this planet is to some degree recycled. The air we breathe, the water we drink, the products we use (plastics are simply recycled plankton from hundreds of millions of years ago, and most of the gold currently in circulation was probably first made into products at least 200 years ago), even ourselves, who are likely recycled molecules from the food we and our ancestors ate. Nature recycles efficiently and endlessly, so it is about time we got serious about repurposing the stuff we make, use and throw out. We may be seeing a technological revolution in the effectiveness and efficiency of our recycling story, but we still have a long way to go to ensure that our landfills are a thing of the past rather than one of the few human-made things easily seen from space.

METALS

Metal recycling is no big deal. From commodity steels to high-performance alloys such as titanium to precious metals like platinum, standardized processes and optimal percentages of scrap concentration ensure that most of what we use can be used again. Construction, automotive, heavy industry, consumer products— all use metals that can be recycled to a greater or lesser degree, and also use high-recycled-content metals in their production. Recycling glass is similar, though it tends to be a down-cycling process, since the composition of a lot of performance glasses is so hard to replicate with the addition of recycled material.

opposite Mieke Meijer collects misprints and unsold copies of her local paper in Eindhoven, the Netherlands, to make NewspaperWood. The durable, recyclable material introduces an alternative to the waste stream for newsprint.

PLASTICS

Plastics recycling is a different matter. As a material plastic is less hardy, more prone to contamination than metals or glass, and reduced in performance every time it is mechanically shredded before remelting to produce recycled granulate. Recycling of beverage bottles requires several stages of cleaning and decontamination to be usable; by contrast, the heat used in melting scrap steel is enough to remove any contaminants and kill any bacteria left on the material. Thus, it is in the area of plastics recycling that innovations lead to the biggest advances for viable recycled raw material content. We have seen over the past few years a steady increase in the range of plastics types, along with more specified color ranges and food-safe options, that suggest that recycling as an end-of-life option is an economically viable one. There are biobased plastics that can now mix safely in recycling streams, and chemical recycling—dissolving the plastic rather than cutting it up—that can maintain physical and mechanical performance of the virgin plastic even after multiple recycling lives.

Beyond simple consumer willingness to accept plastics recycling as an integral part of waste disposal, the major barrier to better choice in recycled plastics is sorting of the different types at the recycling facility. X-ray spectroscopy and buoyancy sorters (some plastics float, others sink), though an improvement on hand sorting, cannot separate some of the variations within plastics families. More accurate sorting of plastics is being achieved through processes such as Near Infrared (NIR) imaging, which can sort the major commodity and engineering plastics consistently, accurately and efficiently, leaving only color as a final sort (also achieved using NIR) to further improve recycled content selection.

CERAMICS AND OTHERS

Recycling of ceramics and stoneware has to date been based entirely on mechanical crushing: thus the second life for ceramics has tended to be as road underlay or gravel for pathways, because minimal crushing is needed to get the products down to such coarse particles. More recently, some countertop manufacturers are using old sanitaryware as aggregate for hardwearing solid surfacing slabs, but thanks to its unique aesthetic, this will only be of limited appeal. Japan, owing to a shortage of certain raw materials for ceramic production, has implemented a project called "Re-Tableware" that uses finely crushed used tableware mixed with pottery clay and fired to create new ceramic articles.

Paper has many of the same issues as plastic regarding contamination, and, similarly, recycling reduces the physical and mechanical properties of paper fibers. Most paper fibers can go through the process five to seven times before they become too short; the paper from orange juice cartons has the longest, cleanest fibers, while tissue paper tends to be at the bottom of the recycling hierarchy. Unfortunately, unlike plastics, there is no chemical way in which the fibers can be reconstituted, though potentially they could be used for the production of other materials such as cellulose acetates or rayon yarns.

The future is likely also to include more use of plasma material processing. High enough in energy to reduce literally anything to atoms, this process is able to quickly break down waste into different classes of material for further use. Currently used commercially by companies such as Plasma Waste Recycling Inc. as a way of converting plastic waste to usable gas fuel at an efficiency of 99 percent, it can also

Designed by Starbucks Creative Group and sold in Starbucks, each mug was made with 20 percent finely ground tableware along with raw clay and rainwater to create a zero-waste mug with a unique gritty texture.

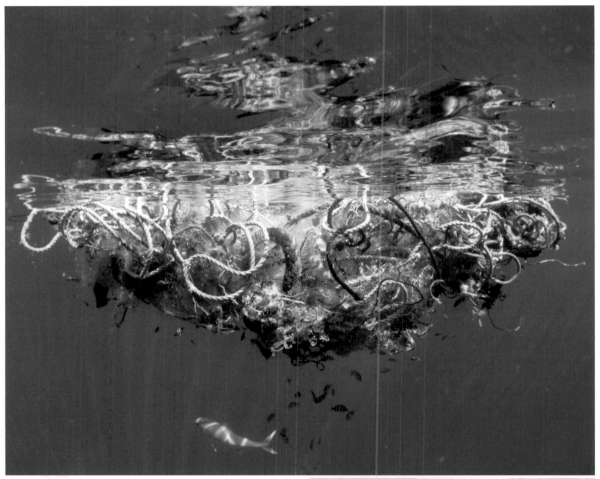

above Sunlight gradually degrades floating plastic waste from watersheds and fishing vessels until the particles are too small to see—but no less buoyant—and are easily ingested by seabirds and marine mammals.

right Plastics need to be sorted by hand to remove impurities such as ink-laden paper before their chemical composition can be detected with infrared or X-ray spectroscopy.

separate metals from other types of waste, with an ideal result (not yet achieved) of sorting all waste into elemental piles for reuse as raw materials in new products. The main limiting factor is its use of power, since to create the plasma, very high temperatures are required.

Recycling is inevitable and essential. There will likely be a time when *nothing* can be thrown away and everything will have a secondary purpose, whether to create more of the same product or a different product, as a filler for something, or just as fuel to burn. The sooner we start to imagine a second—and third, fourth, fifth—life for the materials in our products, the better this time will be.

GREEN CHAIR

DESIGNER
Javier Mariscal
www.mariscal.com

MANUFACTURER
Mobles 114
www.mobles114.com

MATERIAL
Recycled polypropylene

DESIGNER BIOGRAPHY
Javier Mariscal's work defies easy categorization. Working solo, in collaboration, and since 1989 as principal of Estudio Mariscal, he has contributed to the creation of the Barcelona Zoo corporate image, online animations, textiles for Nani Marquina, furniture for Memphis, and the theatrical production *Colors*. Called the Peter Pan of Spanish design for his simple, dreamy, child-like aesthetic informed by an underlying social commentary, he created the corporate identity for the 1992 Barcelona Olympics. Interior design and graphics projects for retail, hospitality, and public spaces include H&M, Moroso, Alessi, Phaidon, and Artemide.

MATERIAL PROPERTIES
Sustainable Solutions, Recycled, Simplification

Mariscal's sketch highlights the polygonal geometry of the seat. The faceted structure is ergonomic and simple to manufacture.

Spanish designer Javier Mariscal wears many hats, ranging from graphic designer and comic artist, which led to an Academy Award nomination for the animated film *Chico & Rita*, to industrial designer (Moroso, Santa & Cole, Artemide, Casina and Uno number among his collaborators). He is also a skilled painter, as demonstrated by his lyrical patterned carpets for Vondom and Nani Marquina.

With the Green Chair he designed for Mobles 114, Mariscal turns his attention to a chair whose seat is made from 100 percent recycled plastic and is, in turn, 100 percent recyclable. Using only a few flat planes, the designer has created a piece of ergonomic comfort derived from the polygonal geometry of the seat. High-relief ribbing across the seat celebrates the material properties of polypropylene that is generated from the recycling of industrial waste, resulting in a charcoal-gray color. Limited variation is introduced depending on the choice of wood or painted metal legs.

The design of the chair is in keeping with its intended role for contract sale and clients with a small budget. The seat's overall form has an austere linearity that plays with diagonals, especially when viewed from the back, where a vertical spine adds solidity and reinforces the stripped-down ethos. Despite the chair's rough, brutalist appearance, its intention is tender—to provide a sustainable option for seating that improves the quality of life and helps to preserve the planet.

MATERIAL INSIGHT
The encouraging aspect of the material and manufacturing choice for this chair was the decision to consider its entire life cycle, from raw material selection, through production and shipping to end of life. One hundred percent recycled polypropylene was used for the injection-molded seat, which

can be easily recycled again into another seat or similar product. The construction of the chair also allows easy assembly and disassembly, encouraging recycling, which is possible for every part of the product. The use of standard spare parts that were the same for other furniture products reduced waste, and in addition, the entire manufacturing process complies with ISO 14006, the internationally recognized ecodesign management system.

The high-relief engraving on the seat (**right**) contrasts with the back of the chair (**left**), where one can more clearly see the mottled dark-gray color of the injection-molded recycled polypropylene.

PAPILLON CUTLERY SET

DESIGNER
FaddaSantos
www.faddasantos.com

MANUFACTURER
Aladdin
www.aladdin-pmi.com

MATERIAL
eCycle®

MATERIAL MANUFACTURER
Pacific Market International (PMI)

DESIGNER BIOGRAPHY
FaddaSantos was formed by Caterina Fadda and Fran Santos to design products and furniture. A thorough understanding of materials and manufacturing processes sustains the studio's creative approach. Caterina Fadda graduated in Ceramics from the University of Westminster, London, and obtained a master's degree at the Royal College of Art, London. Fran Santos studied Furniture Design and Cabinet Making at the London College of Furniture and has degrees from Middlesex University and the Bartlett School of Architecture at University College London.

MATERIAL PROPERTIES
Sustainable Solutions, Lightweight, Recycled, Simplification

above and opposite Much of the post-consumer plastic sourced for the cutlery set is from beverage bottle caps and food-safe polypropylene tubs used for refrigerated packaging of dairy products.

References to meals taken in pastoral settings can be found in the ancient writings of Ovid, Plutarch, and Seneca. For modern-day workers, outdoor dining is more likely a park bench in obliging weather. But the idea of a portable meal necessitates an ease and practical invention consistent with our mobile world, and the Papillon Cutlery Set speaks to both. Its compact nested solution allows fork, spoon, and knife to stack neatly within an easy-to-hold case designed to slip into a handbag or backpack. The rounded container alludes to the contents, encouraging the user to appreciate the cutlery's elemental geometry.

Objects speak for their time and place, as do materials. Just as our fast-food, disposable culture produced the ubiquitous Styrofoam clamshell container, the Papillon (French for butterfly) discourages disposable tableware with a product made from 100 percent recycled material containing up to 25 percent post-consumer content.

MATERIAL INSIGHT

Aladdin has been a pioneer in the development of post-consumer recycled polypropylene (PP). Although this commodity plastic is widely used, there is still no viable high-volume recycling stream for its use in consumer products, at least in the United States. Individual manufacturers and brands have made attempts to create sufficient supply from in-store collection, but unlike polyester (beverage bottles), or HDPE (milk bottles), municipal recycling still is not able to easily determine what is PP and what is some other plastic. eCycle® is an FDA-compliant resin that can be molded into attractive recyclable or potentially biodegradable food service products containing 25 percent post-consumer content. Acceptance by the FDA that the resin may contain this recycled material requires considerable process control including tests of all sources of plastic and also the certification of recycling plants.

NEWSPAPERWOOD

DESIGNER / MANUFACTURER
Mieke Meijer with Vij5
www.vij5.nl

MATERIAL
NewspaperWood

DESIGNER BIOGRAPHIES
Studio Mieke Meijer is the outcome of a close cooperation between Mieke Meijer and her partner Roy Letterlé. Combining their skills resulted in designs that are high quality in both concept and technology. Innovative materials, a constructive form language, elegant lines, and an industrial character are the key elements in their design. The designs are mostly hand made in their Eindhoven-based workshop. Mieke Meijer graduated from the Design Academy Eindhoven in 2006, where she also teaches. Roy Letterlé has an architectural and educational background and is also a teacher of interior design.

MATERIAL PROPERTIES
Sustainable Solutions, Recycled, Composite

Bound together with solvent- and plasticizer-free glue, logs of NewspaperWood are milled into planks, adding value to surplus newsprint and making eventual recycling a relatively simple process.

Invented by Mieke Meijer in 2003 while she was a student at the Design Academy Eindhoven in the Netherlands, NewspaperWood delivers a sly commentary on the ability of one material to masquerade as another. Stacks of discarded newspaper are transformed into thin slivers of color and a densely layered composition that replicates wood grain, mimicking the rings of a tree to suggest the organic nature of real wood. The paper can be cut, milled, sanded, and generally treated like any other type of wood.

NewspaperWood exemplifies one of the Design Academy Eindhoven's major themes: developing a sensitivity to social phenomena as an engine for innovative design. With the user as the focal point, design operates at the service of social developments which offer jumping-off points for the posing of critical questions and the innovation that ensues. The collaboration between Mieke and Vij5, which developed a special machine and process for producing NewspaperWood, began in 2007 when Vij5 discovered the material in Mieke's portfolio. NewspaperWood was introduced in 2008 at the Dutch Design Week Eindhoven (NL), and since then Vij5 and Mieke have continued to refine the material while advocating the concept of upcycling—when discarded objects or material are reused to produce a product of higher quality than the original.

The material also reveals the power of multiples. Just as a single living cell takes on a new purpose and potential when it is joined with others to form a larger organism, so individual items, replicated, become part of a greater whole, investing the mundane with new meaning.

MATERIAL INSIGHT
Recycling paper into molded parts is nothing new—egg cartons, shoeboxes, wall panels (Homasote), even countertops (All Paper Recycling Inc.). The method for

this recycling process, however, reminds us of the material's original purpose, as a newspaper, which also acts as a visual cue in the final product. The striations caused by the multiple layers of individual news sheets adds a "grain" to the parts, especially when cut at right angles. The parts have considerable strength, greater than if the paper had gone through the standard recycling stream, because the cellulose fibers do not get reduced in length through the mechanical action of the recycler.

Paper Frames by Ontwerpduo (**top**), Breg Hanssen's Framed cupboard (**right**), and From A to Z by Greetje van Tiem (**below**) embellish NewspaperWood's aesthetic with contrasting hues and laser-cut grips.

IN-EI LIGHT
COLLECTION

DESIGNER
Issey Miyake + Reality Lab
mds.isseymiyake.com

MANUFACTURER
Artemide
www.artemide.com

MATERIAL
Retreated fiber made from recycled PET plastic bottles

DESIGNER BIOGRAPHY
Issey Miyake established the Miyake Design Studio in Tokyo in 1970. He began experimental work on pleating in 1988, and PLEATS PLEASE started in 1993. In 1998 Miyake developed A-POC (A Piece Of Cloth), a new way to combine traditional ideas with digital technology. In 2004, he established the Miyake Issey Foundation to archive his vast body of work and develop new talent in all areas of design. Today, Miyake continues his relentless search for more advanced twenty-first-century designs.

MATERIAL PROPERTIES
Sustainable Solutions, Lightweight, Recycled, Simplification

below and opposite The Mendori shade, made with one piece of recycled PET cloth, is unfolded from its flat-packed original form and fitted with aluminum base modules to stand firmly on the floor.

The dazzling creativity and startling originality of Japanese fashion designer Issey Miyake are expressed through the technical virtuosity of his micropleating and the incorporation of cultural references into sculptural garments that reconfigure a woman's form. Rare among designers, he has been able to see beyond fashion's physical constraints to its innovative possibilities. The perpetual quest for new fiber technologies, structural ingenuity and highly original designs is evident in his latest endeavor, a collection of LED lights conceived in collaboration with Italian lighting brand Artemide. The freestanding, table and hanging IN-EI lights possess a dimensional complexity derived from mathematics, which is combined with a design inheritance from traditional Japan.

Striking and sustainable, the seven geometric shapes in the series glow like lanterns. This is the result of a translucent fiber made from recycled PET bottles that emerged from Miyake's Reality Lab, a select team of both experienced and young staff whose work on new designs includes the development of environmentally friendly and resource-conscious materials. With the exquisite precision of Japanese architecture, each piece comes collapsed, expanding like a children's pop-up book into a voluminous shape without the need for an interior frame. Layers, twists, and folds create alternating moments of light and dark that suggest forms found in nature, including shells, crevasses, pine cones, and spirals.

Japan's rich visual heritage has long served as a foundation for aesthetic innovation. For all their dynamism, the lamps have a weightless serenity.

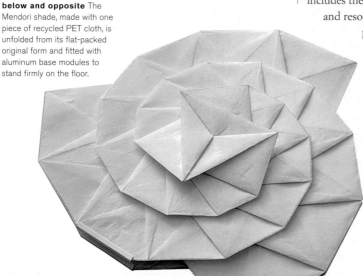

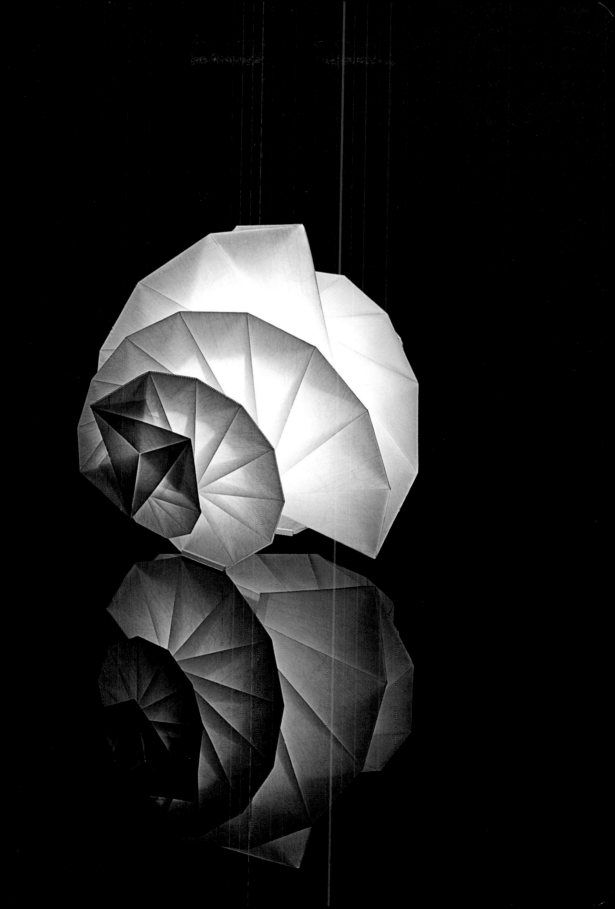

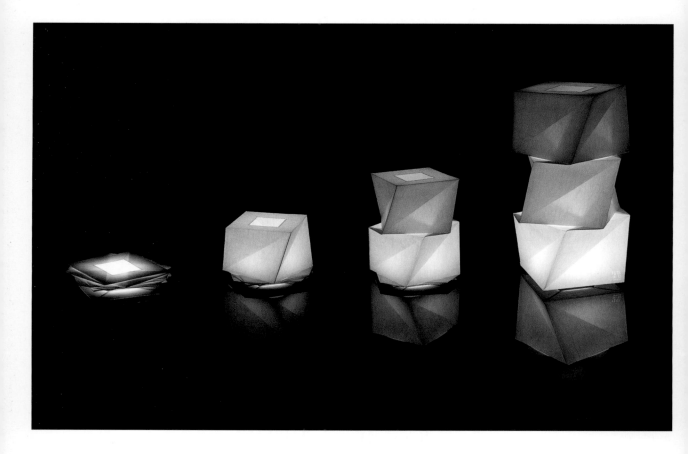

above The Mogura lamp, like each light shade, was created with computer scientist Jun Mitani's ORI-REVO software, which allows designers and mathematicians alike to explore methods of folding a two-dimensional plane to create three-dimensional structures.

opposite The Fukurou (**top**) and Mencori (**bottom**) shades transfer origami paper-folding techniques to recycled PET, a thoroughly unnatural but comparably fibrous material.

MATERIAL INSIGHT

The non-woven fabric used in these lightshades achieves its unique light-transmitting properties through the exact fiber density and color of the recycled fibers. The source of the post-consumer recycled polyester is beverage bottles, an amorphous polyester known as PET. Artemide claims that the recycling and subsequent fabric production reduces energy consumption and CO_2 emissions by up to 40 percent compared to new construction of the material. The use of clear bottle plastic ensures a translucent yarn. Recycled polyester remains the most highly recycled plastic for yarn production, predominantly because of this reliable, clean, and high-volume supply of used drinks bottles, and is being used currently in non-woven, woven, and knit form by a number of apparel brands.

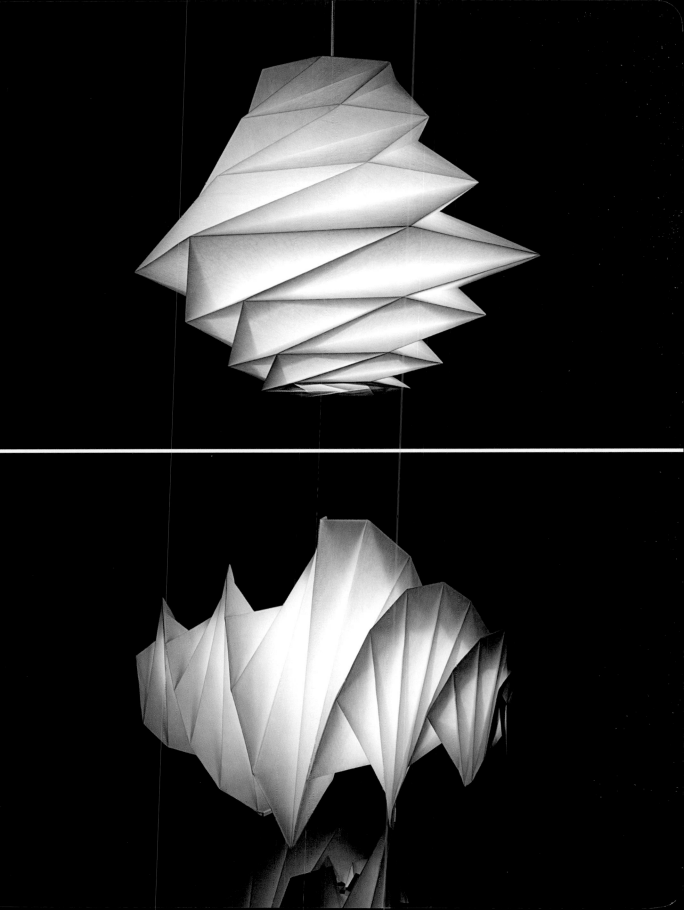

VAC FROM THE SEA

DESIGNER / MANUFACTURER

Electrolux

www.electrolux.com

MATERIAL

Plastic waste collected from the world's oceans

DESIGNER BIOGRAPHY

Electrolux is a global leader in household appliances and appliances for professional use, selling more than 50 million products to customers in more than 150 markets every year. The company focuses on innovations that are thoughtfully designed, based on extensive consumer insight, to meet the real needs of consumers and professionals.

MATERIAL PROPERTIES

Sustainable Solutions, Recycled, Composite

Electrolux's green range (**left**) of vacuum cleaners is made from 55–70 percent recycled plastic. The Pacific Edition demo (**right**), filled with specks of plastic that washed ashore in Hawaii, shows how pernicious plastics that are not recycled can be.

The Electrolux Vac from the Sea project superbly confirms to any doubters that floating in the middle of our oceans are giant islands of plastic trash. What is riveting about the appliance company's response to ocean conservation is that it has chosen a household tool whose primary function is cleanliness as the canvas across which to magnify our communal filth. To accomplish this so that users are engaged rather than repulsed, the Stockholm-based company sent volunteers out to salvage ocean trash from different bodies of water, organized the trash by color, cut it into different shapes, and then created a limited-edition collection of products that provide a visual map linking refuse to location.

The Pacific, the Indian Ocean, the Atlantic, the Mediterranean, the Baltic, and the North Sea are all represented. The North Sea Edition contains circles of primary-color plastic that are—disturbingly—almost celebratory. Conversely, the Indian Ocean is represented by white debris from beaches and seabeds near Thailand that includes Styrofoam, plastic bags, and household garbage.

Storytelling is central to the design. The ritual of cleaning is overlaid with tangible evidence of our failure to properly care for our environment, making the link between our immediate surroundings and the effect of our actions on the planet as a whole. The simple act of putting garbage on display prompts the user to envision a better future and highlights the potential for design and industry to address urgent needs. Electrolux will auction off each of the vacuum cleaners to benefit pollution research.

MATERIAL INSIGHT

Though unlikely to make much of a dent in the incredibly large volumes of scrap plastics currently floating in our oceans, these vacuum cleaners effectively call attention to the challenge we have with our lax approach to handling and

disposal of the material. Focusing on six different saltwater collection points, each design highlights particular plastic forms that are prevalent in these areas. Rather than melting the individual waste parts down after collection, they were incorporated in their found state into molded shells for the vacuums, highlighting the size, form, and degradation state of the materials collected. The waste? Mostly packaging, household products, beverage bottles, and "tourist litter."

above For the North Sea Edition designers rid waterborne trash of oil, then sorted it by color (**top right**) and cut it into small discs (**top left**). The finished version (**bottom right**) and the Baltic Edition (**bottom left**) have the brightest colors because they were exposed to the least light.

overleaf left The Mediterranean region's plastic waste comes predominantly from tourists and beachgoers.

overleaf right For the Indian Ocean Edition, fishing nets were cut loose from coral reefs, then shredded and cut into strips.

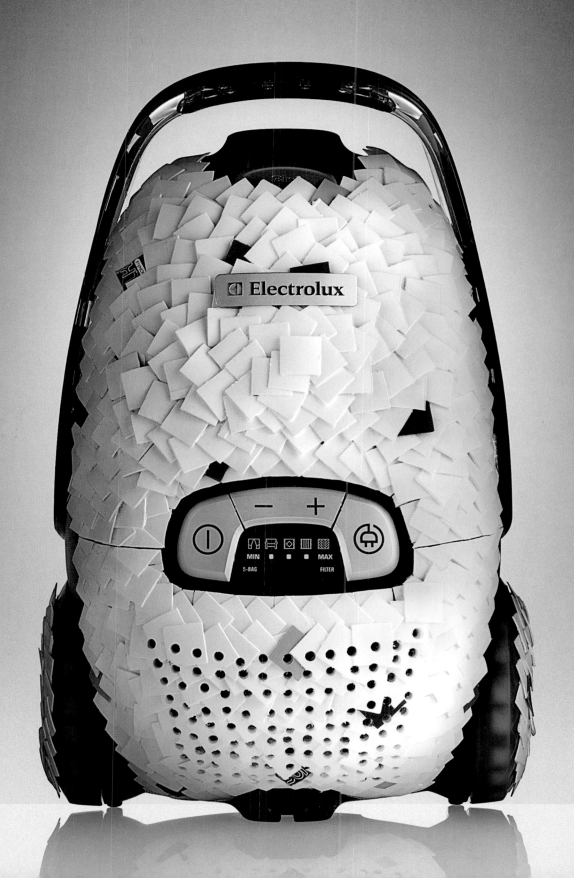

ÇURFACE COMPOSITE PANELS

DESIGNER / MANUFACTURER
Adam Fairweather, Re-worked
Nick Rawcliffe, Rawstudio
www.re-worked.blogspot.com

MATERIAL
Recycled coffee grounds and post-consumer
high-impact polystyrene (HIPS)

MATERIAL MANUFACTURER
Axion Polymers

DESIGNER BIOGRAPHY
Adam Fairweather started Re-worked in 2003 with
the intention of creating sustainable products that
would have a positive impact on the world around
him. Re-worked recycles and manufactures products
made out of coffee, which began with an experiment
to make takeaway cups for coffee shops out of coffee.
A passionate arts and craftsman, Fairweather found
that crossing his hobbies with industrial design and
manufacturing resulted in environmentally conscious,
innovative creativity.

MATERIAL PROPERTIES
Sustainable Solutions, Recycled, Composite

The knobs and side panels are made with 99 percent recycled materials, 30 percent of which is coffee grounds.

If our needs, wants, concerns, and creativity are revealed in the objects we produce, what does it tell us that in today's culture few beverages are as revered as coffee? Worldwide, we drink an estimated 500 billion cups every year. That is a lot of beans—and a lot of left-over coffee grounds.

"Coffee was one of several materials that I looked at recycling when I began exploring ways to add value to waste streams," explains Adam Fairweather, founder of Re-worked, a non-profit design company that specializes in green technology. "Interestingly, it is one of the only commodity materials in contemporary culture that has such a high perceptual value. What nobody really understands is that we only use a small fraction of this material that has a relatively pure waste stream." Fairweather's fascination with upcycling ultimately led to the development of Çurface (pronounced "surface"), a coffee grounds/plastic biocomposite produced with British plastics reprocessor Axion Polymers.

To produce Çurface, coffee grounds from offices, cafés, and factories throughout London are cleaned and then mixed with recycled waste plastic. The mix becomes pellets, the pellets become composite board, and the board becomes chair seats and backs with a finish "reminiscent of a combination of chocolate, leather and stone," says Fairweather. It also gives off a faint whiff of coffee.

Nick Rawcliffe of Rawstudio, whose company shares a similar focus on sustainability, brought a special touch of originality to the design of the Çurface Chair. The legs and back supports have an organic quality that speaks to their origins, wood from trees felled in London's parks.

MATERIAL INSIGHT
Suggestions of what to do with used coffee grounds abound in product design concept workshops, with some coffee

companies creating competitions to elicit the best ideas. This solution stands out thanks to the collaboration with Axion Polymers, an innovative resource recovery company in the UK, whose knowledge both of the resources and of the performance of post-consumer content enabled it to determine the best resin to combine with the grounds on both a performance and a resource availability level. Çurface biocomposite is both waterproof and scratchproof.

Nick Rawcliffe from UK-based Rawstudio helped Adam Fairweather's team at Re-worked to introduce their biocomposite to the market through the design of this chair and table.

PAOLA NAVONE

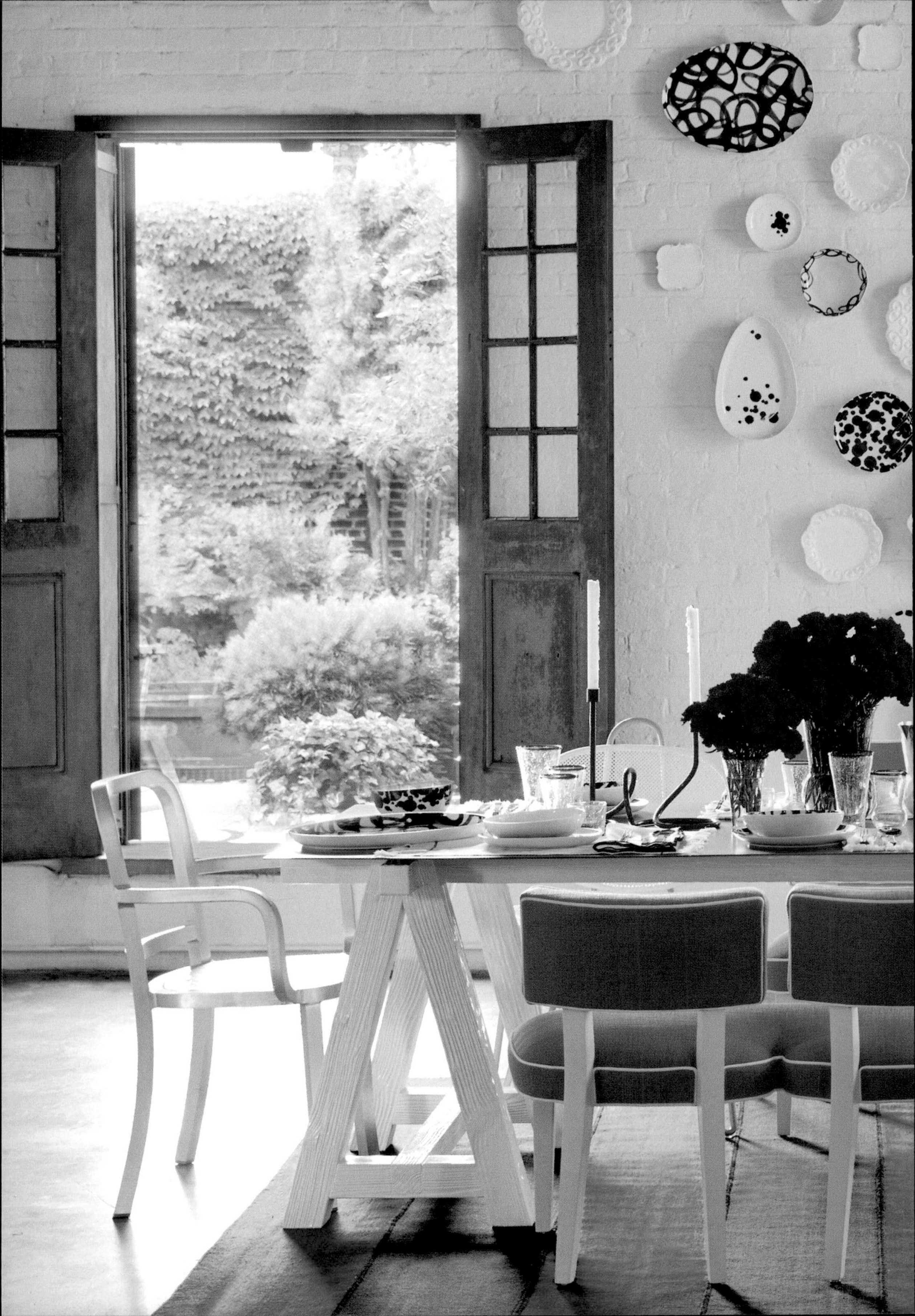

CHAPTER 6
EMBEDDED TECHNOLOGY

opposite Printechnologics'
Touchcode technology is based
on the interaction between
paper printed with a proprietary
type of reflective ink that stores
information and the capacitive
touch screens that register the
printed graphics as points of
contact on the device's surface.

When the "internet of things" is fully realized, everything will talk to everything else, effortlessly updating and regulating, warning and warming, checking and chilling, scanning and simmering. Refrigerators, toothpaste tubes, carpets, trash bins, all of the objects with which we interact can purportedly be improved by making sure that they are working optimally. Professional coaches will know every movement, heartbeat and sweat pH level of their players during a game, instantaneously transferred back from sensors through smart textiles.

For this to happen, all these products must contain some form of electronic transmitter or receiver, some *intelligence*, so that they can be heard by or can listen to all the other things around us. The more intelligent the device, inevitably, the more complex the electronics needed to drive it, thus the need to keep reducing the size of our electronic components such that they do not too obviously reduce the functionality of the device through affecting its form. Traditional electronics are struggling to keep up with this increase in complexity: the "electronic architecture" can no longer cope. We need a new way of building this intelligence.

There are several directions in which this reduction in materiality is being achieved, and each has its advantages and its limitations. The three major thrusts have been printing of electronic circuitry; weaving or knitting the circuitry into smart fabrics; and the intimate and intricate melding of structural material and electronics through plating, composite materials, and new polymer chemistries.

PRINTED CIRCUITRY

Printing is inexpensive and relatively accurate and there are multiple methods to achieve the same effect, each offering unique qualities. Printing of conductor or semiconductor lines onto paper, plastic film and molded parts increases speed, enables thin multilayering of components, and enables greater flexibility if a suitable substrate is used. Examples such as T-Ink's printed molded headliner console for the Ford Fusion and Printechnologics' printed batteries show what is possible when careful control of print line composition, pattern, thickness and interrelationship between different layers can create fully functioning circuits in a fraction of the thickness of traditional parts. Laying down thicker layers of ink also allows the plastic films to be thermoformed and drawn into three-dimensional parts that move beyond the simple idea of a printed film and into complex structural parts. Capacitive touch surfaces can be created, and because printing is both small format (fine type on a page) and large format (billboard signage), these functions can be easily scaled to go from finger- to hand- to house-sized gestures.

E-textiles, or smart fabrics, have also evolved substantially in the past few years, giving way to less obtrusive, more "textile-like" technologies that are finally giving the producers of garments functionality that they can use that does not render the shirt or coat too cumbersome. Capacitive touch is possible with e-textiles, as is pressure sensing, power acquisition and generation, lighting through washable electroluminescent films and seamless integration of LED lighting and OLEDS, and sensing of environmental and personal indicators. Though inevitably more expensive to produce than printed electronics, smart fabrics offer something not yet viable for the printed circuit: an ability to move well with our bodies, enabling enjoyable wearable technology that can maintain the freedom of both movement and expression we expect from our clothes.

A final thrust in this reduction in weight, thickness, and materiality has been a blurring of the line between what is an electronic component and what is the actual product. If the wires, resistors, capacitors and battery, rather than separate components, are in fact the structural and shell materials themselves, this truly integrates the intelligence with the product. Companies such as Mid-Tronic are laying down intricate conductive pathways on complex molded parts by first laser etching the desired path then selectively metallizing the textured surfaces. To incorporate circuitry onto three-dimensional parts, Neotech Services are creating aerosol jets of conductive materials and depositing these in fine lines using a six-axis sprayer.

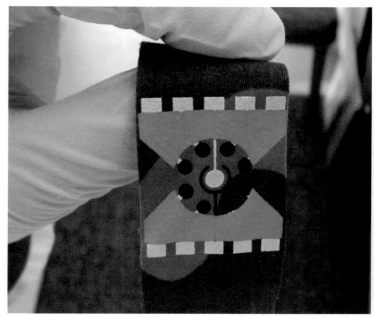

Electrozyme can make temporary biosensors (**left**) and tattoos (**below**) by screen-printing proprietary ink blends that conform to the skin and enable chemical analysis of the wearer's sweat.

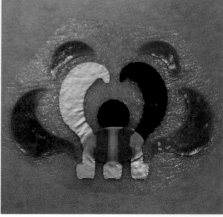

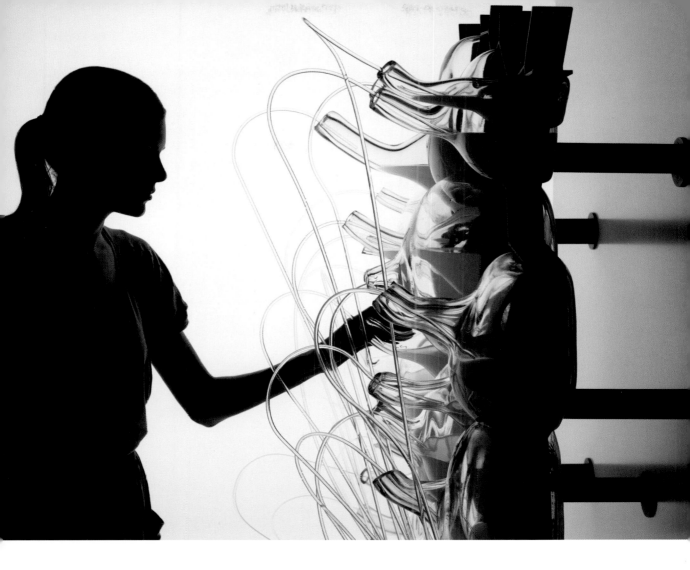

SELF-ASSEMBLING PLASTIC CIRCUITS

The future potentially lies in plastics that are able to self-assemble as they are molded into their final form to create internal "wiring" of conductive plastic filaments. These may be straight, running through the molded part, but may also form bends, junctions, layers and cylinders, equivalent to existing wiring, but "inherent" in the part itself. This begins to mimic biology (and biotech is also attempting to create molecular electronics with the controlled growth of cell structures), in the way that nerves run through the limbs of the body integral to the total structure of the arm or leg. Because these conductive lines are still plastic, they can be recycled with the body of the part they inhabit.

It is likely that each of these new methods for "dematerializing" electronics so that they integrate more seamlessly into our products will find its niche need, whether

The Bio-Light from Philips: Hand-blown glass vessels hold pools of bioluminescent bacteria that produce luciferase, an enzyme that gives off ambient light, as they metabolize waste.

for wearables, packaging or supply chain management, or simply to enable smaller, more flexible devices that no longer look like electronics at all.

We must of course add to these innovations the revolution in wireless power. With almost all information now being delivered wirelessly, there are numerous technologies that are able to charge our devices without cables, mainly through induction charging, with companies such as Powermat, but there are also examples that use magnetic fields (Witricity) to achieve powering over larger distances. Expect all devices and appliances to head in this direction, making our great-grandchildren wonder how we ever survived with everything attached to a wall.

ENERGY COLLECTION

DESIGNER / MANUFACTURER
Marjan van Aubel
www.marjanvanaubel.com

MATERIAL
Titanium dioxide-coated glass pigmented with
natural photosynthetic dye

MATERIAL MANUFACTURER
Solaronix Lausanne

DESIGNER BIOGRAPHY
Marjan van Aubel is a Dutch designer with an
inquisitive, almost scientific perspective. She
graduated in 2012 from the Design Products
course at London's Royal College of Art and is
based in London. Van Aubel comes from a family
of chemists and this background has left its mark
on the way she perceives the world. She has
collaborated with many different companies and
other designers, including EPFL-Lab, Solaronix,
the American Hardwood Export Council, and
Joris Laarman.

MATERIAL PROPERTIES
Biomimicry

opposite top Berry-stained conductive
glassware sits in charging reservoirs
within the cabinet. The vessels, each with
a different wavelength depending on their
color, conduct different currents picked up
by TiO_2-coated channels.

opposite bottom At the Laboratory of
Photonics and Interfaces in Lausanne
(EPFL) Professor Micheal Graetzel
developed a dye-synthesized solar cell
(**middle**) to which the designer added a
system (**right**) that can charge a mobile
device (**left**) in any sunlit room.

Solar panels that convert sunlight into electricity
are among the simplest, cleanest, and most reliable
ways of harnessing the energy of the sun to provide
inexpensive power. When exposed to daylight, solar
cells encased in glass generate electricity, which can charge a
battery. This low-tech process is at the heart of a humble set
of tableware with, literally, powerful possibilities.

Through a collaboration between designer Marjan
van Aubel and Michael Graetzel of the Ecole Polytechnic
Federale Lausanne, Switzerland, a collection of glasses, jugs,
and vases has been outfitted with colored solar cells that emit
different wavelengths and collect different energy currents.
Whether resting or in use, the glassware continually gathers
light. When a vessel is then placed on the accompanying
shelving unit, the energy is collected and stored, allowing
the cabinet to serve as a charging station for a power-driven
device, such as a phone or small lamp.

The design speaks to our concerns about global
resources as it potently reminds us that materials and the
natural world can also be harnessed toward solutions.

MATERIAL INSIGHT

Given the popularity of incorporating photovoltaic (solar)
cells into glazing for residential and commercial spaces, it is
good to see similar cells incorporated into everyday interior
objects. Marjan van Aubel with Michael Graetzel worked
with dye-sensitized solar cells from Solaronix of Switzerland
to create the photovoltaics. Using a porous titanium dioxide
(TiO_2) layer soaked with photosensitive dye—a pigment
extracted from blueberries or spinach—these cells even
work in interior diffused light, unlike standard silicon cells.
The different-color pigments absorb different wavelengths
of light and the TiO_2 converts it to an electric current. The
power is drawn off when the glassware is placed in recessed
shelf locations through copper wiring on the bottom.

The Energy Collection

MICROBIAL HOME PROBE

DESIGNER / MANUFACTURER

Philips Design
www.philips.com/design

MATERIAL

Microbial cultures that metabolize waste

DESIGNER BIOGRAPHY

Philips Design is a recognized global leader in people-centric design, applying creative expertise to ensure that innovations are meaningful. Through intensive collaboration and co-creation with stakeholders in and outside Philips, Philips Design aims to understand people's true needs and desires and translate these into relevant solutions and experiences for people and business. Its creative force of more than 500 professionals is comprised of designers across various disciplines, as well as psychologists, cultural sociologists, anthropologists, and trend researchers in Europe, North America, and Asia.

MATERIAL PROPERTIES

Sustainable Solutions, Biomimicry

opposite The glass shell of the urban beehive filters light through the same orange wavelength that bees use for sight.

overleaf Cast iron transfers heat fast and evenly through pipes that reach from the biodigester hub (**center**), in which bacteria synthesize methane gas for the larder (**left**), where the outer surface of the terracotta cooler maintains a temperature differential for different kinds of fresh food. The waste upcycler (**right**) contains an interior chamber for a strain of mycelium fungi that metabolize plastic.

One way to view the domestic landscape is in purely modernist terms, as a "machine for living" outfitted with labor-saving gadgets whose sleek aesthetic speaks of effortlessness. The smallest task can be accomplished with the push of the proverbial button, seemingly without energy or waste.

An alternative model proposes a home that is active and alive, a self-sustaining ecosystem whose vitality comes from biological processes that view waste as part of a natural order, to be broken down and converted into energy. This paradigm underlies the future-thinking Microbial Home Probe conceived by the Dutch electronics company Philips. Seven organically shaped components—a biodigester kitchen island, a larder, an urban beehive, a bio-light, an "apothecary," a filtering squatting toilet, and a "paternoster" plastic waste upcycler—rely on food and human by-products to generate fuel. In this symbiotic scenario, each element's output is another's input, the entire wood, copper and glass scheme conjuring a rural nostalgia, yet based on rigorous research and insight into new lifestyle concepts.

Designers are understandably preoccupied with a legacy of short-lived products and clear evidence that human existence itself is having adverse effects on the climate. "We need to rethink domestic appliances entirely, how homes consume energy and how entire communities can pool resources," says Clive van Heerden, Senior Director of Philips Design. Seeing waste in a new manner may point the way to a more self-reliant vision of home.

MATERIAL INSIGHT

Bacterial microorganisms play a major part in this concept, in their ability to breakdown organic matter, and also in the case of certain bacteria types, in their property of bioluminescence. Certain animals and plants are bioluminescent—able to produce and emit light through

chemical reactions, and Philips has used bioluminescent bacteria, fed with methane from composted natural materials in a methane digester, as part of its Microbial Home system. Though not generating enough light for task or room lighting, the bio-light does create a mood glow and the process also removes methane from decomposing food. Beyond specific applications, the concept shows how we can harness natural processes from living things that are powered by nothing but waste.

NUUBO INTEGRATED CARDIAC MONITORING GARMENT

DESIGNER / MANUFACTURER
Nuubo
www.nuubo.com

MATERIAL
Textile electrodes proprietary to BlendFix sensor technology

DESIGNER BIOGRAPHY
Nuubo is a wearable wireless medical device company, with headquarters based in Madrid, Spain, and R&D labs and manufacturing facilities in Valencia, Spain. The company designs, manufactures, and sells a proprietary portfolio of innovative wearable wireless medical technologies for cardiac prevention, diagnosis, and rehabilitation.

MATERIAL PROPERTIES
Lightweight, Ergonomic

In the field of healthcare, fiction seems to be turning to fact as technology puts increasing power in the hands of patients. Wearable wireless medical devices that monitor vital bodily activities can now deliver data to medical experts remotely and in real time. Sensors embedded in garments have the potential to track a range of health functions with greater precision, simplifying traditional monitoring and helping to rein in costs.

The Spanish company Nuubo is at the forefront of wearable medical technology with the design of a three-part system that monitors cardiac health to support prevention, diagnosis, and rehabilitation. The strength of the system is based on a wireless ECG (electrocardiographic) remote monitoring platform that incorporates a biomedical e-textile technology called BlendFix sensor electrode technology. Embedded in an athletic shirt is a sleek device able to capture an ECG signal and send it remotely with Bluetooth wireless technology to a computer, where Nuubo's software collects, stores, and displays the data for analysis.

Among the key advances is how the textile adapts to the user's movements, allowing for continuous monitoring without wires. As such, the platform appeals to professional athletes and teams, especially during race training.

MATERIAL INSIGHT

The medical field is leading the way in commercializing e-textiles, creating monitoring systems that are unobtrusive, accurate, and easy to use. The BlendFix sensor electrode technology uses an undershirt that contains textile electrodes that are able to track vital signs such as heart rate, HRV (heart-rate variability), and ECG (electrocardiogram). A device can be easily attached that reads the data collected, storing it on a micro-SD card or feeding it to a physician for analysis. The device is also able to register body position and level of physical activity through a three-axis accelerometer.

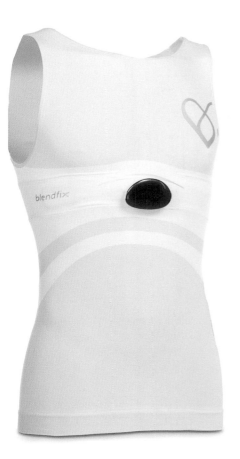

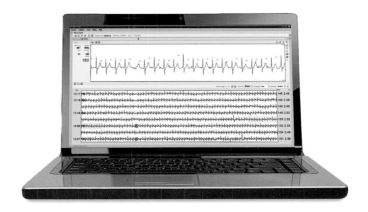

opposite and above Instead of sticking electrodes to the skin and tracing the pattern of a beating heart on a piece of paper, the Nuubo monitoring device allows information to be processed and stored from electrodes embedded into the rECG textile.

below Wearable technology like Nuubo's is based on algorithmically derived data gleaned from the ever more precise measurement of signals received from the movements and heartbeats detected through the textile's natural movements.

MOSS TABLE

DESIGNERS

Carlos Peralta, Alex Driver
Scientific development: Paolo Bombelli
www.carlosperalta.co.uk

MANUFACTURER

Complete Fabrications Modelmakers Ltd, and Institute
for Manufacturing (IfM), University of Cambridge
www.compfab.co.uk, www.ifm.eng.cam.ac.uk

MATERIAL

Biological fuel cells made from moss

DESIGNER BIOGRAPHIES

Carlos Peralta is a Colombian product designer with an
MA in Industrial Design from Domus Academy in Italy.
With more than twenty years experience as a designer and
educator in Colombia, the United Kingdom, Singapore, and
Spain, he is now based in England. Having completed his
PhD at Cambridge University, he works as associate lecturer
at Central Saint Martins College of Art and Design and as a
senior lecturer in design at the University of Brighton.

Alex Driver is an English industrial designer and a
mechanical engineer from the Royal College of Art and
Imperial College London. He worked as an associate
researcher at the Institute for Manufacturing at Cambridge
University and is currently a senior industrial designer at
Native Design in London.

Paolo Bombelli is an Italian scientist with a PhD in
Biochemistry and Plant Sciences from Cambridge
University, where he is researching photovoltaic technology.

MATERIAL PROPERTIES

Sustainable Solutions, Biomimicry

Designers have long viewed the natural sciences as a source of inspiration and potential. To consider the role that designers can play in early-stage scientific research, however, is less common. That question is at the heart of "Design in Science," a research project led by Dr. James Moultrie of Cambridge University's Institute for Manufacturing. Among the outcomes of the project is the prototypically simple, organically modern Moss Table, a piece of futuristic furniture that suggests how natural processes and manmade objects might advocate in years to come for alternative energy solutions.

At first glance, the sleek white design resembles a wide terrarium with a built-in lamp for illuminating dozens of lush miniature plants. In fact, the 112 moss pots visible beneath the transparent acrylic table top operate as bio-electrochemical devices, harnessing a natural biological process that converts chemical into electrical energy. Each moss-filled container represents an emerging technology, BPV (biophotovoltaics), which uses photosynthesis to generate electricity, highlighting in the form of a table its potential application in the domestic landscape.

During photosynthesis plants use sunlight to convert carbon dioxide from the atmosphere into organic compounds, which they rely on in order to grow. As the moss photosynthesizes, it releases some of these organic compounds into the soil, which contains symbiotic bacteria. The bacteria break down the compounds, liberating by-products that include electrons. The Moss Table captures these electrons to produce an electrical current.

Biophotovoltaic technology is in its infancy, with researchers all over the world exploring ways in which the botanical world might offer alternative sources of renewable energy in the future. What cannot be overlooked in the process is the beauty and fascination of working with a material so humble and seductive as moss.

MATERIAL INSIGHT

In the future, placing conducting fibers within the growing moss plants might make it possible for enough energy to be diverted from photosynthesis to power a lamp. The power is achieved by the circuit "harvesting" electrons from bacteria that consume a photosynthetic by-product in the soil, converting the chemical energy of the growing moss into electrical energy. Similar in concept to other BPV technologies, such as those using algae or bacteria, it heralds new ways of thinking about where we can source our energy.

top, left to right Conductive fibers were used to test the connection between each node. Each moss plant pot houses an electrical cell that draws current from the biological process.

bottom, left to right Biotechnologists, biochemists, and plant scientists helped to create the system in the table. The lamp pictured requires too much power for the moss at the moment, though the designers did make a proof-of-concept where the moss modules powered a digital alarm clock. The creators see potential at larger scales, for example as solar panels for power stations.

SPACETOP

DESIGNER / MANUFACTURER
Jinha Lee
www.leejinha.com

MATERIAL
Transparent OLED display

MATERIAL MANUFACTURER
Samsung

DESIGNER BIOGRAPHY
Jinha Lee is an interface designer, engineer, and researcher working at the boundary of the physical and digital world. He is exploring ways to employ our innate kinesthetic and sensory skills to interact with the world of data by seamlessly weaving digital information into physical space and material. He received his bachelor's degree in Electronic Engineering from the University of Tokyo. Taking a leave from his PhD studies at MIT Media Lab, Lee is leading a team to design TV interfaces at Samsung Electronics. In 2013, Lee was selected as a TED Fellow and gave a TED talk.

MATERIAL PROPERTIES
Ergonomic

Evolving computer technologies for further narrowing the distance between the physical and digital worlds are prompting a range of explorations into new forms of gesture-based engagement previously never thought possible. Once rare types of computer interface, such as touch screens that eliminated the need for handheld tools like a stylus, are now pervasive among such small-scale devices as smartphones and tablets.

Interface designer and engineer Jinha Lee, however, believes there is still a big gap to overcome; and he aims to narrow it. His fascination with our natural inclination to absorb information in multiple forms, from text and information graphics to videos and scale models, coupled with the recognition that today's computer screens collapse all forms of data into a single flat surface, has prompted him to explore how a computer might bridge physical space and the digital realm.

From a collaboration with Microsoft's Applied Sciences division has emerged SpaceTop, a transparent, gesture-controlled desktop environment that relies on advanced visualization and interaction techniques to allow users to reach inside and physically interact with 2D digital content in a 3D space as if the objects were real. Users can type, draw, explore, and directly manipulate elements in a physical space suspended above the keyboard. The gestures involved provide a way for people to more intuitively interact with computers by harnessing innate sensory abilities and spatial memory. "It is one of our key human skills to be able to interact with 3D spaces and I wanted to let people do the same with digital content," says Lee.

SpaceTop points to an insatiable curiosity operating at top speed and unlikely to slow down. The possibilities are especially exciting for fields of study that have traditionally relied on 2D and 3D content for sharing complex ideas, such as architecture, medicine or aerospace, to name just a few.

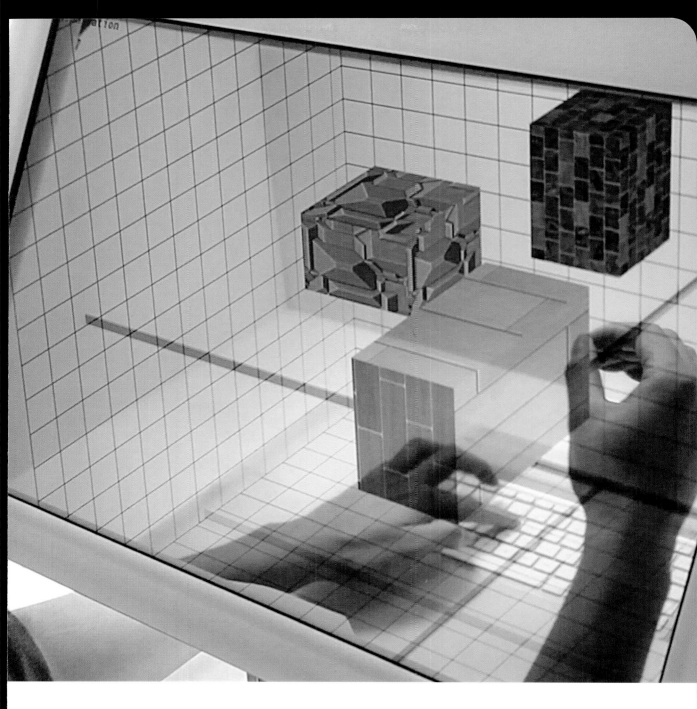

MATERIAL INSIGHT

This interface combines the most dexterous of human tools, our hands, with a 2D screen to increase the functionality of both. Microsoft Applied Sciences, Jinha Lee, and the MIT Media Lab mapped user interactions with digital content behind a transparent display from Samsung. When plugged in, OLEDs between two sheets of glass illuminate the display while sensors recognize such gestures as pinching, stretching, and sifting. It is possible to switch easily to more typical digital interactions such as typing or mouse-clicking.

Combining the exacting inputs of a mouse or keyboard and our natural inclination to gesture with our hands to aid communication, this tool aims to enhance the user experience and deliver information more efficiently.

SWITCH60

DESIGNER / MANUFACTURER
David Horn, SWITCH Lighting
www.switchlightingco.com

MATERIAL
Liquid silicone coolant

DESIGNER BIOGRAPHY
David Horn, Chief Technology Officer at SWITCH
Lighting, has thirty years of experience in high-
technology operations development and management,
and has led all SWITCH activities, from product
research and development to operations. He has
managed planning and preparations for R&D, testing,
validation, and ultimate product commercialization
for the advanced LED lamp solution. He holds
an MSc in Applied Sciences from University of
California, Davis/Lawrence Livermore Labs and a
BSc in Physics from California Polytechnic State
University at San Luis Obispo.

MATERIAL PROPERTIES
Sustainable Solutions, Durable

left Silicone oil—a
food-safe and reliable
coolant for electronic
parts—fills the glass bulb
of the Switch60. From
the top one can see the
delicate ten-finger filament
assembly of LEDs that was
bent with jets of air and
mounted inside.

opposite The patented
LQD Cooling System
consists of a driver that
converts AC to DC voltage
and regulates current
flowing through the LEDs
to reliably cycle warm
liquid silicone away from
sensitive electronics and
toward the glass exterior.

Futuristic and boldly curvaceous, the Switch bulb
cuts a striking figure in the world of lighting.
Designed by a Silicon Valley-based team of
scientists and engineers, the LED-powered bulb
possesses at its core a patented self-cooling system based
on liquid silicone. By devising a way to keep heat away
from the bulb's light-emitting diodes, Switch delivers
a better bulb while dramatically reducing energy
consumption, since LEDs require only a fraction of the
power used by incandescent versions. Furthermore,
monitoring the bulb's temperature helps generate a lifespan
of roughly 25,000 hours, or nearly three years of non-stop
illumination. While that may seem inconsequential in a
residential setting, for commercial use it can potentially
save billions of dollars, decrease dependence on foreign
oil, and reduce greenhouse gases.

MATERIAL INSIGHT
The move from traditional incandescent "Edison" bulbs
has been a contentious one. Compact fluorescents have not
produced the warm bright glow desired, and also contain
small amounts of mercury that has to go somewhere when
the product is discarded. LEDs appear to offer a brighter
future, though because of their size and shape, have tended
to be sold in new devices rather than as replacements for
the hundreds of millions of screw-in bulbs we currently
use. LEDs that fit in standard light-bulb sockets are now
the next generation. This version uses liquid silicone in the
bulb to cool the sensitive electronics, making it more reliable
but heavier than standard replacements. To get the warmer,
less blue hue (it has a color temperature of 2700K), more
electricity is needed, thus the liquid silicone to dissipate
heat. Cost might be this product's current limitation, but it
does offer an ingenious way of prolonging life in a high-tech
lighting innovation.

MICOACH ELITE TEAM SYSTEM

DESIGNER / MANUFACTURER
adidas Wearable Sports Electronics team
www.adidas.com

MATERIAL
Engineered textiles integrated with miCoach
sensor technology

DESIGNER BIOGRAPHY
The miCoach Elite Team System was developed
by the adidas Wearable Sports Electronics team
based in Chadds Ford, Pennsylvania. The team
consists of experts in the fields of user interface,
smart textiles, garment engineering, electronics,
application software, and algorithms. Qaizar
Hassonjee is head of R&D at adidas Wearable
Sports Electronics, the group that spearheaded
the development of miCoach Elite Team System
to enable Smart Soccer.

MATERIAL PROPERTIES
Lightweight, Ergonomic, All-Weather Use

opposite top Embedded in the adizero f50
boot, the miCoach Speed Cell measures direction,
distance, speed, and acceleration for personal
training. A memory chip records performance
metrics, including average and maximum running
speed, stretch and stride rates, and distance, even
at high-intensity levels.

opposite bottom The miCoach Elite base
receives radio (RF) signals from a team of up
to thirty athletes wearing player cells that relay
accurate data to coaches in real time.

A broad-minded yet discriminating approach toward
revolutionizing how technology can meet the needs
of top-tier athletes runs through adidas's miCoach
Elite, an advanced physiological monitoring system
built for professional athletic teams. Designed to help teams
achieve and maintain peak physical performance, the system
comprises five integrated components: a Techfit heart-rate
sensing underlayer; a miCoach player cell, which sits on the
back between the shoulder blades to measure the speed,
distance, acceleration, heart rate, and power of the athlete;
and a base station. The base station houses an internal
computer to which data from the player cell is sent; it then
transmits the data to an iPad so that a coach on the sidelines
can see live information from the athletes on the field. An in-
depth analysis system, where teams can go online and further
analyze data from the day's training session, is also included.

While the system sounds complex, it delivers a highly
calibrated balance of micro-assessment that allows for
practical feedback in real time—during a training session the
miCoach player cell collects data on an athlete's performance
100 times a second.

A prime illustration of how the growth of wearable
technology for athletes is having an impact on sports at the
consumer level can be found in the Speed Cell, an extension
of the miCoach family. A footpod attaches to the shoe to
track not only distance and speed but also multidirectional
movement, thereby giving it an expanded role in a range of
athletic activities beyond simply running.

MATERIAL INSIGHT

The significant material innovation in this system is the
Techfit Elite compression base-layer garment, worn under
the player's team shirt, that acts both as a housing for the
player cell and as an integral sensor that tracks heart rate.
The garment uses yarns for the sensor that are coated

above Coaches can monitor their players' performance metrics and field positions on an iPad to better train their team.

opposite The adizero f50 (**top left**) helps players track their performance with Speed Cell. The Techfit Elite (**top right**) is a durable compression base layer of robust textiles engineered with a scaffold for integrated heart-rate sensors (**bottom right**) and an architecture to fit the player cell between the shoulder blades to stabilize it for accurate readings (**bottom left**).

with a pure metallic silver that makes them highly conductive. Pure silver is a noble metal, so will not tarnish or corrode when in contact with sweat, ensuring a consistent conductivity. The sensor is integrated into the construction of the shirt so that it is able to stretch and move with the polyurethane-based elastic knit fabric, to make sure that the sensors connect well to the skin at all times to ensure accurate readings, even during vigorous movement. The positioning of the sensors on either side of the chest also aids good connection to skin unlikely to be obscured by body hair.

DURACELL POWERMAT

DESIGNERS
Dino Sanchez of frog design (www.frogdesign.com),
Einav Sadan Duschak and Charlie Ozana of Powermat,
Brian Guze, Director of Store Design East for
Starbucks Coffee Company

MANUFACTURER
Duracell Powermat
www.duracellpowermat.com

MATERIAL
Induction coils

DESIGNER BIOGRAPHIES
Dino Sanchez is an Associate Creative Director at frog with
responsibilities around product development, user interaction,
and retail experiences. He has a BFA in Industrial Design
from Carnegie Mellon University, Pennsylvania.

Einav Sadan Duschak, Head of Design at Powermat, is an
Israeli-born industrial designer with a passion for technology,
product innovation, and user-centered design.

Charlie Ozana is an integral member of the design team
at Powermat, where he leads mechanical engineering
and collaborates on product design.

Brian Guze has been directing the new design mission
for Starbucks by creating unique and locally relevant
LEED-certified spaces, while using locally sourced
reclaimed materials.

MATERIAL PROPERTIES
Sustainable Solutions, Durable, Simplification

An induction coil creates
an electromagnetic field
that moves easily through
the laminate cover of the
charging station, where
power can be taken up
by mobile devices and
converted back into
electric current.

A Starbucks is hardly a replacement for a fully
equipped workstation, yet there is ample evidence
that the mobile workforce views any of the Seattle-
based coffee company's thousands of locations
as far more than merely a place to buy an espresso. Ever
since open Wi-Fi networks became standard in restaurants,
libraries, parks, and transit stations, finding new ways to
draw people in and keep them there for longer has been
good for business. The limitation, however, has been power.

No longer. While wireless charging is in its early
days, addressing the power needs of consumers who are
increasingly reliant on battery-draining smartphones is a
goal that taps the inherent capabilities of Duracell. As an
alternative to the bulk that comes with battery cases, the
copper-top battery maker created the Powermat, a sleek
charging station for mobile devices, and teamed up with
Starbucks to take the technology mainstream. Simply placing
a specially encased phone on a Powermat, or a Starbucks
tabletop, will be enough to power it up.

"The Duracell Powermat charging spot is rooted in
user-centered design," says Einav Sadan Duschak, Head
of Design at Powermat. "By doing what we do naturally—
setting down our phone—we are now able to charge it.
And not only does it fit into our habits, the minimalist design
blends seamlessly into many settings."

As wireless charging technology evolves, and
consumer expectations along with it, the tangle of cords
and cables that once promised convenience will, as with
so many modern-era devices, gradually disappear.

MATERIAL INSIGHT
Along with batteries, cables are probably up there as the
most frustrating aspect of the physical side of modern
technology. They both tether us and restrict the boundaries
of what our devices can do. This collaboration between

Duracell Powermat and Starbucks conveniently removes the need for either, at least while you are having a coffee. Using induction charging (the same thing that modern electric cookers use to heat pans safely), the tables in specific restaurant locations contain induction coils embedded beneath their laminate surfaces. These interact with similar, but smaller coils in iPhone cases, so that the phone charges simply while lying on the table—no cables required. This technology can be expanded to other devices such that there is no reason why any of our regular devices in our homes need cables to charge them at all.

top, left to right In the United States, Duracell's technology was rolled out at stores in the Boston, Massachusetts area before expanding to Silicon Valley on the West Coast. The devices are easily integrated into surfaces that people congregate around, such as in cafés, bars, or nightclubs.

bottom Instead of letting devices lose power or obliging customers to find an outlet, induction charging extends battery life and gives public spaces an added convenience.

REVIVAL VEST

DESIGNER
James McNab
www.behance.net/jbmcnab

MANUFACTURER
Footfalls and Heartbeats
www.footfallsandheartbeats.com

MATERIAL
Electrically conductive yarn knitted into
a sensor network

MATERIAL MANUFACTURER
Footfalls and Heartbeats

DESIGNER BIOGRAPHY
New Zealand-born designer James McNab
developed the Revival Vest concept while
studying at Victoria University in Wellington.
Inspired by the death of a family friend, he
set out to solve the problem of shallow-water
blackout while diving. McNab, based in
Tauranga, New Zealand, works as an industrial
designer developing product and furniture for
his newly formed company, Y.S Collective.

MATERIAL PROPERTIES
Lightweight, Ergonomic

The Revival Vest was
designed to lift the
diver when activated
but otherwise remain
unnoticed when
worn by the growing
number of competitive
freediving athletes, who
require safety clothing
to be streamlined and
not cumbersome.

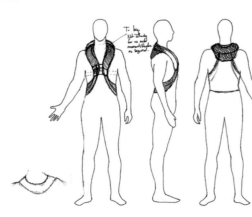

Thrill is the lure for extreme-sport enthusiasts who prefer to play in fluid, uncontrolled, natural environments. For freedivers the rush comes from plunging unencumbered hundreds of feet below the water's surface on a single breath. There are, of course, perils to holding one's breath for extended periods. Out of the estimated 5,000 freedivers in the sport, nearly 100 die each year. The most common threat is shallow-water blackout, a sudden loss of consciousness that typically occurs just prior to resurfacing from a dive.

Motivated by the death of a family friend from shallow-water blackout, New Zealand industrial designer James McNab conceived of a life jacket that would meet the sport's need to locate, retrieve, and resuscitate a diver in trouble without hampering the experience of the dive. The Revival Vest recognizes physiological changes in the wearer, notably those pertaining to drowning, and responds. When triggered, the vest self-inflates and pulls the diver to the surface so that rescue breathing can begin.

The key to the vest is a chest strap that sits around the torso against the skin. Smart fabric technology from the strap monitors the circumference of the chest under water and a wireless transmitter in the front alerts a receiver in the vest should the diver go limp. Once triggered, the vest inflates, placing the diver in a laid-back position that raises the head above water and inhibits further intake of fluid into the lungs.

With this ingenious solution, McNab reveals design's potential for empathy. The vest responds to the freediver's desire for maximum freedom through its streamlined ergonomic form, yet addresses the most urgent safety needs, investing the term "life jacket" with new meaning.

MATERIAL INSIGHT

This combination of smart fabric and deployable life jacket for divers is a noteworthy demonstration of this textile that can detect changes in respiration. The fabric does this by registering small changes in stretch through a nanostructured electrically conductive coating on a knitted fabric. If the wearer either starts hyperventilating or blacks out, the fabric that fits around the chest registers the altered breathing and causes the life jacket to inflate, bringing the diver to the surface. A small CO_2 cylinder is used to fill the jacket, and can be reused.

above Cerebral hypoxia occurs when the brain goes without enough oxygen, and the victim begins to lose consciousness. The vest inflates when the user goes limp and the sensors trigger the outer garment to fill with CO_2.

below A woven network of sensors underneath the wetsuit detects any change in circumference and stretch around the user's chest. When breathing stops under water, textile sensors wirelessly communicate to the bladders on the outside.

SMART BANDAGE BACTERIA SENSOR

DESIGNER / MANUFACTURER
Edgar D. Goluch
www.northeastern.edu/goluchgroup

MATERIAL
Palladium circuitry

DESIGNER BIOGRAPHY
Edgar Goluch attended the University of Illinois at Urbana-Champaign, where he received a BSc in Chemical Engineering, an MSc in Mechanical Engineering, and a PhD in Bioengineering. He went on to complete a two-year postdoctoral fellowship at Delft University of Technology in the Netherlands. Goluch is currently the DiPietro Assistant Professor in the Department of Chemical Engineering at Northeastern University in Boston, Massachusetts. His research interests are in the area of nanobiotechnology.

MATERIAL PROPERTIES
Rapidly Renewable Resource, Lightweight, Biomimicry

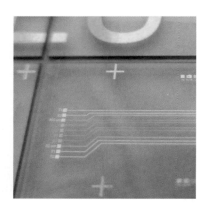

Electrochemical devices with microscale wires were made with palladium to create "stable reference electrodes" for sensing a specific compound created by a harmful strain of bacteria.

Whether inherited or acquired, immunodeficiency diseases affect the body's ability to fight antigens, resulting in a vulnerability to infections, which can be especially problematic during a hospital stay. Early detection is crucial since, if left unchecked, an infection can run rampant and ultimately be fatal. Any wound or opening, for example following a surgical procedure, requires careful monitoring.

Solutions are now emerging in the form of "smart bandages" made possible by a combination of microsensor technology and material science. Smart bandages go beyond keeping a wound clean and protected, to assist healing by detecting molecular changes on the skin that signal the growing presence of an infection. Once identified, the bacteria can then be treated with antibiotics.

The device—a thin blue semitransparent disc threaded with metallic sensors—is the work of Ed Goluch, an assistant professor of chemical engineering at Northeastern University, and graduate student Thaddaeus Webster. Bacteria produce a host of compounds, some of which are electrochemically active. The bandage specifically targets *P. aeruginosa*, a unique bacterium that secretes a molecule that can be detected by an electrochemical sensor. Each gold line in the bandage represents a separate electrochemical device that alerts doctors to microscopic bacteria at very low concentrations.

The novel approach relies on palladium, a rare, lustrous, silvery-white metal. Palladium's ability to be manufactured into miniature wires makes it an ideal material to incorporate into microscale sensors. While researchers have previously been stymied by the exceptionally miniature scale required for smart bandage electrodes, Goluch's Smart Bandage exploits the metal's properties, providing better protection for those at risk for infection.

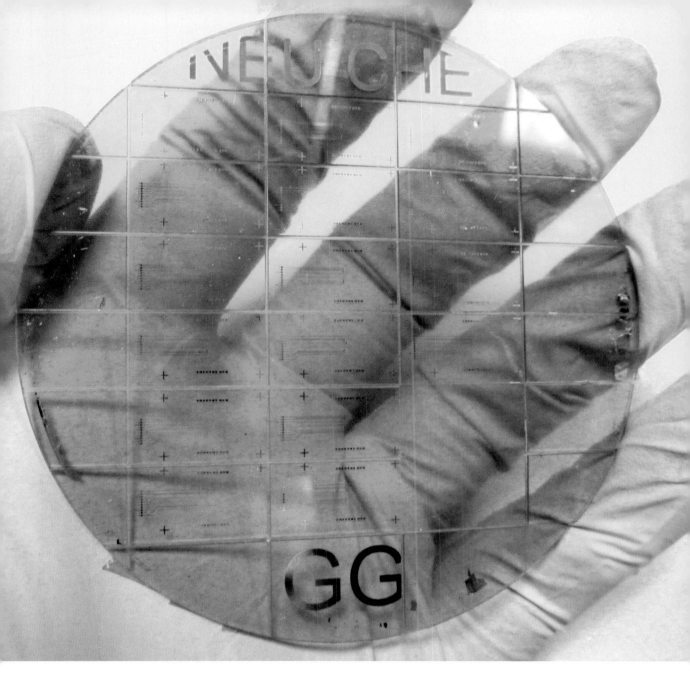

MATERIAL INSIGHT

Bacteria can produce compounds that are electrochemically active. This is the basis for the electrochemical sensor used in a smart bandage that works by detecting these charged molecules. Essential to this miniature innovation is a stable, microscale reference electrode incorporated into the device, made of tiny amounts of palladium, that can detect pyocyanin, present in the *P. aeruginosa* bacterium, which is potentially deadly to those with compromised immune systems. The palladium is shaped into tiny wires that crisscross the bandage and can pick up any sign of the bacterium.

The palladium circuitry is made with the same equipment used to fabricate computer chips. Ease of integration and forthcoming research may soon make this technology an affordable addition to bandages, enabling them to diagnose infection.

K-DRESS

DESIGNER / MANUFACTURER
CuteCircuit (co-founders Francesca Rosella
and Ryan Genz)
www.cutecircuit.com

MATERIAL
LED-laced silk chiffon

DESIGNER BIOGRAPHIES
London-based CuteCircuit is a global leader in
interactive fashion founded by Francesca Rosella and
Ryan Genz. They have brought much innovation to the
fashion arena by integrating beauty and functionality
through the use of smart textiles and microelectronics.
The label launched its ready-to-wear line in 2010,
bringing the first technologically infused casual wear
to major fashion retailers.

Francesca Rosella began her career as a designer for
Valentino in Italy. Ryan Genz is trained as an artist,
anthropologist, and ultimately interaction designer
focusing on wearable technology; he holds patents
and patents pending for wearable technologies.

MATERIAL PROPERTIES
Lightweight, Ergonomic

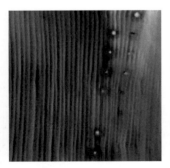

CuteCircuit has made
sophisticated garments
with thousands of LEDs
that emit coordinated high-
speed animations, but the
elegant K-Dress exhibits
the designers' expertise
with programmable lights
scattered over and woven
into silk chiffon.

CuteCircuit has been upending the aesthetic and
technological conventions of apparel since it was
founded in 2004. Inspired by other disciplines
and a desire to incorporate new technologies,
Creative Director Francesca Rosella and CEO Ryan Genz
propose a twenty-first-century reinterpretation of textiles.
Pushing beyond mere embellishment, CuteCircuit's wearable
technology introduces new avenues for fashion design via
smart textiles and microelectronics.

In their eye-stopping creations, the clothes are
enhanced by tiny light-emitting diodes, or LEDs. The
K-Dress uses hand-pleated chiffon incorporating hundreds
of LED lights embedded in the fabric. The LEDs are
powered by a small clip-on controller that recharges via
USB in about two hours. The individual LEDs are sewn
into the garment and connected via flexible wires. The
lights switch on and off in numerous illuminated colors
and patterns as programmed by the wearer.

For CuteCircuit, the human body becomes a
vessel of illumination. The garments are intended for an
adventuresome client who is not merely out to look good
but possesses a desire for surprise and wonder. Although
such complex creations are impressive for their minute
details, each piece appears to have been conceived as a
single gesture, allowing the garment to transcend its purely
functional aspect with striking visual results.

MATERIAL INSIGHT
These energy-efficient light sources have opened up new
possibilities for, literally, seeing light. Their efficiency offers
a further advantage by allowing wires to be thinner and
less insulated, so that they can be embedded in fabrics and
activated with Bluetooth technology. The surface of an LED
is also cool, so they can be knitted into a garment without
producing heat.

MATERIALS DIRECTORY

Material ConneXion is the world's largest library of advanced innovative materials. Our online database gives users access to images, technical descriptions, and usage characteristics, as well as to manufacturer and distributor contact information, all of which has been written and compiled by our international team of material specialists. The content is intended to meet the needs of engineers and scientists as well as architects and designers by providing advanced material expertise in an accessible, user-friendly format. Each material in the database is catalogued with a six-digit MC number: the first four digits identify the manufacturer and the last two indicate how many unique materials are included in the library. Each entry has been juried by a panel of material specialists, architects, designers, and technicians from diverse manufacturing backgrounds. The jury determines whether or not a material warrants inclusion in the library by assessing its inherent innovative qualities. Material innovation is not limited to new materials and technologies. It also includes significant improvements in performance that pave the way for future development, and materials previously used in specialized fields that become more accessible to designers. Innovation also applies to sustainable materials that perform as well as commonly used products with a greatly reduced impact on the environment. To learn more, visit: www.materialconnexion.com/books.

MC# 0027-19
VESTAMID® *Terra* DS
Evonik Industries
www.vestamid.com

Continuing the evolution of plastics from biobased raw materials, this nylon is produced from castor seed oil, a renewable plant source. The resin has a very low carbon footprint while retaining the desirable properties of nylon. It is comparable to nylon 12 (a high-performance version of the plastic) in many attributes, such as: high mechanical strength, low water absorption, medium–high temperature resistance, and good transparency in thin profiles. The resin is suitable for use in fiber, filament, injection molding, extrusion, and 3D-printing systems. **Properties:** Rapidly Renewable Resource; High Strength; Sustainable Solutions

MC# 0664-05
pebax® Rnew
Arkema Inc.
www.arkema-inc.com

This high-performance biobased elastomer (TPE) is made from up to 95% plant-based materials (namely oil from the castor plant). It has reduced greenhouse gas emissions by up to 30% compared to an equivalent petroleum or fossil fuel-based product. Its low density gives it flexible fatigue performance, good energy return, and power transmission. Durable, recyclable, injection-moldable, overmoldable, and extrudable into films or sheets, it is one of the lightest elastomers, with good resilience and suitability for consumer products, sports equipment, and footwear. **Properties:** Sustainable Solutions; Durable

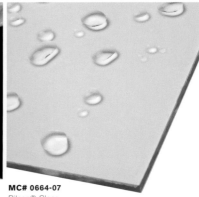

MC# 0664-07
Rilsan® Clear
Arkema Inc.
www.arkema-inc.com

A transparent biobased engineering resin designed for injection-molding applications, this polyamide (nylon) is made from 54% biobased raw materials with transparency similar to glass. It is the lightest engineering resin available, with lower density than water. The material exhibits better chemical resistance than previous generations of transparent polyamides, with a high level of alcohol and hydrocarbon resistance. Applications include eyewear frames, ski masks, industrial filters, athletic shoes, mobile phone casings, and lenses. **Properties:** Sustainable solutions; Durable

MC# 4780-08
Perennial Wood™
Eastman Chemical Company
www.perennialwood.com

Acetylation, the process of treating wood with a vinegar-like substance to harden and waterproof it, has been around since the 1930s but has only recently become economically viable. Leaving a slight vinegar smell after treatment, it enables softwoods to act as though they were durable hardwoods. This gives protection, even uncoated, against decades of outdoor exposure. Acetylation does not stop the wood being sawed, nailed, screwed, or otherwise worked like any other lumber. There may, however, be a darkening in the color of the wood over time. **Properties:** Sustainable Solutions; Rapidly Renewable Resource; Durable

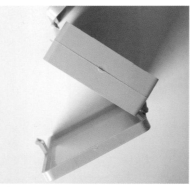

MC# 5008-04
reSound™
PolyOne Corporation
www.polyone.com

These patent-pending compounds combine a minimum of 30% bioderived content, biobased polymers such as PLA, PHB, PHBV, and biopolyesters with compatible engineering thermoplastic resins. Key improvements over unfilled biopolymers include levels of heat tolerance (up to 120° C / 248° F) and impact resistance, bringing performance levels in range with ABS and high-impact polystyrene (HIPS). Processing characteristics are similar to traditional engineered resins. Applications are found in interior automotive components, medical devices and equipment, electronics equipment, and consumer durable goods. **Properties:** Sustainable Solutions; Durable

MC# 5842-03
Transform™ Worksurface
e2e Materials, Inc.
www.e2ematerials.com

Using locally sourced waste agricultural materials, this proprietary soy-based resin process creates stiff, strong biocomposite panels and parts that can be dyed with water-based pigments. The addition of a proprietary natural additive creates "cross-linking" of the soy, resulting in a stiffer resin than normal. Compared to particleboard, these are stronger, 66% lighter, inherently flame-retardant, and petrochemical-free, use 60% less energy to create, contain zero formaldehyde, and are completely biodegradable. It is used to produce smaller industrial parts and solid surfacing. **Properties:** Sustainable Solutions; Durable; Composite

MC# 6419-01
Solanyl® BP
Rodenburg Biopolymers B.V.
www.biopolymers.nl

One of the increasing number of starch-based bioplastics, this compostable resin is made from potato starch reclaimed from the food-processing industry. Mechanical properties are roughly the same as polyester (PET) or polystyrene (PS) but require 65% less energy to produce than polyethylene (PE). Degradation periods of between three months and two years are established but use of coatings, such as beeswax, can decrease the biodegradation rate. Applications are found in the agricultural, packaging, construction, and automotive industries and in consumer products. **Properties:** Sustainable Solutions; Compostable

MC# 6573-02
Biotex Flax / PLA
Composites Evolution Ltd.
www.compositesevolution.com

This composite material is made of flax fibers in a polylactic acid (PLA) resin matrix. The flax fibers are highly aligned, allowing faster wet-out and impregnation. This structure also takes advantage of flax's inherent mechanical properties in loadbearing applications with stiffness comparable to glass fibers at nearly half the density. As PLA is derived from 100% renewable resources (plants, e.g. corn), these composites can be recycled or composted. Applications are found in the automotive, construction, and marine industries. **Properties:** High Strength; Composite; Compostable

MC# 6573-03
Biotex Flax / PLA Preconsolidated Sheet
Composites Evolution Ltd.
www.compositesevolution.com

Great leaps are being made in the development of high-performance natural-fiber composites. These sheets consist of flax fibers and polylactic acid (PLA) utilizing a proprietary "Twistless Technology," where the long natural fibers are woven specifically to gain high-tensile strength compared to other natural composites. They exhibit loadbearing performance with lower weight and ease of processing compared to glass-reinforced materials and can be composted or recycled. Applications include automotive parts, furniture, doors, interior walls, and cabinetry. **Properties:** High Strength; Composite; Compostable

MC# 6669-01
Cocofelt
Natural Composites, Inc.
www.naturalcompositesinc.com

These thermoformable high-performance panels, composed of coconut fibers and polypropylene (PP), are used as a replacement for synthetic polyester (PET) fibers found in traditional compression-molded composites. The board is made by shredding the whole husk of the coconut into a brown dust-like substance. It is then placed on a hot press, which adds the right combination of heat and pressure, compressing the dust together to form a sheet of particleboard. The panels are used in packaging, automotive interiors, luggage construction, furniture, signage and appliances. **Properties:** Composite

MC# 6670-01
Biodegradable Plastic Products
Reangwa Standard Industry Co., Ltd.
www.reangwa.co.th

This polylactic acid (PLA)-based biopolymer is suitable for injection-molding, thermoforming, and blow-molding applications. PLA is an aliphatic polyester resin that is made from a polymerized lactic acid, which in turn comes from a renewable resource, such as cornstarch or sugarcane, using a chemical synthetic process. It is FDA approved for food- and microwave-safe containers, insulated ice coolers, and other food packaging items. Applications are for packaging, food storage, and various household items. **Properties:** Sustainable Solutions

MC# 6702-01
Absorv®
Zeus Inc.
www.zeusinc.com

Any plastic used in the human body needs to be biocompatible. These polyester-based plastics have many properties similar to polyethylene (PE) and polypropylene (PP), and are designed to be implanted in the body to hold open an artery, deliver a time-release drug, or as a medical tool that can be left in during surgery and harmlessly absorbed back into the body over time. They have modulated degradation rates (from days to years) and varying strength and hardness, and may be extruded into numerous shapes with exacting tolerances. **Properties:** Biodegradable; Biomimicry

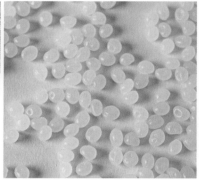

MC# 6738-01
Green Polyethelene
Braskem
www.braskem.com.br

The first high-volume production bioplastic produced from sugarcane, which removes CO_2 from the atmosphere. This high-density polyethylene (HDPE) uses plant material as a renewable alternative to petroleum for a plastic that is physically and mechanically equivalent to standard HDPE. The resin can be pigmented with standard colors and effects, and can be extruded, blow and injection molded, and made into films. Applications are for all forms of HDPE packaging and consumer products that may be substituted with this renewable version. **Properties:** Sustainable Solutions; Rapidly Renewable Resource

MC# 6753-02
TRAVERSE® Prime
Solegear Bioplastics Inc.
www.solegear.com

As an alternative to talc- or glass-filled plastics, this high-performance hybrid material contains biobased fibers. This hybrid plastic is a combination of virgin (new) conventional plastic (PP, PE, PET, nylon) and a customized percentage of biobased fiber content. Using wood, hemp, bamboo, rice husks, or other natural fibers, along with virgin polymer, it can have between 20% and 60% natural fiber content, and is durable and easy to process. It can be injection molded or extruded and finds applications in consumer products. **Properties:** Lightweight; Durable

MC# 6753-05
POLYSOLE®XD
Solegear Bioplastics Inc.
www.solegear.com

This high-performance biodegradable thermoplastic allows manufacturers to create polylactic acid (PLA) products with better flexibility, strength, and impact capacity. Made using entirely natural materials and organic additives. PLA is an aliphatic polyester resin that is made from a polymerized lactic acid, which in turn comes from a renewable resource, such as cornstarch or sugarcane. Strong, easy to process, and cost-competitive, it can be processed on conventional equipment for use in film, sheet, and blow- and injection-molding applications. **Properties:** Rapidly Renewable Resource; Lightweight; Compostable

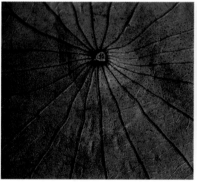

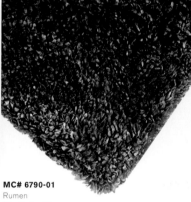

MC# 6757-02
Natural Bedding Foam
FXI
www.fxi.com

This flexible polyurethane (PU) foam is made partially of plant-based polyols instead of petroleum-based polyols. While conventional foaming methods require toxic chemicals to control foam properties, variable pressure foaming (VPF) uses pressure to modify the foam's physical properties. The resulting foam requires fewer toxic ingredients, emits fewer toxins, and has more consistent foam densities and more overall controlled properties than traditional foam processes. Applications include interior cushioning and bedding. **Properties:** Sustainable Solutions; Rapidly Renewable Resource

MC# 6784-01
Preserved Lotus Leaf
Sirada Products Co., Ltd.
www.siradaproducts.com

This preserved lotus leaf may be used as a paper-like covering for stationery, book and file covers, and in packaging. Through fermentation, drying under sunlight, and treatment for mold resistance, this leaf looks and feels like a fresh lotus leaf and has a shelf life of four to five years. It is water-resistant, and when dry, can be softened with body lotion or polished with a leather gloss agent. The leaves are available in five diameter ranges and custom colors are available using natural dyes. **Properties:** Sustainable Solutions, Rapidly Renewable Resource; Compostable

MC# 6790-01
Rumen
Mandy den Elzen
www.mandydenelzen.com

This original leather is made of cattle stomach. The first two chambers, the rumen and the reticulum, are the largest of the four chambers of cattle stomachs and are used to make this textured leather material, which requires two months of tanning. It has small, paper-thin, finger-like folds, in addition to a hexagonal honeycomb structure that gives the leather its resemblance to fur. The leather is slightly translucent, resilient, and not flammable. Applications are for wall panels and artwork. **Properties:** Sustainable Solutions; Biomimicry

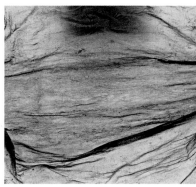

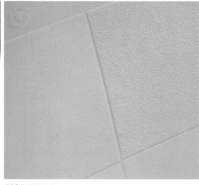

MC# 6790-02
Algae
Mandy den Elzen
www.mandydenelzen.com

Dried algae leaves (kelp) have been used for centuries as food, medicine, and industrial raw materials. This version has leaves that are approximately 10–20 cm (4–8 in.) wide and 30 cm (12 in.) long. The algae are boiled, then processed while still moist and molded into the desired shape. They are then lacquered with an acrylic resin, increasing the durability of the plant for added strength and resilience. The leaves come in shades of green and brown, and each strand is different. The material's translucency allows it to be used in lighting but also finds application in indoor wallpanels and in artwork. **Properties:** Sustainable Solutions; Rapidly Renewable Resource; Durable

MC# 6839-01
Riceware
out of the GREEN box Co., Ltd.
www.greenvolutions.com

These hard, natural-fiber and polymer composites are composed of waste materials from rice harvesting and production in Thailand. They can be thermoformed from a blank, but cannot be injection molded at this stage. The formed parts can withstand a wide temperature range, including dishwasher and microwave environments. Virtually impervious to rot and insects, the material is claimed to be recyclable and biodegradable. It is used in the food industry (tableware), chemical industry, and agricultural applications. **Properties:** Durable; Composite

MC# 6899-01
Arnitel® Eco
DSM Engineering Plastics
www.dsm.com

Furthering the evolution of bioplastics, this thermoplastic co-polyester elastomer uses rapeseed oil in its composition. A widely available non-food harvested resource, it is used as a substitute for up to 50% of the petrochemical oil, which compared to standard co-polyesters shows up to a 50% reduction in GWP (global warming potential). It combines the processing characteristics of thermoplastics with the performance of rubbers. The resin is used in automotive interiors and exteriors, sports equipment, consumer electronics, furniture, and alternative energy. **Properties:** Sustainable Solutions; Rapidly Renewable Resource

MC# 6926-02
Studio Biofoam®
Malama Composites
www.malamacomposites.com

A biobased rigid polyurethane (PU) foam made with vegetable polyols from castor oil. Confirmed to be carbon neutral in its manufacture, it sequesters 1.18 kg (2.6 lbs) of CO_2 for every 0.45 kg (1 lb) of foam. It has a very fine and consistent cell size offering high-quality secondary processing, such as carving, sanding, and painting. A version is also sold as a blank for lower-environmental impact surfboards. Additional applications include 3D modeling and prototyping, stage and film sets, museum exhibits, trade show displays, retail environments, signage, and POP displays. **Properties:** Rapidly Renewable Resource

MC# 6968-01
Organoid Technologies and Materials
Organoid Technologies GmbH
www.organoids.com

These large- and small-format biocomposite forms are made from natural fibers with a natural binder that changes properties depending on the composite. This material is processed by an inflatable inner form that can be shaped as desired, with the fiber/binder mixture sprayed on. The still damp and flexible material is covered with another vacuum film and hermetically sealed. Lastly, a defined negative pressure is applied to compress and harden the biocomposite into its final form. Applications include interior design, industrial design, and architecture. **Properties:** Sustainable Solutions; Compostable

MC# 7037-01
DuraPulp
Södra
www.sodra.com

This pulp biocomposite, which can be colored, is composed of wood fibers and polylactic acid (PLA) fibers from renewable, non-fossil-based raw materials. It can be "activated" or "non-activated"—each changes its properties. The pulp is activated with heat and pressure, becoming strong, rigid, and dimensionally stable with low water absorption. Non-activated pulp is used in specialty paper for high folding resistance, high tear strength, and high dimensional stability. Applications include furniture and accessories. **Properties:** Sustainable Solutions; Rapidly Renewable Resource; Durable

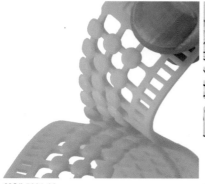

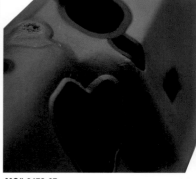

MC# 5321-02
LYNX™ XOLOK™
Chittenden Research and Development, LLC
www.lynxfast.com

In an approach to the challenge of "the next Velcro," this elastomeric, non-grabbing polymer closure is a potential alternative to hook and loop fasteners. The open-matrix structure allows for easy cleaning and ventilation, or impermeability to water when closed. This closure has high flexibility and a low profile, and is self-engaging (hermaphroditic), self-cleaning, soft, silent and durable. It may be integrally molded as a fastening zone within a larger component, or it can be overmolded onto an open weave fabric. Applications include closures of nearly any kind.
Properties: Ergonomic; Simplification

MC# 5548-03
Mille-feuille
HORIE
www.horie.co.jp

A proprietary titanium-etching process for creating thin perforated foils of 0.1 mm (0.004 in) that are stacked into piles and bonded together for strength but allow air to pass through with very controlled flow rates. The titanium can be colored with an anodizing process that gives it light-interference properties where the color shifts or changes depending on the direction and angle of the light. There are no pigments or dyes involved. Titanium can be used outdoors and is suitable for wet environments (spa, marine sports) because it will not rust. Applications are for accessories.
Properties: Lightweight; Simplification

MC# 6472-07
Terocore®
Henkel AG & Co. KGaA
www.henkel.com

Rigid foam can offer stiffness and volume with lower weight. These high-strength structural reinforcement foam products are intended to enhance the structural integrity and mechanical strength of various architectural, automotive, and industrial components. They strengthen hollow structures and reinforce panel surfaces, creating high-performance hybrid foam-plastic/metal pieces that have low weight, strong stiffness, dent resistance, and strong crashworthiness. They are typically used to reinforce frame rails, body cavities, or body panels in the automotive industry.
Properties: Lightweight; Durable; High Strength

MC# 6572-01
UVMax®
DVUV, LLC
www.dvuv.com

These UV-cured powder coating finishes for wood and medium-density fiberboard (MDF) are among the thinnest. The process involves first pre-heating the MDF to draw moisture out of the wood, which attracts the powder electrostatically. The entire process is completed in less than twenty minutes. The UV-curing process is energy-efficient, resulting in 40–60% savings over paints or laminates. The powder formulation has no solvents, generates zero VOCs (volatile organic compounds), and is PVC-free. Applications include retail, healthcare, architectural elements, and specialty products.
Properties: All-Weather Use; Durable

MC# 6603-02
Blushing Bottles
Americhem
www.americhem.com

A photochromatic (changes color with light) plastic made of 80% high-density polyethylene (HDPE) and 18% thermoplastic elastomer (TPE). The TPE is the outer layer of the sheet, containing photochromatic pigment that enables the bottle to blush (in this case, turn red) when exposed to sunlight or UV radiation. The hues, shades, and color of the bottle as well as the color change can be customized. This two-layer sheet can be used in processes such as blow molding, injection molding, and extrusion. Applications for the molded pieces are for packaging and electronics.
Properties: Biomimicry; Simplification

MC# 6677-01
nanoMAG
Thixomat Inc.
www.nanomag.us

Magnesium is the lightest structural metal in common use. This process creates injection-molded magnesium parts without the need of die-casting to create ultra-thin shaped parts as thin as 0.5 mm (0.02 in.). The process creates isotropic (the same properties in all directions), fine-grained strengthening, increased ductility, greatly reduced grain size, reduced edge cracking, and improved mechanical properties. It has the strength of carbon steel at quarter the weight and significantly improved corrosion resistance. Applications include consumer and commercial electronic devices.
Properties: Nanotech; Lightweight

MC# 6732-01
Cerakote™ H-series
NIC Industries
www.nicindustries.com

These durable, ceramic-loaded polymer coatings have the look of high-end ceramic parts thanks to a spray coating that does not peel. They have excellent resistance to chemicals, scratches, and wear thanks to the tiny ceramic particles. They are available in both clear and high-gloss colored coats and are able to withstand temperatures in excess of 537° C (1000° F) as coatings for the automotive industry. The surface exhibits resistance to grease, oil, solvents and most industrial chemicals, and is suitable for the coating of firearms, exhaust systems, watches, and other high-wear applications. **Properties:** All-Weather Use; Durable; Stain-Resistant/Easy-Clean

MC# 6812-01
Easy Supply Tube
CTL Packaging
www.turboplastctl.com

This in-mold labeling process fabricates single material polypropylene (PP) plastic container tubes (sleeve and cap), making it easier to change print design and recycle. A novel technique, it allows for the incorporation of customizable high-quality decorative labels into the storage tubes' outer layer, enabling the creation of different head, closure and cap options. This technology reduces inventory and processing steps, lowering costs by enabling a quicker changeover between label types. **Properties:** Lightweight; Simplification

MC# 6832-01
Metal / Plastic Hybrid PMH
Lite-On Mobile
www.liteonmobile.com

The development of adhesion molding and nanomolding technologies has resulted in the creation of novel bonding techniques that enable the joining of metal and plastic parts without the use of mechanical fixtures. To integrate these dissimilar materials directly, a modified injection-molding process creates a hybrid metal plastic (PMH) structure. This eliminates the need for an additional assembly process or mechanical fasteners. It is used in the construction of cell phones and other electronic equipment. **Properties:** Composite; Simplification

MC# 6833-01
MICRALOX®
Sanford Process Corporation
www.micralox.com

Adding heat and corrosion resistance to decorative aluminum parts, this patented anodizing process incorporates a microcrystalline barrier surface that offers much greater resistance to corrosive environments such as dishwashers, sterilization procedures, and sanitizing. This coating increases resistance to wear and chemical corrosion and eliminates color fading thanks to superheated steam. It is being used in medical-based applications as well as industrial and marine applications. **Properties:** All-Weather Use; Durable

MC# 6866-01
Printed Case
P & TEL Inc. / People & Telecommunication Inc.
www.pntel.co.kr

Capitalizing on our desire for customized accessories for our products, this printing process is able to render high-quality graphics on plastic films. A sublimating dye transfer embeds the graphic into the polymer layer very much like a tattoo, so that it is not removed by surface scratches. It can be applied to three-dimensional curved and angled profiles with no distortion of the image. Applications include films applied to curved surfaces of mobile phone cases, laptop cases, consumer product shells, and other printed surfaces. **Properties:** Stain-Resistant/Easy-Clean; Durable

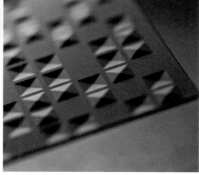

MC# 6973-04
White Porcelain
Nissha USA
www.nissha.co.jp

Taking the technology of in-mold decoration (IMD) to a more advanced level, these four-layer constructions give a ceramic or porcelain surface texture and effect. The molding is used to create rigid decorative parts that have a base-molded rigid layer with mold texture, a "backup" layer on top, with a base color layered on top of this, and a top coat to give a soft-touch surface. Applications include consumer electronics, home appliances, automotive, consumer healthcare, cosmetics, and toys. **Properties:** Stain-Resistant/Easy-Clean

MC# 6973-06
Injection Molding Decoration (IMD)
Nissha USA
www.nissha.co.jp

These multiple-layered printed graphic films are for two-shot injection-molding decoration (IMD) of plastics. This process imparts a sense of depth and three-dimensionality by layering graphics and a clear and a colored resin within the molded part. The simultaneous molding of two different resins allows for back surface molding and front surface molding for process step reductions and lower costs. Applications include casings for consumer electronics, home appliances, car interiors and exteriors, cosmetic packaging, and toys. **Properties:** Simplification

MC# 6980-01
UVMax®
Keyland Polymer, Ltd.
www.keylandpolymer.com

Powder coatings offer a low-impact way of protecting a range of different surfaces such as metals, plastics (UV curing means lower-melting-point parts can be coated), and now wood-based materials and composites. The coatings are available in a wide range of finishes, including pearl, metallic, opaque, or solid surface finishes and can be color-matched through Pantone, RAL or existing paint or laminates. Applications are for furniture, consumer products, and composite parts. **Properties:** All-Weather Use; Durable

MC# 7002-01
Silmade® Digital Print
Silcos GmbH
www.silcos.com

As silicone becomes more prevalent in our molded products, processes are being developed to improve and add functionality to this wonder material. Abrasion-resistant, sterilizable, and resistant to cleaning detergents, the silicone-molded parts are surface-activated to provide adhesion, printed with an industrial printer, and spray-coated with a protective layer of polyurethane (PU). The printed parts can endure harsh environmental conditions in the automotive, medical, industrial, and aerospace industries. **Properties:** All-Weather Use; Durable

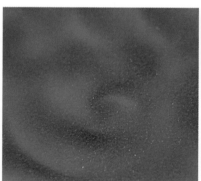

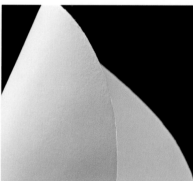

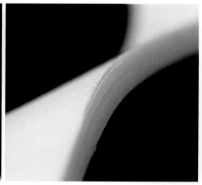

MC# 7007-01
Magne-View®
USWP Manufacturing
www.magnerite.com

This film responds to magnets with a color change. The film is flexible and can be cut to any size, though the only color option at this time is green. Popular uses for the film are quality control, product demonstration, reverse engineering, product authentication, and education. **Properties:** Stain-Resistant/Easy-Clean

MC# 7033-01
Highly-filled Sinterable Paper
Papiertechnische Stiftung
www.ptspaper.de

This paper-like sheet can be folded, cut, shaped and otherwise worked like paper, but sinters into a ceramic when fired at high temperatures. The paper is loaded with ceramic particles integrated within the wood pulp fiber layers. This semi-finished ceramic material offers a smooth surface and printability, with uniform wall thickness and customizable porosity. Applications include filtration media, household, kitchen and consumer products, accessories, and packaging. **Properties:** All-Weather Use; Durable

MC# 7039-01
Shape Retaining Plastic
Sekisui Seikei, LTD
www.inabataamerica.com

This multi-layered plastic sheet can be shaped repeatedly by hand in multiple directions and retain that shape, giving easy formability to soft metals and wire. Plastic sheets are stretched and oriented, giving them a directional grain, and then they are laminated together in a variety of orientations to create multiple directional properties. Applications include food packaging, packaging, fashion, accessories, custom-fit bands, sports protection, and nose bands. **Properties:** Durable

MC# 0027-14
ACRYLITE® EndLighten
Evonik Cyro LLC
www.acrylite.net

This transparent acrylic (PMMA) with light-diffracting particles provides uniform glow to the edge when illuminated. The sheets and rods are embedded with colorless light-diffusing particles that cause the acrylic to accept light through its edge and channel it through to the other side, providing directional illumination. If no light is fed in, the material offers a clear view without disturbing optical effects due to clouding halftone printing or inscribed textures. Applications include illuminated shelving, interior panels, thin-profile signs, and poster panels for commercial spaces. **Properties:** All-Weather Use

MC# 1254-03
QISO™ Triaxial Braiding
A&P Technology
www.braider.com

Triaxial woven carbon-fiber reinforcement reduces weak points for composite parts. Increasing the number of fiber directions from two to three, and changing the orientation of the fibers from orthogonal to 60 degrees increases the damage tolerance and also improves energy absorption. The yarns are quasi-isotropic and balanced in a single layer of braid, making it thinner and lighter than most laminates while allowing for decreased lay-up time. Applications are for composite reinforcement in aerospace, engineering, sports equipment, and automotive racing. **Properties:** High Strength; Composite

MC# 2492-04
Coremat® XM
Lantor Composites
www.lantor.nl

This polyester non-woven fabric for composites reduces the amount of resin needed. It is a cost-effective solution for spray-up open-mold processing, allowing for fast thickness build-up. It conforms well into contoured corners, and is compatible for use with standard resin types, including polyester, vinylester, phenolic, and epoxy. Reduced resin and glass usage saves weight and labor, and allows for high-quality surface finishes. These membranes are currently used in marine areas, transportation, mass transit, kayaks, surfboards pools, and tubs. **Properties:** Lightweight; High Strength

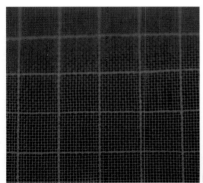

MC# 4832-05
TST 1/2/3
Gruppo Creamoda
www.ideascudo.com

This decorative screening textile for electromagnetic waves (EMI) is comprised of polyester (PET), steel alloy, and shantung "nubby" screening yarn. It can be cut, sewn, dyed, and embroidered. The fabric is non-allergenic and can be machine-washed at low temperatures without affecting its functionality. Applications include curtains. **Properties:** Lightweight

MC# 4914-02
Exogrid®
VyaTek Sports, Inc.
www.vytex.com

This process is used to make lightweight, high-strength composite tubes through the use of an exterior aircraft-grade aluminum extruded tube that has been lase cut to remove geometric sections from the walls of the profile. The tube can be any geometry, such as square, elliptical, round diamond, or teardrop. A secondary process inflates a carbon-fiber tube onto the inner walls for an additional strengthening layer. Applications include sports equipment, baseball bats and ski poles, and high-performance structural pieces in other consumer products. **Properties:** Lightweight; Composite

MC# 6404-01
IsoTruss
Novatek, Inc.
www.novatek.com

This process, based on geometry that extrapolates the traditional 2D triangle-based truss to a 3D truss made up of pyramids formed by isosceles triangles, creates lightweight, 3D composite structures. This provides a redundant load path, and high stiffness and damage tolerance. It is an alternative to wood, steel, or aluminum, and is non-toxic, and low-maintenance. Applications include bicycle frames, civil infrastructure, and pre-assembled reinforcement for concrete, aircraft and satellite structures. **Properties:** High Strength; Biomimicry

MC# 6439-01
Innegra™ S fiber
Innegra Technologies, LLC
www.innegratech.com

This lower-cost, high-performance fiber is used in combination with carbon, glass, quartz, or aramid fibers to create lightweight, high-strength fabrics and composites. This fiber has high tenacity, tensile modulus, and dimensional strength, and excellent dielectric properties. It has good water, chemical, and UV resistance, and excels in performance under cryogenic and high-speed impact conditions. Applications include police and military vests and helmets, composite armor for aircraft and vehicles, and ropes and cords. **Properties:** Lightweight; High Strength

MC# 6469-03
HyPerform®
Milliken Chemical
www.clearpp.com

This additive to polypropylene (PP) offers improved stiffness and part quality with lower loading amounts than glass fiber or other fillers. The filaments have a high aspect ratio and are much smaller than standard glass fibers. They do not degrade molding equipment, and are soluble if inhaled, making them non-hazardous to humans. Parts that utilize this additive have faster processing speeds, higher productivity, and reduced warpage, among other benefits. It is used in automotive interior surfaces, and various consumer products. **Properties:** High Strength; Composite

MC# 6524-03
Seconect
PolymerPark materials GmbH
www.seconect.de

These lightweight, durable, and recyclable foamed thermoplastic panels are laminated with a woven, non-porous polypropylene (PP) anti-slip surface developed specifically for commercial vehicle floors. It weighs 20–50% less than conventional vehicle flooring, is easy to handle and install, and reduces vehicle weight, consequently decreasing fuel consumption. Rot-proof, abrasion-resistant, and water-resistant, the panels are produced in a one step process, lowering cost. FDA-certified for food contact, applications are for commercial vehicle floors and construction. **Properties:** High Strength; Composite

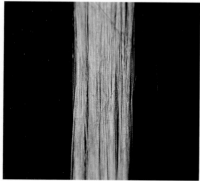

MC# 6579-03
SupraTene
Fuesers Garne GmbH
www.fuesers.com

This ultra-high-molecular-weight polyethylene (UHMWPE) offers the highest strength-to-weight ratio of any fiber, with 10–15 times the strength of drawn steel wire thanks to extremely long polymer chains. It is cut-, chemical-, and UV-resistant with extremely low moisture absorption. It has the same density as water (it floats) and a melting point of 144–155 °C (291–311°F). Applications include apparel, ropes, and military equipment. **Properties:** Lightweight; High Strength

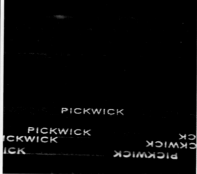

MC# 6579-04
Anti-Counterfeit Tape
Fuesers Garne GmbH
www.fuesers.com

This narrow anti-counterfeit tape made from 100% polyester (PET) can be sewn or molded into products. A trademark or text is imprinted on the film which is then micro-slitted to make a tape. These tapes are hard to reproduce and completely customizable. Color, metallization, holographic features, and glow under UV light are all custom. Applications are for protection against brand piracy by means of a safety thread in woven fabrics, knitted fabrics, seams, or labels. **Properties:** Lightweight; All-Weather Use

MC# 6590-01
Radius Pultrusion™, gebogene Endlosprofile aus CFK und GFK
Thomas GmbH + Co. Technik + Innovation KG
www.thomas-technik.com

A process for the continuous manufacturing of curved fiber- and fabric-reinforced profiles, this technology is based on the modification of pultrusion, but allows for the continuous manufacturing of circular and screw arcs with nearly any angle and rise up to coil springs. Pultrusion is typically only able to reinforce straight profiles. Applications are found in the automotive and transport industries, roof construction, aircraft bodies, interior and exterior structure profiles, springs, and roof, building, marine and machine construction. **Properties:** Lightweight; High Strength; Composite

MC# 6600-02
Tegris® LM
Milliken & Company (Tegris)
www.tegris.milliken.com

This stiff thermoplastic 100% polypropylene (PP) woven textile composite is fully recyclable and has good impact resistance and stiffness with two to fifteen times the impact resistance over typical thermoplastic and thermoplastics composites. It is intended for panel or molded applications such as in transportation (truck liners, floors), automotive (underbody shields, air dams), water sports (small boats, watercraft), construction (architectural panels), consumer products (helmets, luggage, outdoor furniture, playground equipment), and ballistics. **Properties:** Composite; Simplification

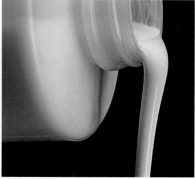

MC# 6609-01
Acrodur®
BASF - Performance Products
www.basf.com

This non-toxic, non-solvent-borne, water-based resin/binder system has a small environmental footprint and offers high bonding performance for a wide variety of fibers. Highly compatible and efficient when used with natural fibers (wood, kenaf, jute, flax, hemp, sisal, bamboo), it can also be used with glass, polyethylene, and polyamide. The binder system can adopt any desired color but the manufacturer offers easy-to-use stir-in systems for a wide color range. Applications are for the manufacturing of two- or three-dimensional composite materials. **Properties:** Sustainable Solutions

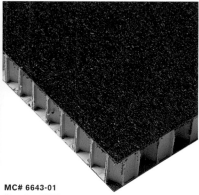

MC# 6643-01
Thermhex PP Cores
ThermHex Waben GmbH
www.thermhex.com

These stiff, lightweight, honeycomb-structured panels are a lower-cost alternative to existing honeycomb composites. They are produced via a patented fold-and-cut process applied to flat sheets of polypropylene and other plastics (including PET). Surfacing with polymer films (PP, PET, PE, etc.), woven textiles (glass-fiber-reinforced polymers, woven PP textiles) or non-woven fabrics to give the structure integrity and stiffness. Applications are found in the automotive, furniture, construction, consumer product, and packaging industries as lightweight stiff panels. **Properties:** Lightweight; Simplification

MC# 6719-02
Armordon® Consolidated Panel (srPP)
Don & Low Ltd.
www.donlow.com

This rigid composite self-reinforced polypropylene (SRPP) sheet has high stiffness and good impact resistance. Safer to handle than glass-filled composites, it is available in fabric or sheet stock. The fabrics can be formed into various shapes using heat and pressure. It is intended as an alternative to carbon fiber and glass fiber composites in applications such as luggage, helmets, sports equipment, automotive parts and consumer products. **Properties:** Composite; Simplification

MC# 6733-01
barracuda®
Porcher Industries Groupe
www.porcher-ind.com

This aluminized glass-fiber fabric has the appearance and functionality of moldable steel woven mesh, while maintaining the characteristics of high-performance composites. The fabric may be utilized in vacuum forming, hand lay-up, resin transfer molding and autoclave molding. When combined with resin, finished parts made with the glass-fiber fabric maintain a silver sheen similar to formed steel and are strong, durable, and lightweight. Applications include tennis rackets, dashboards, motorcycle helmets, kitchen appliances, luggage, and automotive parts. **Properties:** Lightweight; High Strength

MC# 6756-01
Inorganic Nanofibers
Kertak Nanotechnology s.r.o.
www.kertaknanotechnology.com

Electrospun nanofibers of inorganic materials give properties such as high surface area, good connectivity, and lower inner electrical resistivity. Using an electrical charge to draw microfibers or nanofibers from a liquid, they have excellent surface uniformity and controllable aspect ratio. Applications include electrode materials in lithium batteries, energy converters in solar cells, humidity and gas sensors, inorganic membranes, photocatalytic degradation of bacteria and toxic chemicals, pigment for paints and cosmetics, in solid oxide fuel cells, and in waste water purification. **Properties:** Nanotech

MC# 6780-01
Multi-Axial Multi-Ply Fabric
SGL Group – The Carbon Company
www.sglgroup.com

These glass, carbon, and aramid high-performance fibers offered as uniaxial, biaxial, triaxial, and quadraxial fabrics are for use in prepregs (pre-impregnated composite fibers), woven fabrics, and composites. Curved structures, concave geometries, and textile structures with no thread displacement are possible with 2D braiding with different cross-sectional geometries while connecting surfaces over the length of the fabric. Applications include boat building, rotor-blade construction, and non-woven structures for sports equipment. **Properties:** Lightweight; High Strength; Composite

MC# 6780-03
UDO®
SGL Group – The Carbon Company
www.sglgroup.com

These unidirectional and multiaxial reinforcement fabrics made from carbon, glass, and aramid fibers are processed into composite material components. The unidirectional fiber alignment results in high strength and rigidity. They are lightweight and compatible with different resin systems. The fibers used contain an average or high filament count, but still offer weight and cost savings. Common processing methods include wet lamination, molding, resin transfer molding (RTM), and the production of prepreg (pre-impregnated composite fiber) materials. Applications include low-weight construction materials for speedboats and aircraft. **Properties:** Lightweight; High Strength; Composite

MC# 6853-01
PURE®
Lankhorst Pure Composites bv
www.pure-composites.com

This 100% polypropylene self-reinforcing polymer (SRP) composite material is fully recyclable, created using a hybrid tape welding and extrusion process. It has high stiffness and low density (0.78 g/cm³; compared to a 30% glass-fiber composite, which has 1.1 g/cm³). It has good impact resistance at very low temperatures (up to -40° C / -40° F), does not splinter, and can be thermoformed in various shapes. The material can be obtained in tape, fabric, or sheet form. This material has been used for construction and automotive applications as well as for the fabrication of various consumer products. **Properties:** Lightweight; High Strength

MC# 6858-01
NanoDiamonds
Yüksek Teknoloji Malzemeleri Arastırma ve Gelistirme A.S.
www.nano-tekno.com

Nanodiamonds are nano/micron-scale versions of their larger carbon-based diamond counterparts, with the same material properties, such as high hardness, optical transparency, low thermal expansion, high thermal conductivity, electrical insulation, high resistance to chemical corrosion, and biocompatibility. They find application in the defense, auto, aerospace, information, cosmetic, and health industries, and in industrial lubricants, electrochemical plating, precision machinery, and optical instruments. **Properties:** Nanotech

MC# 6928-01
Kymiera
Audiomasons Design Works, LLC
www.audiomasonsdesignworks.com

Combining a cement-like look and feel with some of the processing ease of polymers, this solid surface is created from 80% recycled inorganic materials bound together with a geopolymer matrix. The material is non-flammable and waterproof, and provides thermal insulation, acoustical absorption, and shock/impact resistance. Applications include solid surfaces, furniture, flooring, roof shingling, outdoor flooring, consumer goods, acoustical panels, electronic housings, and non-load bearing architectural elements. **Properties:** Durable; Composite

MC# 7026-02
SkinTec
AXIAmaterials Co., Ltd.
www.axia-m.com

Unlike standard woven composites, the resin in this version is sprayed on like a powder coat and can be pressed and thermoformed like a regular thermoplastic. The fiber-reinforced-polymer laminate is composed of glass-fiber fabric (40–70%) and modified epoxy resin (60–30%). It can replace metals to provide lower-weight parts with the same strength and modulus. This material can be thermoformed in a press-molding process or with tools used for wood machining. Applications include consumer electronics housings and structural parts for the automotive industry. **Properties:** Durable; High Strength; Composite

MC# 4108-03
ABS-ESD7
Stratasys, Ltd.
www.stratasys.com

This static dissipative polymer is used in rapid prototyping (additive manufacturing) machines. The acrylonitrile butadiene styrene (ABS) resin contains conductive particles (carbon black) that make the part anti-static. It is for use in fused deposition modeling (FDM) machines. The resin is only available in black. Applications are for production of rapidly prototyped parts for electronics applications or other uses that need good static dissipation. **Properties:** Lightweight; Simplification

MC# 5020-04
Tupfenbeschichtung Mineralpunkt
Wunderlich Coating GmbH & Co.KG
www.wunderlich.info

These printed slip-resistant polyvinyl chloride (PVC) dot coatings for textiles can be customized for size, shape, color, and individual dot spacing. The application weight of the coating is 125 g/m², but is lower for dots compared to full coverage of the PVC coating. The coating can be applied to all types of fabrics, natural and synthetic, with a width of up to 1975 mm (77.8 in.). Applications are for interior and exterior anti-slip application and decoration. **Properties:** All-Weather Use

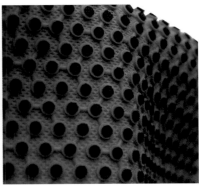

MC# 5086-01
Dual Stencil Fabric
Taica Corporation
www.taica.co.jp

This printing process is used for layering polyurethane (PU) onto a textile using masked stencils. It was first developed for replacing the rubber soles on athletic shoes during the 1988 Seoul Olympics—reducing the weight of the sole by 50%. The PU is melted onto a base fabric to provide traction with lightweight and abrasion-resistant material. Base fabric can be anything that allows melted PU to penetrate. Currently used in sporting shoes, it has potential applications in cars, housewares, accessories, apparel, bags, wristwatches, packing material, stationery, and sporting equipment. **Properties:** Lightweight; Durable

MC# 5594-01
Wovenit
Visictex GmbH
www.wovenit.de

This knitting process can create complex 3D textile shapes with seamless structures using a one-step knitting procedure based on sock heel creation. The 3D shape may be knitted from virtually any yarn material using a computer-controlled textile machine to render objects from CAD files. Meshes, hooks or hollow seams (to allow for stiffening rods) may be incorporated into the structure during knitting. The process is used for producing seat covers, shoe uppers, and shapes for composite part manufacture. **Properties:** Lightweight; Sustainable Solutions; Composite

MC# 5687-02
Alumide®
EOS GmbH Electro Optical Systems
www.eos.info

This aluminum alloy in powder form is optimized specifically for direct metal laser sintering (DMLS). These metallic powders feature excellent mechanical characteristics (strength, hardness) as well as excellent corrosion and temperature resistance. The aluminum alloy has good ductility. Applications are in medicine (implants), high-temperature engineering, aircraft engines, and small batch products. **Properties:** Composite; Simplification

MC# 5687-03
EOS CobaltChrome MP1 / StainlessSteel 17-4
EOS GmbH Electro Optical Systems
www.eos.info

This powder-form stainless steel alloy is optimized specifically for direct metal laser sintering (DMLS). These metallic powders feature excellent mechanical characteristics (strength, hardness) as well as excellent corrosion and temperature resistance. The stainless steel alloy has good ductility. Applications are in medicine (implants), high-temperature engineering, aircraft engines, and small batch products. **Properties:** Sustainable Solutions; Simplification

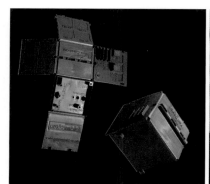

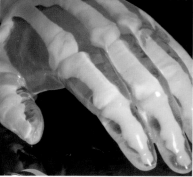

MC# 6460-01
Rapid Injection Molding
Proto Labs, Inc.
www.protomold.com

This rapid injection-molding process is a hybrid of rapid prototyping and conventional injection molding. Based on customer-supplied 3D CAD models, it uses aluminum alloys and three-axis CNC machining to create parts in almost any engineering-grade resin. Compared to conventional injection molding, this process takes one-third of the time and offers a variety of surface finishes and material properties. Applications include prototyping, bridge tooling and low-production runs. **Properties:** Lightweight; Simplification

MC# 6526-01
Objet Pro, Eden & Connex
Stratasys Ltd.
www.stratasys.com

This high-resolution rapid-prototyping printing process with variable material combinations is based on proprietary PolyJet Matrix™ technology and offers the possibility to print individual parts from multiple model materials with different mechanical or physical properties, for example soft–hard or opaque–transparent combinations, in one single step. Each photopolymer layer is UV-cured immediately after the jetting. Applications exist in the automotive, aircraft, footwear, medical, and toy industries, and in mechanical engineering, consumer products, and electronics such as hearing aids. **Properties:** Lightweight; Simplification

MC# 6607-01
Sugru®
FormFormForm, Ltd.
www.sugru.com

A silicone elastomer that can be hand-molded before becoming rigid, this tough, flexible, moisture-curing silicone has a working time of 30 minutes and a cure time of 24 hours. It forms a strong bond to aluminum, steel, ceramics, glass, and other materials, including most plastics. It is waterproof, has good heat resistance, and can be used outdoors. It has good flame and UV resistance and is meant to be shaped manually but can be compression-molded or extruded. It is used as a sculptural material for creating personal additions to products and for encasing products in a waterproof shell. **Properties:** Ergonomic; Simplification

MC# 6608-01
Expancel microspheres
EKA Chemicals AB
www.expancel.com

These tiny plastic hollow spheres expand when heated. The shell contains a gas; when heat is applied, the thermoplastic shell softens and the gas volume increases, expanding the sphere. The average diameter ranges from 6 to 38 microns. Fully expanded microspheres have as much as 40 times their initial volume. Expansion takes place at temperatures ranging from 95 to 148° C (203–298° F). When the microspheres are cooled, the shell stiffens and the microspheres maintain their expanded form. Applications include anti-slip coatings, printing ink, car underbody coatings, and industrial non-woven textiles. **Properties:** Lightweight; Durable

MC# 6900-01
Reticube Technology
Guimer srl
www.guimer.it

This selective laser-sintering (SLS) technology is used for brass and silver alloys in accessory applications. The powder is bonded using a high-powered laser, giving almost 100% solid parts that require minimal final polishing. This 3D concept can be applied on a large scale in metals such as brass, steel, and silver without the cost of making a wax mold. Applications include accessories or parts for interior design, fashion, footwear, eyewear, furniture, cutlery, lighting design, and logos. **Properties:** Sustainable Solutions; Simplification

MC# 7071-01
LAYWOO-D3
CC-Products
www.cc-products.de

Expanding the number of materials that 3D printing can use, this wood fiber-based filament is the first wood/polymer composite to be used in 3D modeling. Fused with heat, it looks, smells, and can be handled like wood. The warmer the temperature, the darker the laid-out filament will be. Printed objects can be cut, ground, or painted. Composed of 40% recycled wood, it has low shrinkage and warp while printing and can be used for bigger objects than standard acrylonitrile butadiene styrene (ABS) or polylactic acid (PLA). Applications include prototyping, architecture models, and decoration. **Properties:** Sustainable Solutions; Durable; Composite

MC# 6174-11

Eco-EVA with Fabric
EXTRAMOLD JOMO Industria de Plasticos Ltda.
www.jomo-online.com.br

This thermoformed fabric-covered panel made from 100% recycled polyester (PET) comes from recycled beverage bottles, with backing made of 50% recycled post-consumer tires. It is available in laminated, embossed, and different thermoformed patterns. Available colors are black, white, and gray. Applications are for computer cases, office materials, shoe uppers, wall decoration, and packaging.
Properties: Sustainable Solutions; Recycled

MC# 6395-03

Grey rubbRe™
Vulcana, LLC
www.vulcana.net

These gray sheet-rubber textiles are made from recycled tires and developed for outdoor use. Comprised of a proprietary compound including 30% crumb rubber from used car tires taken from American landfills, the de-vulcanized tires are compounded with other materials and formed into a slab. They comply with the California Technical Bulletin 117 for flammability for upholstery uses. Applications include acoustical textiles, high-traction textiles for cars or aircraft, and weatherproof footwear, luggage, furniture and other outdoor products. **Properties:** Sustainable Solutions; Recycled

MC# 6559-01

Recyclinggranulate
Exner Trenntechnik GmbH
www.exner-trenntechnik.de

These recycled metals are derived from a new, lower-impact, and non-melting recycling process that is available as aluminum, copper, brass, and zinc granulate with a purity of over 90%. It is derived from aluminum bottle caps, aluminum window laths, and aluminum cans among others. The reprocessed materials comply with the highest standards and are directly used in steel and smelting plants as secondary raw material and can also be used as decoration.
Properties: Sustainable Solutions; Recycled

MC# 6590-02

Naturfaserverstaerkte Endlosprofile
Thomas GmbH + Co. Technik + Innovation KG
www.thomas-technik.com

These natural-fiber-reinforced profiles are produced from sustainable raw material—flax fiber—using pultrusion technology. The fibers are first immersed in resin, then run through a hardening tool. They receive their actual profile in a drawing tool. Benefits of this technology include its lightweight components, decrease in CO_2 emissions, and low thermal conductivity. Applications are found in the automotive and transportation industries, aircraft bodies, shipbuilding, interior and exterior structural profiles, construction, and mechanical engineering.
Properties: High Strength

MC# 6796-02

Eco-Fi
Foss Manufacturing Company, LLC.
www.fossmfg.com

This polyester (PET) staple fiber is made from 100% post-consumer recycled plastic PET bottles. Produced by shredding, melting, and extruding the PET, the fiber is then drawn, cut, and cropped to obtain a strong staple fiber. Finally the fiber is baled and can be processed into a variety of textiles. It can also be blended to enhance fibers such as cotton or wool. It is strong, soft, anti-shrink, and colorfast. Applications include clothing, blankets, carpets, wall coverings, auto interiors, home furnishings, and craft felt.
Properties: Sustainable Solutions; Recycled

MC# 6813-01

Thermoforming of Nonwovens
Volar Plastic Oy
www.volarplastic.fi

Thermoformed non-wovens and felts offer a fabric-like surface with the rigidity of a plastic. The color, thickness, and density of the form can be customized. Additional decorative or protective films can be applied to the back or front of the form. The density of the formed part can be reduced such that the inner core can be almost foam-like, giving lower densities. In addition, other materials can be added within the layers to give different properties. Applications are for headliners, chairs, wall panels, and other interior items.
Properties: Composite; Simplification

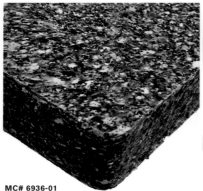

MC# 6936-01
Ecosheet
2K Manufacturing Ltd.
www.ecosheet.com

This rigid, large-format panel is a polymer-based foam sheet used as an alternative to plywood and MDF in construction. It comprises a combination of a number of different recycled polymers pressed into a porous core and solid, waterproof face. The panel can be cut, sawed, nailed, screwed into and otherwise worked like wood. The panels can also be welded together. The panels are currently used for construction, interior and exterior furniture, animal housing, and marine work.
Properties: Sustainable Solutions; Recycled

MC# 6952-01
Linear Low Density Polyethylene
NextLife
www.nextlife.com

Linear low-density polyethylene (LLDPE) pellets processed from certified recycled, post-consumer stretch films. This material can be tailored to specific applications and due to its recycled content is produced with a lower carbon footprint than virgin resins. The post-consumer materials are sorted, cleaned, and then extruded into pellets. The pellets can be ordered by the pound or ton and are available in natural, black, or mixed color (dependent on the material being recycled). Applications include sheet extrusion for durable consumer and commercial plastic products and packaging. **Properties:** Sustainable Solutions; Recycled

MC# 6952-02
Polystyrene
NextLife
www.nextlife.com

These polystyrene (PS) pellets are processed from certified, post-consumer rigid material and can be tailored to specific applications. They have a lower CO_2 footprint than comparable virgin resins. They have been approved by the US Food and Drug Administration (FDA) and Health Canada for use in the manufacture of thermoformed or injection-molded articles for contact with food. Applications include durable consumer and commercial plastic products such as extruded sheets and food packaging and containers.
Properties: Sustainable Solutions; Recycled

MC# 6952-03
Polypropylene
NextLife
www.nextlife.com

These polypropylene (PP) pellets are processed from certified, post-consumer rigid material and approved for use in food contact applications, while creating a lower carbon footprint than virgin resins. Content is sorted, cleaned, and then extruded into pellets. They have been approved by the US Food and Drug Administration (FDA) and Health Canada for use in the manufacture of thermoformed or injection-molded articles. Applications include durable consumer and commercial plastic products such as extruded sheets, food packaging and containers. **Properties:** Sustainable Solutions; Recycled

MC# 6964-01
EnViramid® Post-Consumer Nylon
Ravago Manufacturing America
www.ravagomfg.com

This post-consumer nylon (PA) polymer resin is from recycled residential carpets. The carpet is typically composed of PA, polypropylene (PP), and 4% ash. The face fiber of the carpet (nylon) is separated from the backing (PP) through mechanical grinding. Using a wet mechanical separation process, the fibers are sorted into their pure forms. The fibers are then extruded into pellet form that is suitable for compounding feedstock, extrusion, and injection molding. Applications for the nylon include automotive and industrial parts, lawn/garden equipment, and a compounding additive to enhance prime nylons. **Properties:** Sustainable Solutions; Recycled

MC# 6964-02
EnViramid® Post-Consumer Polypropylene
Ravago Manufacturing Americas
www.ravagomfg.com

This post-consumer polypropylene (PP) polymer resin is from recycled residential carpets. The carpet is typically composed of nylon (PA), PP, and 4% ash. The face fiber of the carpet (nylon) is separated from the backing (PP) through mechanical grinding. Using a wet mechanical separation process, the fibers are sorted into their pure forms. The fibers are then extruded into pellet form that is suitable for compounding feedstock, extrusion, and injection molding. Applications for the PP include consumer products, packaging and automotive, and industrial parts. **Properties:** Sustainable Solutions; Recycled

MC# 6972-01
Demodé
Demodé
www.demode.cl

These compressed, lightweight, solid panels and other objects are made from recycled fabric. The fabric is cut into small pieces and mixed with a modified starch adhesive, before being put into a pressing machine at high temperature, trimmed, and finished. The parts can be made from 100% cotton, 100% polyester, and 50% cotton / 50% polyester mixtures. The basic color available is blue denim, but other color or mixtures become available depending on the types of recycled fabrics. Applications are for wall panels, furniture, and accessories. **Properties:** Sustainable Solutions; Recycled

MC# 6978-01
Polyfloss
The Polyfloss Factory
www.thepolyflossfactory.com

This material uses a unique process for recycling glass-filled plastic parts to create 100% recycled polypropylene (PP) fiber that is easily remolded, a solution to the existing problem of separating composite materials before recycling. The plastic is shredded and inserted into a rotating oven, which spins out the PP while retaining the fiber in the center section. The basic texture is like wool, but can be remelted in a metal mold to copy any surface texture with high precision and create protective, insulating shells. Applications include fashion, packaging, and products. **Properties:** Sustainable Solutions; Recycled; Simplification

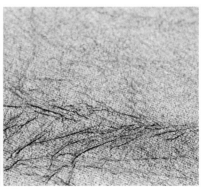

MC# 7012-01
Paper No. 9™
Paper No. 9, LLC
www.paper-no9.com

This flexible and water-resistant fabric is composed of recycled paper, fabric (denim or canvas), natural glues, waxes, oils and emollients. The fabric gently wears as it ages and does not use rubber or plastic to create its visual effects. The paper is cured in a mixture of natural oils and emollients and fused to a fabric backing using a proprietary process. Applications include accessories, bags, luggage, stationery products, trimmings, clothing, and home décor. **Properties:** Recycled

MC# 7019-01
Ncell™ Natural Fiber Composites
GreenCore Composites Inc.
www.greencorenfc.com

This high-performance, lightweight, natural-fiber composite made from 35% lignocellulose fiber, 57% (potentially recycled) polypropylene (PP) and 8% additives has excellent impact strength and flexural properties, and can be engineered to meet specific physical properties by changing polymers (including recycled polymers), adding fillers, and changing the percentage of natural fiber content (25–40%). The fiber is FSC-certified (Forest Stewardship Council) and the polymer can be food-grade if specified. Applications include consumer and industrial products. **Properties:** Sustainable Solutions; Composite

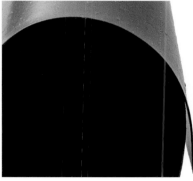

MC# 7035-01
VinyLoop® R-PVC
Vinyloop Ferrara SpA
www.vinyloop.com

This is the only recycling process that can use vinyl-coated fabrics as a source. It separates the polyvinyl chloride (PVC) compound from other materials (other plastics, rubber, metal, and textiles) by selective dissolution (dissolving into parts or elements) and filtration, which creates micro-granules of post-consumer PVC compound. Applications are for garden hoses, membranes, foils, coated textiles, mats, and footwear. **Properties:** Sustainable Solutions; Recycled

MC# 7036-01
SKALAX
Xylophane AB
www.xylophane.com

This biodegradable coating for cardboard and paper products protects against oxygen transmission, grease, printing inks, and scents. Made from rapidly renewable resources, it can add functionality and safety to biobased, recyclable, and compostable materials, while preserving their low environmental impact. Based on xylan, a carbohydrate extracted from agricultural by-products such as seeds and husks, it is mixed with proprietary additives, and then layered onto the surface through dispersion coating. Applications include packaging for food and consumer goods **Properties:** Sustainable Solutions; Compostable

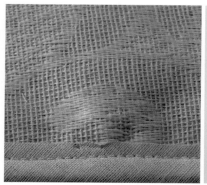

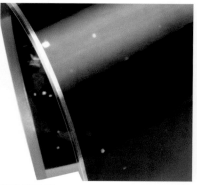

MC# 4832-02
Natural and Artificial Anti-Radiation Mat
Gruppo Creamoda
www.ideascudo.com

This electromagnetic interference (EMI) screening mat is composed of cotton and other natural and artificial materials, and is able to screen electromagnetic and telluric waves. The anti-radiation mat reflects environmental radiation such as that from wiring, household appliances, etc. It can be processed as a standard textile product—cut, sewn, dyed, and embroidered. Applications include mats for bed mattresses. **Properties:** Lightweight; Durable

MC# 5086-15
Silicone Paste
Taica Corporation
www.taica.co.jp

A soft paste-type (grease) gel that has thermal conducting properties, it is made of cross-linked particles that eliminate the running and vaporization seen in traditional grease and phase-change materials. The range offers tapes with a variety of thermal conductivity, spreadability, and electromagnetic absorption characteristics along with the ability to be used over a wide temperature range (-40–200° C /(-40–392° F). Applications are for gaps around heat sources or heat sources without sufficient space for sheet-type thermal conductive materials. **Properties:** All-Weather Use

MC# 5613-02
Printed LED films
SUN-TEC Swiss United Technologies Co., Ltd.
www.sun-tec.ch

These films contain tiny white LED lights that are connected through clear plastic films that run through the sheet, which can be printed with high-resolution graphics. The printed LED films are designed for lamination between glass, plastics such as acrylics, polycarbonates, and flexible polyvinyl chloride (PVC) films. Extremely durable and resistant to fading under UV light, these films are designed to be used for Point of Sale (POS) and Point of Purchase (POP) displays. Applications in automotive interiors are also possible. **Properties:** Lightweight; Stain-Resistant/Easy-Clean

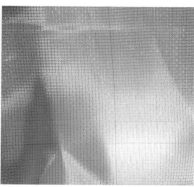

MC# 6337-02
SCHULATEC® TinCo
A. Schulman Inc.
www.aschulman.com

Combining plastic-processing ease with conductivity, this plastic–metal hybrid material exhibits very high conductivity. It offers high electromagnetic shielding and can be used as injection-molded contacts that can be connected with other electronic parts by soldering, clamping, or overspraying. The material is available in gray and is superior to conventional conductive plastic compounds with steel or carbon fibers by a factor of 100–1,000. Applications are for the integration of conducting paths in injection-molded electronic articles. **Properties:** Composite

MC# 6408-02
PowerGlow
Sefar AG
www.sefar.com

This e-textile consists of polyester (PET) and copper fibers in warp and weft direction. The metal wires have a thin insulating lacquer coating so the fabric can be used as a lightweight, extremely flexible and air-permeable substrate for electrical circuits. The material is available in custom sizes and compositions. Partial removal of the insulation creates a custom layout of a flexible circuit board. It is mainly used as a lightweight, highly flexible substrate for electrical circuits. **Properties:** Lightweight; Durable

MC# 6717-01
HYPERION R-Lite System™
Lumificient Corporation
www.lumificient.com

A modular LED lighting system developed specially for "channel letter" and "contour lighting" signage applications, the system uses a continuous flexible conductor carrier to electronically connect the AC LED modules (AC LEDs do not require a transformer like more traditional DC systems). The LEDs are mounted on adhesive-backed, high-performance, flame-retardant polyester (PET) film that can be cut to size. Available colors are red, blue, green, amber, orange, and white, and there are three white color temperatures: warm white, cool white, and mid-white. **Properties:** Lightweight; Durable

MC# 6727-01
Philips Lumiblade
Philips Technologie GmbH
www.lumiblade-experience.com

This extremely thin light source based on organic LEDs (OLEDs) emits from its entire surface and exhibits diffuse radiating characteristics. The part consists of glass and very thin layers of aluminum, indium tin oxide (ITO) and hydrocarbon. When switched off, the module exhibts mirror optics. Applications are for interior design, esthetic light accents, advertising, and mood lighting. **Properties:** Durable

MC# 6860-01
Conductive Rubber
Zyvex Technologies
www.zyvextech.com

This version of conductive rubber is made from a synthetic silicone rubber that has metal powder or conductive carbon particles suspended within its composition. It can still bend and flex like traditional rubber and has many of the same characteristics as traditional rubbers, such as resilience, high temperature stability, and general inertness. When stretched, the electrical conductivity decreases and when compressed, its electrical resistance decreases. Several uses include bendy, electrically charged aircraft wings, artificial muscles, and wearable computers. **Properties:** Durable

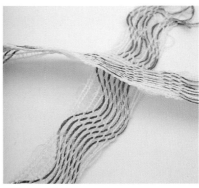

MC# 6961-01
AMOTAPE® CONDUCT
AMOHR Technische Textilien GmbH
www.amohr.com

Adding stretchability to conductive fabrics, this woven tape made from polyester (PET) yarn and seven tin-plated copper strands enables the wire to "float" in wavy lines along the tape, allowing for small amounts of elasticity. The tape contains hot-melt material on the backing that can be heat-pressed or ironed onto any textile and other surfaces. Applications include flat and flexible conductors for the automotive and construction industries, and smart textiles.
Properties: Lightweight; Ergonomic

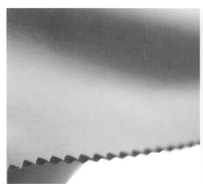

MC# 6977-05
Ariaprene™ Max
Tiong Liong International Co., Ltd.
www.ariaprene.com

Closed-cell synthetic rubber foam for sports apparel and equipment from thermoplastic elastomer (TPE). It is thermoformable and has high compression and elongation. The foam is non-toxic, hypoallergenic (rubber- and latex-free), waterproof, and readily recyclable, and outperforms synthetic rubber by providing better insulation, lighter weight, and hot and cold temperature tolerance. It can be perforated for added breathability, or thermomolded and embossed after lamination. Applications include bags, footwear, laptop sleeves, apparel, and sports apparel and equipment. **Properties:** Ergonomic

MC# 7032-01
SMP Tagnologies™
BAM Federal Institute for Materials Research and Testing
www.bam.de

This thermoplastic polyurethane (TPU) has shape-memory properties (SMP). As such when the TPU is deformed, the printed QR (quick response) code is unreadable, but owing to the nature of the SMP, the material will revert to its original form when heated, thus allowing the QR code to be read. The labels could be deformed and affixed to products, thereby storing information to mark and identify products in a way that is very difficult to counterfeit. Potential applications are found in the automotive, aerospace, toy, textile, and sports industries as well as in leisure products. **Properties:** All-Weather Use

MC# 7106-01
Thinfilm Memory™
Thin Film Electronics ASA
www.thinfilm.no

These sticker-like labels with a passive memory system can store rewritable data to make objects "smart." Data is physically recorded and retained within a ferroelectric polymer by altering the position of its molecules. This creates "non-volatile" data, which retains information without needing to be powered, lessening the need for electronic infrastructure. The printed tags can be a cost-effective alternative to radio-frequency identification (RFID) tags. Applications include data storage for gaming, toys, shipping and transport, value cards, frequent shopper cards, and product tracking.
Properties: Lightweight; Nanotech; Simplification

RESOURCES

PROFESSIONAL ORGANIZATIONS

Associazione per il Disegno Industriale
(ADI, Industrial Design Association)
Via Bramante 29
20154 Milano
Italy
T: 39 02 33100164
E: info@adi-design.org
www.adi-design.org

Danske Designere/Danish Designers
Republic
Vesterbrogade 26
1620 Copenhagen
Denmark
T: 45 33 13 72 30
E: design@danishdesigners.com
www.danishdesigners.com

Design Forum Finland
Erottajankatu 7
00130, Helsinki
Finland
T: 358 9 6220 810
E: info@designforum.fi
www.designforum.fi

Hong Kong Designers Association
Unit 216A, InnoCentre
72 Tat Chee Avenue
Kowloon Tong, Kowloon
Hong Kong
China
T: 852 24272968
E: info@hongkongda.com
www.hongkongda.com

Industrial Designers Society of America
(IDSA)
555 Grove Street, Suite 200
Herndon, VA 20170
United States
T: 1 703 707 6000
E: jennifers@idsa.org
www.idsa.org

International Council of Societies of
Industrial Design (ICSID)
455 St-Antoine Ouest, Suite SS10
Montreal, Quebec H2Z 1J1
Canada
T: 1 514 448 4949
E: office@icsid.org
www.icsid.org

Product Development and Management
Association (PDMA)
330 North Wabash Avenue
Suite 2000
Chicago, IL 60611
United States
T: 1 312 321 5145
E: pdma@pdma.org
www.pdma.org

Swedish Industrial Design Foundation
(SVID)
Sveavägen 34, 6 tr
111 34 Stockholm
Sweden
T: 46 8 406 84 40
E: info@svid.se
www.svid.se

TED
250 Hudson St.
Suite 1002
New York, NY 10013
United States
T: 1 212 346 9333
www.ted.com

Verband Deutscher Industrie Designer
(Association of German Industrial
Designers)
Markgrafenstraße 15
10969 Berlin
Germany
T: 49 307 407 85 56
E: vdid@germandesign.de
www.vdid.de

TRADE SHOWS AND EVENTS

January

Consumer Electronics Show (CES)
www.cesweb.org

Maison et Objet
www.maison-objet.com

February

Ambiente Frankfurt
www.ambiente.messefrankfurt.com

March

Ipex
www.ipex.org

April

Salone Internazionale del Mobile
www.cosmit.it

May

Hospitality Design Exposition
www.hdexpo.com

International Contemporary Furniture
Fair (ICFF)
www.icff.com

POINT
www.pointconference.com

Product Design + Innovation
Conference
www.pdesigni.com

June

Designer's Days
www.designersdays.com

August

IDSA
www.idsa.org

Magic
www.magiconline.com

September

100% Design
www.100percentdesign.co.uk

WEBSITES

Materials Research

MTRL
www.mtrldesign.com

Networks for Product Designers

Dexigner
www.dexigner.com

Blogs

CAD CAM News
www.cadcamnews.in

design boom
www.designboom.com

Design East
www.designeast.eu

design mind
www.designmind.frogdesign.com/blog

Design Observer
www.designobserver.com

Embody 3D
www.embody3d.com

Fast Co. Design
www.fastcodesign.com

Industrial Design Sandbox
www.idsandbox.blogspot.com

Industrial Design Served
www.industrialdesignserved.com

Inhabitat
inhabitat.com

Monkee Design
www.monkeedesign.com

Planet Industrial Design
www.planet-industrial-design.org

Product Design Hub
www.productdesignhub.com

Yanko Design
www.yankodesign.com

MAGAZINES
(DIGITAL AND PRINT)

Core77
www.core77.com

Curve Magazine
www.curvelive.com

Fast Company
www.fastcompany.com

I.D. Magazine
www.id-mag.com

Metropolis
www.metropolismag.com

Surface Magazine
www.surfacemag.com

Wallpaper
www.wallpaper.com

ADDITIONAL READING

Alesina, Inna and Ellen Lupton. *Exploring Materials: Creative Design for Everyday Objects.* Princeton Architectural Press, New York, 2010

Ambasz, Emilio. *Italy: The New Domestic Landscape.* Museum of Modern Art, New York, 1972

Ashby, Michael F. and Kara Johnson. *Materials and Design: The Art and Science of Material Selection in Product Design.* Butterworth-Heinemann, Oxford, 2nd edition, 2009

Bell, Victoria Ballard and Patrick Rand. *Materials for Design.* Princeton Architectural Press, New York, 2006

Benyus, Janine M. *Biomimicry: Innovation Inspired by Nature.* Morrow, New York, 1997

Beylerian, George M., Andrew Dent and Anita Moryadas. *Material ConneXion: The Global Resource of New and Innovative Materials for Architects, Artists, and Designers.* Thames & Hudson, London and Wiley, Hoboken, 2005

Braungart, Michael and William McDonough. *Cradle to Cradle: Remaking the Way We Make Things.* North Point Press, New York, 2002

Caplan, Ralph. *By Design: Why There Are No Locks on the Bathroom Doors in the Hotel Louis XIV and Other Object Lessons.* Fairchild Publications, New York, 2005

Eissen, Koos and Roselien Steur. *Sketching: Drawing Techniques for Product Designers.* BIS Publishers, Amsterdam 2009

Fiell, Charlotte and Peter. *Industrial Design A–Z.* Taschen, London and Cologne, 2006

Hara, Kenya. *Designing Design.* Lars Müller Publishers, Baden, 2nd edition, 2007

Henry, Kevin. *Drawing for Product Designers (Portfolio Skills: Product Design).* Laurence King, London, 2012

Honoré, Carl. *In Praise of Slow: How a Worldwide Movement is Challenging the Cult of Speed.* Orion Books, London, 2004

Hudson, Jennifer. *Process: 50 Product Designs from Concept to Manufacture.* Laurence King, London, 2nd edition, 2011

Katz, Barry M. and Lukic Branko. *Nonobject.* MIT Press, Cambridge, Mass. and London, 2010

Kelley, Tom. *The Art of Innovation: Lessons in Creativity from IDEO, America's Leading Design Firm.* HarperCollinsBusiness, London, 2001

Laurel, Brenda and Peter Lunenfeld. *Design Research: Methods and Perspectives.* MIT Press, Cambridge, Mass. and London, 2003

Lesko, Jim. *Industrial Design Materials and Manufacturing.* Wiley, New York and Chichester, 1st edition, 2011

Loewy, Raymond. *Industrial Design.* Fourth Estate, London, 1988

Maeda, John. *The Laws of Simplicity (Simplicity: Design, Technology, Business, Life).* MIT Press, Cambridge, Mass. and London, 2006

Mallick, P.K. *Fiber-Reinforced Composites: Materials, Manufacturing, and Design, Third Edition.* CRC Press, 2007

Milton, Alex and Paul Rodgers. *Product Design.* Laurence King, London, 2011

Moggridge, Bill. *Designing Interactions.* MIT Press, Cambridge, Mass. and London, 2007

Morris, Richard. *The Fundamentals of Product Design.* AVA Publishing, Lausanne, 2009

Norman, Donald A. *The Design of Every Day Things.* MIT Press, London, 2002

Papanek, Victor. *Design for the Real World: Human Ecology and Social Change.* Academy Chicago Publishers, 2009

Peters, Tom. *Design.* Dorling Kindersley, London, 2005

Peters, Sascha. *Material Revolution: Sustainable Multi-Purpose Materials for Design and Architecture.* Birkhäuser, Basel, 2011

Reis, Dalcacio. *Product Design in the Sustainable Era.* Taschen, Cologne, 2010

Roberts, Kevin. *The Lovemarks Effect: Winning in the Consumer Revolution.* PowerHouse Books, New York, 2006

Schröpfer, Thomas. *Material Design: Informing Architecture by Materiality.* Birkhäuser, Basel, 2010

Stumpf, Bill. *The Ice Palace that Melted Away: Restoring Civility and Other Lost Virtues to Everyday Life.* Pantheon Books, New York, 1998

Sudjic, Deyan. *The Language of Things: Understanding the World of Desirable Objects.* W. W. Norton, New York and Penguin, London, 2009

Thompson, Rob. *Manufacturing Processes for Design Professionals.* Thames & Hudson, London and New York, 2007

Ulrich, Karl. *Product Design and Development.* McGraw-Hill, New York, 2011

GLOSSARY

ABS plastic (acrylonitrile butadiene styrene)
A stiff, durable, and easily processed copolymer made from the polymerization of styrene and acrylonitrile in the presence of butadiene. Many different grades can be produced by varying the amount of each chemical, offering a wide range of features and applications. It can be blended with other plastics and is used widely in consumer goods.

aliphatic and aromatic hydrocarbons
Compounds containing hydrogen and carbon (hydrocarbons), which are the building blocks of polymers, are divided into two types: aromatics, which have a ring of molecules such as benzene rings, and aliphatics (non-aromatics), which do not.

aramid
A hybrid of nylon, aramids are high-performance yarns and fabrics that offer exceptional properties. There are two main types: meta-aramids such as Nomex that are heat- and fire-resistant, and para-aramids such as Kevlar that are impact-absorbent enough to be used in bullet-proof vests.

Arduino board
An Arduino board is an open-source electronic prototyping platform used to create interactive electronic objects.

bast fiber
A class of natural fiber that is strong, woody, and durable found in the phloem of certain plants, especially flax, hemp, and jute. It is used in the manufacture of woven goods and cordage, such as rope and baskets, and in natural-fiber-reinforced composites.

BPA (bisphenol A)
A chemical produced in large quantities primarily for the production of polycarbonate plastics and epoxy resins. Polycarbonate plastics are used in sports sunglass and safety-glass lenses, architectural skylights, mobile phones, and until recently in baby bottles and beverage containers. BPA is a known hormone disruptor and has been banned for use in baby bottles in Canada and Europe.

CNC (computer numerical control)
Computer Numerical Control (CNC) is the computer-controlled automation of tooling. CNC converts a design produced by Computer Aided Design software (CAD) into numbers. These numbers form the coordinates of a graph and control the movement of the cutter tool. In this way the computer controls the cutting and shaping of the material.

HDPE (high-density polyethylene)
A polyethylene thermoplastic made from petroleum, HDPE has a slightly higher density than standard polyethylene. It is known for its large strength-to-density ratio. The material has excellent corrosion, abrasion and impact resistance. Commonly recycled, it can be easily heat-formed, welded, cut and drilled, and is widely used in the production of plastic bottles, corrosion-resistant piping, geomembranes, and plastic lumber.

isotropic
The same property in all directions. These can be any physical, mechanical, or electrical properties. A golf ball has isotropic impact properties as it will travel the same distance and direction no matter where on its surface it is hit.

LCP (liquid-crystal polymer)
A class of aromatic polyester polymers that can form highly ordered (almost crystal) structures while still in the liquid phase. They have excellent mechanical properties, can withstand extreme temperatures, and are resistant to most chemicals even at elevated temperatures. This polymer molds easily using standard equipment and is used for electrical equipment, baking molds, and as a high-tenacity yarn for high-performance fabrics.

nylon 4, nylon 6
Nylon, chemical name polyamide (PA), was the first commercially successful thermoplastic polymer, initially used as a replacement for silk and now used for machine screws and gears, packaging, carpet fiber, apparel fabrics, and in composites. Nylon 4 and nylon 6 are versions of the polymer: the numbers relate to the number of carbon atoms in the molecular chain of the nylon.

OLED (organic light-emitting diode)
A thin, organic polymer-based electroluminescent film that can be flexible and transparent. The device emits light in response to an electric current, similar to the way an LED (light emitting diode) works, but using an organic film rather than a semiconductor to create the display. OLEDs are used as displays for mobile phones, tablets, TVs, and gaming devices.

PE (polyethylene)
The most widely used polymer, based on the simple hydrocarbon molecule C_2H_4. This lightweight translucent thermoplastic is used in grocery bags and geomembranes. High-density formulations (HDPE) are used for milk containers, pipes, and toys, and low-density versions (LDPE) in films and rigid containers. It can be foamed, and cross-linked to make it more durable, or blended to make rubbery elastomers.

PET, PETE (polyethylene terephthalate)
The chemical name for the polyester widely used as a fabric fiber and in transparent beverage bottles as well as some food packaging. Polyesters are a family of thermoplastics and thermosets that contain an ester in their polymer chain. These can be naturally occurring or synthetic materials, some of which are biodegradable.

plasma
A phase of matter distinct from liquid, solid, or gas. It is a collection of free (negatively) charged electrons and positive ions that responds strongly to electromagnetic fields, taking the form of gas-like clouds or ion beams. It is electrically neutral, can be hot (stars, nuclear fusion) or cold (fluorescent lamps), and is a good electrical conductor. Plasmas have numerous uses, including for heating, cutting, and coating.

PMMA (polymethyl methacrylate)
Also known as acrylic, this is a synthetic resin produced from the polymerization of methyl methacrylate. It is a transparent and rigid plastic often used as a substitute for glass, especially for shatterproof windows, skylights, illuminated signs, and aircraft canopies. It is commonly sold under the trademarks Plexiglas, Lucite, and Perspex.

polyol
An ingredient in the manufacture of chemicals, especially polymers, that is based on alcohol but with multiple hydroxyl (oxygen covalently bonded to a hydrogen) groups. Polyols are an essential component in the manufacture of polyurethane foams used in seating and mattresses.

post-consumer recycled, post-consumer content
Post-consumer content is produced by the end consumer of a material stream—the waste that individuals routinely discard, for example in a waste receptacle, recycling bin or a dump, or by littering, incinerating, or pouring down the drain. By contrast, post-industrial, or pre-consumer, waste is typically manufacturing scrap, such as defective parts or trimmings, which is recycled within the existing manufacturing process.

PP (polypropylene)
A low-density, low-cost translucent polymer based on the hydrocarbon molecule C_3H_6, used for yoghurt cartons, carpet fibers, some shampoo bottles, reusable food containers, and plastic chairs. It is one of the most commonly used thermoplastics and provides a combination of durability, light weight and resistance to fading. It can be foamed (for use in toy aircraft and bike helmets) and blended to make rubbery elastomers.

PTFE (polytetrafluoroethylene)
A fluoropolymer (contains fluorine) that is best known by its brand name Teflon. It is exceptionally durable, inert, resistant to UV, acids, and bases (alkalis); and is both oleophobic (oil aversion) and hydrophobic (water aversion). This highly soil-resistant plastic is commonly used as a non-stick coating for pans and other cookware and as a breathable membrane for outdoor clothing (Gore-Tex). It is also used extensively in industry for bearings, seals, and valves.

pultrusion
A method for creating long-fiber composites where the strengthening fibers, typically glass or carbon, are pulled along with the binder resin (typically an epoxy resin) through a die. The resin-infused, fibrous pultrusion is heated to cure and harden it. This creates straight, stiff parts of different profiles with fibers running the length of the piece. Pultruded composites are used in architecture, for wind turbine blades, as aircraft components, and as ski poles.

PVD (physical vapor deposition)
A process for the coating of parts by depositing high-purity materials in their vapor state. Metals such as titanium, chromium, and aluminum are evaporated by heat or by bombardment with ions (sputtering) and deposited onto the part as a thin, highly adherent coating whose properties (hardness, structure, chemical and temperature resistance, adhesion) can be accurately controlled.

shot-peening
Hardening of a metal surface by bombardment with small shot, typically steel balls. Metals exhibit the property of "work hardening," where deformation by bending, hammering, or otherwise distorting a part will cause it to harden, much as a piece of copper wire stiffens when repeatedly flexed. Shot-peening uses this phenomenon to harden the top few millimeters of a part by hitting it with hard steel or ceramic shot.

sintering
The production of solid, dense objects by fusing powders at high temperatures. Metals and ceramics, when pressed together at heats just below their melting temperature, will bond on an atomic level much like ice cubes in water. If powders are used, these can be shaped into specific forms before this process, resulting in a solid form that has the equivalent properties to parts produced by casting or forging.

Tynex
A brand name from DuPont, Tynex is a range of brush bristles that have been chemically or mechanically tapered.

UHMW, UHMWPE (ultra-high-molecular-weight polyethylene)
A type of thermoplastic polyethylene that contains exceptionally long polymer chains, making it extremely tough. It is resistant to most corrosive chemicals and when extruded into yarn has fifteen times the strength to weight of steel. Spectra and Dyneema are commercial high-performance yarns made from UHMWPE.

VOC (volatile organic compound)
These are organic compounds that evaporate in large amounts from a product owing to the compound's low melting point. These gases are not acutely toxic, but some, over a period of time, can have harmful effects on humans and animals, and are regulated. Glues, binders, and paints can contain VOCs such as formaldehyde or solvents that have melting points below room temperature; VOCs are also emitted from plants such as wood. Most scents and odors we smell are VOCs.

CONTRIBUTOR CONTACTS

AB Electrolux
St Göransgatan 143
SE 105 45 Stockholm
Sweden
T: 46 8 738 60 00
E: info@electrolux.com
www.electrolux.com

adidas AG
Adi-Dassler-Strasse 1
91074 Herzogenaurach
Germany
T: 49 93 284 0
www.adidas.com

Enrico Azzimonti
C.so Sempione 100
21052 Busto Arsizio
Italy
T: 39 331 380673
E: info@enricoazzimonti.it
www.enricoazzimonti.it

Bespoke Products
3D Systems, San Francisco Office
431 Tehama Street
San Francisco, CA 94103
United States
T: 1 803 326 3900
E: info@bespokeinnovations.com
www.bespokeinnovations.com

BioCouture Ltd.
E: info@biocouture.co.uk
www.biocouture.co.uk

BIOMOOD Srl
Via Ungheria, 4
Monte Urano
Italy
T: 39 02 058640448
E: info@inature.it
www.inature.it

Bogobrush
Do., LLC,
PO Box 3614
Saint Paul, MN 55101
United States
T: 1 313 806 0675
E: contact@bogobrush.com
www.bogobrush.com

Carnegie Mellon University
5000 Forbes Ave
College of Fine Arts Building (CFA) 212
School of Architecture
Carnegie Mellon University
United States
T: 412 268 2000
E: info@code.arc.cmu.edu
www.code.arc.cmu.edu

Central Standard Timing
E: info@centralstandardtiming.com
www.centralstandardtiming.com

CuteCircuit Ltd.
144 Shoreditch High Street
London E1 6JE
United Kingdom
T: 44 20 7502 1994
E: cute@cutecircuit.com
www.cutecircuit.com

David Trubridge Ltd.
PO Box 15 Whakatu
Hastings 4161, Aotearoa
New Zealand
T: 64 6 6500 204
E: office@davidtrubridge.com
www.davidtrubridge.com

Dikini
6630 Hutchison #100
Montreal, QC H2V 4E1
Canada
T: 1 514 508 3300
E: info@studiodikini.com
www.studiodikini.com

Dirk Winkel Design Office
Eberswalder Str. 29
10437 Berlin, Germany
T: 49 17 088 07 107
E: dw@dirkwinkel.com
www.dirkwinkel.com

Disney Research
4720 Forbes Ave Ste 110
Pittsburgh, PA 15213
United States
T: 1 412 623 1800
E: drinfo@disneyresearch.com
www.disneyresearch.com

Duracell Powermat
14 Research Drive, Bethel
CT 06801, United States
T: 1 203 796 4000
E: info@duracellpowermat.com
www.duracellpowermat.com

ECCO Design
900 Broadway, 5th Fl.
New York, NY 10003
United States
T: 1 212 989 7373
E: contact@eccoid.com
www.eccoid.com

Ergon / RTI Sports GmbH
Universitätsstr. 2
56070 Koblenz, Germany
T: 49 26 189 999 80
E: info@ergon-bike.com
www.ergon-bike.com

Estudio Mariscal
C/ Pellares 30-38
08019 Barcelona, Spain
T: 34 93 303 69 40
E: estudio@mariscal.com
www.mariscal.com

FaddaSantos
Unit 11,
81 Southern Row
London W10 5AL
United Kingdom
T: 44 20 8964 3725
E: info@faddasantos.com
www.faddasantos.com

Footfalls & Heartbeats Ltd.
Ground Floor, Shed 20
139 Quay Street, Princes Wharf
Auckland 1010
New Zealand
T: 64 93779689
E: info@footfallsandheartbeats.com
www.footfallsandheartbeats.com

Ganymed GmbH
Breitenloh 7
82335 Berg
Germany
T: 49 81 51 953 235
E: info@ganymed.eu
www.ganymed.eu

Global Surf Industries
T: USA: 1 855 474 6821
T: Australia: 62 1300857791
T: New Zealand: 64 98896050
E: info@globalsurfindustries.com
www.globalsurfindustries.com

Ed Goluch, PhD
313 Snell Engineering Center
Northeastern University
360 Huntington Avenue
Boston, MA 02115
United States
T: 1 616 373 3500
E: e.goluch@neu.edu
www.sites.google.com/site/goluchgroup

Idris Skis
Post 199 Chemin Verney du Fouilly
74310 Les Houches
France
T: 33 6 28 32 19 20
E: info@idriskis.com
www.idriskis.com

Inter IKEA Group
Olof Palmestraat 1
2616 LN Delft
The Netherlands
T: 32 2 357 41 11
E: contact.group@inter-IKEA.com
www.inter.ikea.com

Jerry Mejia Design Studio
1312 Puritan Avenue
Bronx, NY 10462
United States
T: 1 646 410 6065
E: mejia.jerry@gmail.com
www.jerrymejia.com

Kammok
8301 Lakeview Pkwy, Ste. 111
Rowlett, TX 75088
United States
T: 1 214 901 8420
E: info@kammok.com
www.kammok.com

Layerwise NV
Kapeldreef 60
3001 Leuven
Belgium
T: 32 16 298 420
E: info@layerwise.com
www.layerwise.com

Jinha Lee
MIT Media Laboratory
E14-348 75 Amherst St.
Cambridge, MA 02139
United States
T: 1 617 253 5960
E: jinhalee@media.mit.edu
www.leejinha.com

Legacy Effects
340 Parkside Drive
San Fernando, CA 91340
United States
T: 1 818 782 0870
E: info@legacyefx.com
www.legacyefx.com

Logitech International SA
Moulin Du Choc
1122 Romanel-Sur-Morges Vaud
Switzerland
T: 41 21 863 5111

Logitech Americas Headquarters
7600 Gateway Blvd
Newark, CA 94560
United States
T: 1 510 795 8500
E: info@logitech.com
www.logitech.com

Julia Lohmann
Am Reisenbrook 37
22359 Hamburg
Germany
T: 49 17 647 05 0131
T: 44 7909 882545
E: julia@julialohmann.co.uk
www.julialohmann.co.uk

Marvel
135 West 50th St.
New York, NY 10016
United States
T: 1 212 576 4000
E: info@marvel.com
www.marvel.com

Miyake Design Sudio
1-12-10 Tomigaya Shibuya-ku
Tokyo 151-8554

Japan
T: 81 3 5454 1710
E: info@mds.isseymiyake.com
www.mds.isseymiyake.com

MYKITA GmbH
Brunnenstrasse 153
10115 Berlin
Germany
T: 49 30 204 566 45
E: mail@mykita.com
www.mykita.com

Paola Navone
paola.navone@paolanavone.it

Nervous System
561 Windsor St., Suite A206
Somerville, MA 02143
United States
T: 1 347 637 8311
E: press@n-e-r-v-o-u-s.com
www.n-e-r-v-o-u-s.com

Nike
1 SW Bowerman Dr.
Beaverton, OR 97005
United States
T: 1 503 671 6453
E: info@nike.com
www.nike.com

Nonobject
2453 Ash Street
Palo Alto, CA 94306
United States
T: 1 650 473 9040
E: info@nonobject.com
www.nonobject.com

Nordisk Company A/S
Papirfabrikken 74
8600 Silkeborg
Denmark
T: 45 73 73 40 00
E: info@nordisk.eu
www.nordisk.eu

Nuubo
Paseo de Recoletos n° 21
28004 Madrid
Spain
T: 34 91 36 04 431
E: info@nuubo.com
www.nuubo.com

Patagonia, Inc.
259 W. Santa Clara St.
Ventura, CA 93001
United States
T: 1 805 643 8616
E: info@patagonia.com
www.patagonia.com

Carlos Peralta
E: purplecamaleon@yahoo.co.uk
www.carlosperalta.co.uk

Philips
High Tech Campus
Build ng HTC-33
5656 AE Eindhoven
The Netherlands
T: 31 40 274 92 00
E: philips.sustainability@philips.com
www.philips.com/sustainability

Plantronics
345 Encinal St.
Santa Cruz, CA 95060
United States
T: 1 831 426 5858
www.plantronics.com

POC Sports / POC Sweden AB
Nackagatan 4
116 41 Stockholm
Sweden
T 46 8 717 40 50
E: info@pocsports.com
www.pocsports.com

Polisport Plásticos, SA
Avenida Ferreira de Castro, 818
Fontanheira
3720-024 Carregosa
Portugal
T: 351 2 5641 0230
E: polisport@polisport.com
www.polisport.com

Re-worked Ltd.
The Round House, Rock Mill
Powys
Wales SY15 6NN
United Kingdom
T: 44 20 8133 4276
E: info@re-worked.co.uk
www.re-worked.co.uk

Samuel Wilkinson Studio
49 Hackney Road
London E2 7NX
United Kingdom
T: 44 207 7293 694
E: info@samuelwilkinson.com
www.samuelwilkinson.com

Sanford Process Corporation
1 Shorr Ct.
Woonsocket,
Rhode Island 02895
United States
T: 1 877 899 2734
E: tpcabot@sanfordprocess.com
www.micralox.com

Sierra Designs
6235 Lookout Road, Suite C
Boulder, CO 80301
United States
T: 1 800 736 8592
E: canadacustomerservice@
americanrec.com
www.sierradesigns.com

Studio Aisslinger
Heidestraße 46-52
10557 Berlin
Germany
T: 49 30 315 05 400
E: studio@aisslinger.de
www.aisslinger.de

Studio Dror
175 Varick St., 8th Fl.
New York, NY 100 4
United States
T: 1 212 929 2196
E: info@studiodror.com
www.studiodror.com

Studio Geenen
Ottho Heldringstraat 3, room 2.03
1066 AZ Amsterdam
The Netherlands
T: 31 61 650 509 0
E: info@studiogeenen.com
www.studiogeenen.com

Studio Mieke Meijer
De Graal 7
5625 CZ Eindhoven
The Netherlands
T: 31 61 125 4354
E: info@miekemeijer.nl
www.miekemeijer.nl

Switch Bulb Company, Inc.
225 Charcot Ave.
San Jose, CA 95131
United States
T: 1 650 298 9910
E: info@switchlightingco.com
www.switchlightingco.com

Teague
2727 Western Ave., Ste. 200
Seattle
WA 98121
United States
T: 1 206 838 4200
E: info@teague.com
www.teague.com

Tumi, Inc.
1001 Durham Ave.
South Plainfield, NJ 07080
United States
T: 1 908 756 4400
E: info@tumi.com
www.tumi.com

Union Binding Co. (Distributed by C3 Worldwice)
2700 W Commodore Way
Building A1, Suite 301
Seattle
WA 98199
United States
T: 1 206 632 1601
E: info@c3-worldwide.com
www.c3-shop.com

Marjan van Aubel
70 County Street
London SE1 4AD
United Kingdom
T: 44 7775 448967
E: mail@marjanvanaubel.com
www.marjanvanaubel.com

Dirk Vander Kooij
Hallenweg 3, 5615 PP Eindhoven
The Netherlands
T: 31 85 876 96 29
E: info@dirkvanderkooij.nl
www.dirkvanderkooij.nl

Vivian Chiu Designs
T: 1 401 212 0953
E: vchiu@risd.edu
www.vivianchiudesigns.com

Material ConneXion®
1271 Avenue of the Americas
17th Floor
New York, NY 10020
United States
T: 1 212 842 2050
E: info@materialconnexion.com
www.materialconnexion.com

Material ConneXion® Bangkok
Bangkok, Thailand
www.materialconnexion.com/th

Material ConneXion® Beijing
Beijing, China
www.materialconnexion.cn

Material ConneXion® Cologne
Cologne, Germany
www.materialconnexion.com/de

Material ConneXion® Daegu
Daegu, Republic of Korea
www.materialconnexion.com/kr

Material ConneXion® Istanbul
Istanbul, Turkey
www.materialconnexion.com/tr

Material ConneXion® Italia
Milan, Italy
www.materialconnexion.com/it

Material ConneXion® Seoul
Seoul, Republic of Korea
www.seoul.materialconnexion.com

Material ConneXion® Shanghai
Shanghai, China
www.materialconnexion.cn

Material ConneXion® Skövde
Skövde, Sweden
www.materialconnexion.com/se

Material ConneXion® Tokyo
Tokyo, Japan
www.materialconnexion.com/jp

While this series is intended for both the academic and the professional reader, its primary goal is to reveal for the young practitioner the extraordinary range of advanced materials and their influence on the creative process. This knowledge provides the foundation for how to use materials as a vehicle for addressing many of today's creative challenges.

Each chapter is separated by a spread in the form of a visual narrative. The purpose of these pages is to graphically depict the journey a designer takes from conception to completed design, recognizing that engagement with a material is part of an extended process of exploration and invention. These pages have been generously provided by a handful of outstanding individuals and firms that, in many cases, have produced a body of work that reflects their intimate working knowledge of a particular material type or process. Our hope is that by acknowledging the exploratory process inspired by the possibilities of material science, especially as they apply to a specific commission or set of conditions, we can foster greater material innovation across all creative disciplines.

DAVID TRUBRIDGE (PAGE 12)
Hastings, New Zealand

"Ideas begin with the land—wild rugged beaches or windy mountaintops. Empty space gives thoughts the freedom to roam, to alight on new and delicate possibilities. Words capture these thoughts, and the pencil wanders off to doodle feelings and responses, patterns and rhythms that resonate with the land. Perhaps these will go no further, or they will wait until the time is right, or evolve into a new form. Only then is the computer engaged, and an iterative design process refines the idea until it is fully resolved. From the computer it is an easy jump to the CNC machine, which follows the immateriality of those lines, turning them into solid reality. In homage to its source, the product comes full circle to be photographed in nature, its original inspiration."

SAMUEL WILKINSON (PAGE 40)
London, UK

"'Blown' is a new glass lamp that aims to convey 'industrialized craft,' a mass-produced product with the complexity and detailing of something handmade. Initially inspired by seeds, berries, and antique ceramics, the lamp explores the refractive qualities of glass by breaking up the light without compromising its function. The twisted quilted texture was 3D modeled in CAD to control the inflation of each of the bubbles. This produces a flatter profile at the top and bottom with an inflated 'blown' effect on the sides. To enhance the glass surface a unique manufacturing tool was designed to hide the parting line within the reliefs of the pattern. This quality, combined with the die-cast aluminum bulb holder, results in a product where every detail has been painstakingly considered."

STUDIO DROR (PAGE 66)
New York City, USA

"One of Italian furniture manufacturer Cappellini's iconic designs, the Peacock Chair speaks to the physical and metaphorical meaning of a peacock's feathers—they are inviting and structured. Three sheets of thick colored felt, a matted rather than woven fabric, are given structure and strength by their undulating, peacock-like folds, which results in a comfortable lounge chair without any sewing or upholstery. The base is in metal, powder-varnished in a dark-brown color. The Peacock Chair is in the permanent collection of the Metropolitan Museum of Art, New York."

ERIC CHAN OF ECCO DESIGN (PAGE 96)
New York City, USA

"The act of sitting forms a narrative between the human body and the material it touches. This ergonomic interaction speaks to comfort and gentleness, as well as strength and resilience. Each material has its own physical property to express its natural visual language. As designers, we are driven to discover the sensitive elegant rhythm between human and nature through each unique material, from bamboo, metal, and leather to fabric."

DIKINI (PAGE 124)
Montreal, Canada

"'Water Journeys' creates vibrant public spaces by providing a gathering place to play, socialize, and contemplate. Inspired by a flowing stream, a set of game modules leads to a giant chain reaction of play. Water runs through a network of channels, beds, and pools in which the user can engage and interact with a range of props (gates, strainers, watermills, pumps, and jets) to transform the flow. The multi-generational game is a collective experience where the action of one user impacts someone else's downstream. Based on an equilateral triangular grid, a modular system of fiberglass-reinforced concrete allows for multiple configurations. Connected together, the modules rise into a topography that constitutes both the ground surface and the game interface."

PAOLA NAVONE (PAGE 146)
Milan, Italy

"I don't believe in the isolated product design as a museum object that stands alone. Interest comes from creating stories, establishing connections between objects. Often this results from unexpected pairings of things that are at times opposites. This room can be read as a landscape of different elements that relate to each other: warm and cool, handcrafted and modern, simple and sophisticated. While I mix things, I never think of a shape without its material. For me, innovation comes from combining familiar materials—glass, ceramic, wood, tile, marble—in unexpected ways."

PICTURE CREDITS

a = above
b = below
c = center
l = left
r = right

1: credits for images on this page are listed under the relevant projects; 2–3: Courtesy of Studio Geenen; 6: Material ConneXion; 8: 3D Systems, Bespoke Products; 10: Karen Ostertag; 11: Material ConneXion; 12–13: © DAVID TRUBRIDGE; 14: Images by Sam J. Bond; 16al, 16ar: Luis E. Fraguada; 18, 19a, 19b: Michael Bonvin; 21al, 21ac, 21bc, 21b: BioCouture Ltd.; 21ar, 23: Santiago Arribas, BioCouture Ltd.; 22: Gary Wallis, BioCouture Ltd.; 24–25, 25a, 25r: Photos by Mike Glinski, © Do., LLC; 26, 27a, 27b: Jerry Mejia; 28, 29a, 29bc, 29br: © Julia Lohmann Studio; 29bl: © Petr Krejci/V&A; 30bl, 30bcl, 30bcr, 30br, 31l, 31r: Patagonia Inc and Yulex Corporation; 32, 33 all images: Biomood Srl; 34, 35, 36–37, 37a, 37r: Global Surf Industries; 38, 39l, 39r: Arc Fotografia; 40–41: © Samuel Wilkinson 2013; 42: Material ConneXion; 44l, 44r: © by nanopool GmbH; 45l: Hoowaki, LLC; 45r: Material ConneXion; 46, 47: © Plantronics. Photograph by Bruce Ashley; 48, 49a, 49r, 49b: Courtesy of Sanford Process; 51a, 51b: Sandra Luoni; 52, 53: Courtesy of Union Binding Co.; 54, 55, 56, 57a, 57l: Central Standard Timing; 58, 59bl, 59br, 59ar, 60–61: Courtesy of Ultimate Ears; 62; 63a, 63bl, 63br: Kammok; 64, 65a, 65b: Courtesy of Logitech; 66–67: © Studio Dror; 68–69: Cicli Pinarello spa; 70l, 70r: Ridea Skis; 71: Material ConneXion; 73: Courtesy of Tumi, Inc.; 74, 75: Karen Ostertag; 77a, 77b: Studio Geenen; 79a, 79l, 79r, 79b, 80–81, 81: RTI Sports; 82, 83l, 83r, 84, 85a, 85b: Vivian Chiu; 86 all images, 87a, 87b: POC Sports; 88, 89a, 89bl, 89bc, 89br: Sierra Designs; 90, 91bl, 91btr, 91bbr, 91r: Nordisk Company; 92bl, 92ar, 93: Wästberg; 94, 95al, 95ar, 95b: Idris Skis; 96–97: © ECCO Design Inc.; 98: Images Courtesy NikeInc.com; 100a: Photo: Universe Architecture; 100b: © KOR EcoLogic, photo: Dana McFarlane;

101l: © Kristof Vrancken – Z33 / artist: Unfold / Tim Knapen; 101r: Susan Smart Photography; 103al, 103ar, 103b: TEAGUE; 104, 105, 106, 107: 3D Systems, Bespoke Products; 108, 109l, 109a, 109r, 109b: © LayerWise; 110, 111: Jessica Rosenkrantz; 112, 113a, 113bl, 113br: Studio Dirk Van der Kooij; 114, 115a, 115bl, 115br: Photo by Jason Lopes, Legacy Effects; 115bc: © 2010 Marvel Studios; 117a: Photographer: Mitchell Feinberg, Prop Stylist: Megan Caponetto; 117bl, 117br, 118–19, 119: Images Courtesy NikeInc.com; 120, 121al, 121ar, 121b: Disney Research, Pittsburgh; 122, 123: MYKITA; 124–25: © Dikini; 126: Vij5; 128: Starbucks Coffee Company; 129a: Lindsey Hoshaw; 129b: Mark Skalny Photography and Waste Management; 130, 131: Estudio Mariscal & Mobles 114; 132: FaddaSantos; 133: Joff Lee, Aladdin; 134, 135a, 135r, 135b: Vij5; 136, 137, 138, 139a, 139b: Photo by Hiroshi Iwasaki, © Miyake Design Studio 2012; 140, 141al, 141ar, 141bl, 141br, 142, 143: Courtesy of Electrolux; 144, 145a, 145b: Adam Fairweather; 146–47: © Crate & Barrel; 148: Printechnologics GmbH; 150l, 150r: Electrozyme; 151: © Philips – Microbial Home Design Project; 153a, 153bl, 153bc, 153br: Wai Ming Ng; 155, 156–57: © Philips – Microbial Home Design Project; 158, 159al, 159ar, 159b: Courtesy of Nuubo; 161al, 161ac, 161ar, 161bl, 161bc, 161br: Carlos Peralta; 163: Courtesy Microsoft / MIT; 164, 165a, 165b: Nicklas Hellborg; 166, 167: James Wade Photography; 169a, 169b, 170, 171al, 171ar, 171bl, 171br: adidas group; 172, 173al, 173ar, 173b: Starbucks Store Design; 174, 175a, 175b: James McNab; 176, 177: Edgar D. Goluch; 178, 179: CuteCircuit; 180, 182–99: all images in the Materials Directory courtesy of Material ConneXion

THE AUTHORS

Dr. Andrew H. Dent, Vice President, Library & Materials Research, plays a key role in the expansion of Material ConneXion's technical knowledge base. His research directs the implementation of consulting projects and the selection of innovative, sustainable, and advanced materials for Material ConneXion's Library, which to date contains more than 7,000 materials. From Whirlpool and Adidas to BMW and Proctor & Gamble, Dr. Dent has helped numerous Fortune 500 companies develop or improve their products through the use of innovative materials. A prominent speaker, he has presented at many international events on sustainable and innovative material strategies. He has contributed to numerous publications and is co-author of *Ultra Materials: How Materials Innovation is Changing the World* and *Material ConneXion: The Global Resource of New and Innovative Materials for Architects, Artists and Designers*. He received his Ph.D. in Materials Science from Cambridge University in the United Kingdom.

Leslie Sherr is a writer, editor, and brand strategy consultant focusing on architecture, design and innovation. She is the former Director of Marketing and Business Development at C&G Partners; before that she worked for the Carbone Smolan Agency and Desgrippes Gobé Associates. In addition, she has consulted with leading architecture and design firms, including Assouline, Chandelier, Munder-Skiles, The 7th Art and YARD, among others. She has written for many design publications and is co-author with Dr. Andrew Dent of *Material Innovation: Architecture* (Thames & Hudson). She has a Bachelor of Fine Arts from SUNY Purchase and a Master of Science in Landscape Design from Columbia University.

Material ConneXion (materialconnexion.com) is a global materials and innovation consultancy that helps clients create the products and services of tomorrow through smart materials and design thinking. Material ConneXion, a Sandow company, is the trusted adviser to Fortune 500 companies, as well as to any forward-thinking agencies and government entities seeking a creative, competitive, or sustainable edge. With eleven locations—in Bangkok, Beijing, Cologne, Daegu, Istanbul, Milan, New York, Seoul, Shanghai, Skövde, and Tokyo—Material ConneXion's international network of specialists provides a global, cross-industry perspective on materials, design, new product development, sustainability and innovation. Material ConneXion maintains the world's largest subscription-based materials library, with more than 7,000 innovative materials and processes—an indispensable asset to a wide audience of users. The consulting division, ThinkLab, works with clients to strategically incorporate trends, service and innovation into their business models and products, while sister company Culture + Commerce represents the world's leading designers, including Philippe Starck and Marcel Wanders, in licensing their groundbreaking new products and projects.

ACKNOWLEDGMENTS

Although we appear as the authors of this book, it is in fact the work of many hands. The project has been in every sense a team effort, which would not have been possible without the vision of George M. Beylerian, founder of Material ConneXion, together with the knowledge, skills, hard work, and dedication of many colleagues. The book is the culmination of many people's work and we would like to take this opportunity to thank those who were most closely connected with the project. We are grateful to Michele Caniato, president, for bringing Material ConneXion and Thames & Hudson together to realize the full potential of this ambitious project, and to Adam I. Sandow, founder, chairman, and chief executive officer of Sandow, for his support. Our extended thanks go to the Material ConneXion marketing department—Gabriella Vivaldi, Daniel Swartz, Carlo Grioli and, William Nichols, Assistant Editor—for working tirelessly to help bring this book to life. For his guidance: Matthew Kalishman; for contributing to the editorial team: Tiffany Vasilchik, Maider Irastorza, Fiona Anastas, Elizabeth Peterson, Sarah Hoit, and Alejandra Kluger. Thank you also to the sales team at Material ConneXion who have given their time and resources and whose dedication is reflected in these pages.

We owe a special debt to the outstanding product, design and innovation consulting firms whose human-centered visions have enriched and expanded our understanding of what is materially possible in the field of product design, and who have given so generously of their time, knowledge, and insight, especially Allan Chochinov for his introduction to this volume. Our endless thanks also go out to the many contributors, including photographers, media contacts, engineers, scientists, and manufacturers, whose creativity, research, and knowledge inform every chapter in the book. It has not been possible here, for reasons of space, to include every single individual by name, but that does not lessen our gratitude to them.

Material Innovation has been created in collaboration with Thames & Hudson. Without Jamie Camplin's championing, this series would not have been possible. We would like to extend our warmest appreciation to him, as well as to Ilona de Nemethy Sanigar, who offered invaluable editorial direction, patience and support. We are also grateful to Johanna Neurath, design director, and Samuel Clark, senior designer, for the publication design, to Kirsty Seymour-Ure for her sensitive copyediting, and to Paul Hammond for his production control.

Andrew H. Dent
Leslie Sherr